Black Days,
Black Dust

T0168162

BLACK DAYS, BLACK DUST

The Memories of an African American Coal Miner

Robert Armstead

As Told to S. L. Gardner

THE UNIVERSITY OF TENNESSEE PRESS

Knoxville

Library of Congress Cataloging-in-Publication Data
Armstead, Robert.
Black days, black dust: the memories of an African American
coal miner/Robert Armstead; as told to S. L. Gardner.— 1st ed.
    p. cm.
Includes bibliographical references and index.
ISBN 1-57233-175-5 (cl.: alk. paper)
ISBN 1-57233-176-3 (pbk.: alk. paper)
1. Armstead, Robert.
2. African American coal miners—Biography.
3. Coal miners—United States—Biography.
I. Gardner, S. L.
II. Title.
HD8039.M6152 U62 2002
622'.334'092—dc21   2001005652

This book is dedicated to West Virginia coal miners, past and present.

"You have all left a mark on our state's history which can never be erased by anyone, anytime, for any reason. You are part of the heritage, the strength and the power of West Virginia."

Gov. Jay Rockefeller,
April 1, 1982
UMW Local 4047 luncheon
honoring forty- and fifty-year
veteran miners
Grant Town, West Virginia
Times West Virginian

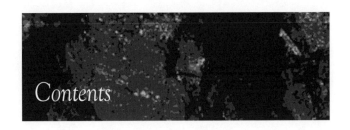

Contents

Illustrations

Foreword

I n 1860 fewer than fifteen thousand African Americans lived in western Virginia. Three years later this region broke away from secessionist Virginia, joined the North, and became West Virginia, a free state with voting rights for all men. By 1920, forty-five thousand African American immigrants had migrated west from Virginia and the Carolinas, and north from Alabama and Mississippi, into West Virginia. The post–Civil War Great Migration of African Americans to the northern industrial cities had little to do with this massive influx into West Virginia. Few factories existed in this mountainous, rural state. One industry inspired tremendous growth in the African American population: coal.

Coal operators leased land for as little as fifteen cents an acre from poor, inexperienced farmers, built above ground coal works, and started digging shafts wherever they found this profitable mineral. The coal industry needed wood for coal works, mine-tunnel supports, and to build coal towns. Sawmills flourished, stripping the hillsides bare of trees. Deforestation was so complete, the only large accessible stand of virgin trees remaining in West Virginia now grows protected in Cathedral State Park, a 132-acre reserve in Preston County.

Rail spurs meandered deep into remote river and stream valleys. As the last foot of track went down, the train backed in and took on its first load of coal. Vast deposits and rapid development of the industry generated a tremendous demand for laborers. Immigrants from Europe accepted free train tickets to West Virginia, on the promise of work, and headed to the coalfields.

Thousands of struggling African American farmers and sharecroppers from Virginia and the Carolinas flowed into the state for mining jobs. Mining companies imported African Americans from the South by the trainload to fill in for striking white miners. If the strikers and coal operators couldn't resolve their issues, African Americans kept their jobs. Some stayed on, regardless of the outcome, because mining jobs were available everywhere. Laid-off or dissatisfied miners, African American and white, could easily relocate for work (Lewis 1989).

Though considered inferior, even beneath the status of non–English-speaking immigrants, the African American population in some southern West Virginia counties grew to become the majority. Many native white miners fought this intrusion, fearing African Americans would take over the job market and move into their white communities. In some areas Ku Klux Klan activity discouraged mine operators from hiring African American miners.

Intimidation and violent incidents were not as prevalent in the northern West Virginia coalfields. African Americans were assimilated into the mining industry and permitted to live on the edge of white society. They were still segregated, but with more acceptance and individual rights. The wage scale, though slightly depressed for African Americans, was not as bad as the double standard in the South. African American men, as a whole, were industrious workers in the mines. Because they were used to backbreaking farm work and possessed a strong work ethic, African American miners didn't slack off when tired, did what they were told, and didn't complain about conditions.

Impressed by this new work force, coal operators sent promoters to Alabama and Mississippi to recruit disgruntled African American sharecroppers and coal miners. It wasn't difficult for promoters to find experienced miners weary of labor disputes, meager pay, and the oppressive harness of segregation. Slavery, tied to the southern justice system, continued in mines in the South. "Free" tickets and the promise of a better life in the North lured family after family to board trains with nothing more than a bag of clothes. Miners soon discovered, however, that employers deducted travel costs from their first months' paychecks. The migration continued into the 1920s. Job opportunities remained plentiful as more mines opened up.

Bob Armstead's family joined this Great Migration near its end, in 1924. Four generations came together. His great-grandmother, a former slave, was the oldest generation. His grandfather, the son of the former slave and the white plantation owner who sharecropped a portion of his land to their family, was the second generation. Bob's parents were the third generation, and their growing family made up the fourth generation.

They paid their own way to the northern West Virginia coalfields from Alabama. With fierce determination and hard work, Bob's father carved a new life in West Virginia for his family. Bob did the same after the example of his father. As we shall see, it wasn't easy. ■

Acknowledgments

When I moved into the Appalachian coal-fields in 1991, the history of the region captured my attention. In southern West Virginia my husband and I traveled the back roads into Keystone and Welch, witnessing historical Mine War plaques, dying coal camps, and mountains of gob piles that filled ravines and scarred the landscape at every turn. I read everything I could find about coal, forming my own opinions, most of them negative.

We moved to the northern West Virginia coal-fields in 1996. As I dodged huge coal trucks on narrow roads, the spark of interest returned. I devoured local histories, began exploring, and talked to anyone asso-ciated with coal. My opinions began to change, posi-tive mingled with negative.

I found coal to be the past and, in many cases, the present lifeblood of the area. Yes, the coal trucks tear up the roads. Yes, the mine closings continue, causing high unemployment and family hardships. On the positive side, I discovered that many former coal miners have pride in the work they did in the past, and that some would give their eyeteeth to be part of it again. Regardless of past exploitation, there's a certain reverence for what mining did, and still does, for the area.

Gaps in the local histories compelled me to write several feature articles on old coal camps for the *Times West Virginian*, the Fairmont daily newspaper. John Veasey, editor of the paper's Marion Pride section, welcomed my work, complete with pictures, and encouraged me to do more. He has my thanks for his interest, advice, and encouragement.

After my in-depth article appeared on Dakota, a former coal camp outside Fairmont, Bob Armstead called me to discuss his father's work in the mine there. He spoke of a possible article on his life for the paper. As he recounted several of his stories, I knew that even a series of articles would not do justice to his fascinating life. We discussed working together on a book and mapped out a plan.

Thankfully, Bob had already started writing down his experiences since his retirement. With his work, interviews, and thousands of questions and answers, we brought the project to completion within a year and a half. He was always willing and available to give me details. I appreciated his patience. The stories in this book are Bob Armstead's. As his collaborator, I recorded his stories; organized his writings; interviewed miners, his family, and his supervisors for details; and pulled everything together. I did not modify events or interject my opinions into his observations or conclusions.

The reference staffs of the Marion County Public Library and Fairmont State College Library, and the United Mine Workers Association District 31 office provided much-needed assistance in helping me dig for dates, statistics, confirmations, and historical background.

Several individuals deserve recognition for assisting me with this project. They have my limitless gratitude. Author Gerald D. Swick gave me priceless advice and counseling, especially in the beginning. After reviewing the first four chapters, his declaration, "This story is definitely a book, and you can do it!" spurred me on. Doug Henderson, an experienced West Virginia coal geologist and family friend, helped to edit the glossary. Ronald L. Lewis, West Virginia University professor and author, reviewed the first half of the manuscript and provided valuable advice and suggestions. Author Teresa Hearl poured over every word and phrase, questioning and advising. Her incredible contribution—words can't say it here.

My husband, Joe, served as my editor, critic, computer expert, and ever-present support system. His encouragement and patience held me up as I lived and breathed coal for months and months. Thank you for everything.

S. L. Gardner

Black Days,
Black Dust

Preface

This is the story of my life, the circumstances I could and could not control, and the choices I made. My choice, as a child, would not have been to enter the coal mines. I saw how my father suffered physically. When I did go into the mines, it was because I felt I had no choice. The opportunity came, and I took it. I made it my life's work because, from the very first day, it fascinated me. I wanted others to know what it was like to work in the coal mining industry.

Drastic changes occurred from one generation to the next. The contrast between working and living conditions, then to now, is almost unbelievable. When my father became a miner in the South, coal mining was extremely dangerous and very primitive. In the late 1920s in West Virginia, he often worked fourteen hours a day for less than five dollars. When I started in 1947, making ten dollars for an eight-hour day, machines did much of the work. Between us, we worked almost ninety years underground in the most dangerous industry in the world. Sharing my work experiences, and those of my father, is important to me.

Much emphasis is placed on life in a West Virginia coal camp in the 1930s. It was a hard life, and I have tried to recall interesting stories, both good and bad. The coal industry has always been unstable, dependent on demand. As a result of this instability, changes in our lives came abruptly. Thanks to my parents, we survived and remained a close-knit family.

I would like to thank all the Consolidation Coal Company foremen and top supervisors I worked with during my years as a United Mine Workers contract miner and as a salaried supervisor. Some names have been changed so as not to offend anyone, but all statements are truthful.

I also feel indebted to my wife, Gay, for being dedicated and for understanding my feisty frustrations during our forty-year marriage. An unstable work environment made this very challenging for both of us.

My gratitude goes to my parents, and to my sisters and brothers, with whom I share a great deal of pride and closeness. Born of a large and church-going family, we clung to each other for strength and assurance in times of peril, sickness, heartaches, and death.

Bob Armstead

Part 1

1927–1947

CHAPTER ONE

Lessons in Life

As I stepped inside the Koppers Coal Company office and stomped the snow from my boots, I felt pride swelling up inside. I approached the payroll window like a man. In 1932, I was short and scrawny for a five year old. The window and counter were so high off the floor that I had to stand on my toes to present my dad's scrip card.

A gigantic white woman filled the window and blocked the light from above. She frowned down at me and barked, "What do you want?"

"Please, ma'am. I'd like to have three dollars' worth of scrip to buy food," I said, using my polite manners. Scrip was coal company money, credit from my father's payroll earnings.

Taking her time, she opened the four-foot-long payroll book to check my father's record. With a disgusted look, she shuffled back to the window and grumbled, "109, right?"

"Yes. Armstead." I emphasized our last name. My father's payroll number was 109.

Koppers Coal Company store, Grant Town, West Virginia, 1998. Photograph by S. L. Gardner.

"109 can only have two dollars."

"What do I do?" I asked as the cold melted away. I felt my cheeks getting hot.

The secretary glared at me for what seemed like an hour. "Do you want the two dollars or not?"

Confused at first, I studied those hostile eyes and then decided. "Yes, ma'am. I do." She dropped the card and two pieces of scrip into my cold, outstretched hand and walked away.

Dazed, I left the office and walked slowly across the mine road and tried to think what to do. I climbed the steep, slippery iron steps to the company store. The three-story brick building had a tiny porch, high off the ground, that was snow-packed and icy. I stepped into a corner away from the howling wind to make my decision. Should I go inside or go home?

My mother's voice came back to me. The night before, as she tucked the covers under my chin and gave me a warm kiss, she had whispered in my ear, "Bobby, you'll have to miss school tomorrow morning. I need you to run to the store and get me a few things. Delivery time is too late for what I need. Good night now."

Queen Esther Armstead at age twenty-nine, 1922. Courtesy of Sister Louise Britton.

Strange that Mom wanted me to miss school. I had just started pre-primer at the black school near our house. We were learning to color and draw and to get along with other kids before going to first grade. Mom's confidence in me to do this important task pleased me and made me proud. She couldn't take my two-year-old brother out in the cold weather, and she was expecting a new baby. My older brother, Bill, was hard to trust. "If I want something done, I'll call on Bobby" were familiar words.

During the night a blizzard had dumped four inches of snow on the ground. The wind blew hard and rattled the windows. Where we lived in the mountains of West Virginia, the winters were bitter cold. Snow covered the ground in late October and seemed to stay until late spring. Storms came often. Usually, I enjoyed watching the snow build up on the windowsills and on the steep wooden steps to our front porch. The ice caked on the windowpanes was so thick, I couldn't see through them. I'd learned long ago to stand next to the wood stove to warm my bones before going outside when it was cold.

As I finished my last bite of butter-smothered biscuit, Mom wrapped a heavy scarf around my ears and neck and helped me into my coat and boots. She pushed my dad's scrip card and the grocery list deep into my pocket. I loved having her fuss over me. Then she got very serious. "Bobby, listen. Ask at the office for three dollars' worth of scrip for food. Take the card and this list to the store. Get everything on the list. And don't lose this card!" When Mom opened the door, a blast of cold air hit us. "You're going to be all right," she said, but she looked troubled.

Nothing was going to stop me from helping her. Before I stepped outside, I grabbed her around the knees, smiled at her from underneath my scarf, and said, "I'll be fine." After I slid down our hill on my bottom, I made a new path up the road. Snow pelted my face, and the wind tried to knock me over. The temperature with the chilling wind felt like ten degrees.

I'd walked the mile through Grant Town many times to the mine and the company store, but this time, the blowing snow nearly froze my eyes shut. It took me an hour to walk up and down the steep hills. I had to keep my head down and couldn't see any of the beer joints or food places along the winding road. I don't know if they were open. I passed no one. After all that, the mean old woman told me there wasn't enough money to buy what was on the list. The only thing in my mind was that Mom was counting on me to help her.

With my back pressed against the porch wall, I decided. "I have to buy *something*." I blinked back tears and opened the door to the company store. The smells of new merchandise and coal heat pulled me inside. I walked past the women's nightgowns, the household goods, and the racks of guns. Since I felt prying eyes watching me across the wide center aisle, I didn't even make my usual stop to look over the big display of toys.

Clumping down the inside cement stairs to the grocery store in the basement, I felt the panic coming. "What should I do?" My voice echoed in the narrow stairwell. Thankfully, a friendly clerk worked in the store that day. She knew my mother and selected what she felt were the most important items to buy with my two dollars. Her understanding and kindness made me feel warm inside my frosty clothes.

The walk home was a little easier with the wind at my back, but the snow was deeper, and I had my arms full. I arrived an hour later, clutching my father's scrip card and my mother's groceries. My fingers were numb from the cold. When I came into the house, Mom hugged me, kissed me, and rubbed me warm.

I told her why I couldn't get all she wanted. For a moment we looked at each other. "You couldn't know that. You did just fine. I'm so proud of you." I knew she meant it because she hugged me again, but she wasn't smiling.

After I'd changed into dry clothes, Mom gave me a bowl of hot soup and sent me to school.

In 1932 life was hard. The nation was deep into the Great Depression, but we knew little of that. We were too busy struggling to live day to day. Harsh winter weather was an accepted fact. We dressed warmly and went about our business. No one had much to live on, and parents expected all able-bodied children to run errands and work hard to help the family.

I was cold and discouraged that day. I knew my father worked to exhaustion in the mine, usually six days a week, and we still didn't have enough money for groceries. He must have been frustrated and angry. I became determined not to let that happen to me. Though I was only five years old, the experience of not having enough money was humiliating. It changed me.

I got into the lifetime habit of hoarding change. If my father or an older brother gave me a nickel or a dime, I didn't spend it all. Like any kid, I might buy candy or gum, but I saved the rest. I kept the change in my socks in a dresser drawer or stored it in cans and boxes under my bed or deep in a closet. And I became a hustler. Hustlers watch and listen for a chance to make money, even if it's just a nickel. I'd take any job for money. I carried water, coal, and wood and ran errands for neighbors who needed help. If someone offered me the opportunity to make a dollar, I'd mop a floor or do whatever it took. I eventually sold newspapers, washed store windows, and shined shoes. Anything to make money. Some might call this greed, but I never felt I wanted lots of money. I simply didn't ever want to be caught without it, like I was at the company store that day. I needed to pay my own way.

Growing up poor, I also learned to be tough physically and mentally. In everything I did, I took care of myself and tried never to get hurt. Very simply, if I got hurt, I couldn't work, and work kept me independent.

Pain and death were all around us in the coal camps during the Depression. Miners getting seriously injured, or killed, was not unusual. Doctors didn't have many effective medicines to treat illnesses. Sometimes

I wonder how we survived childhood. My first recollection of pain, and my first experience with death, occurred when I was only three years old.

"Give me that pan right now, Bobby! I need it!"

My response, typical for a young child, was to turn the oatmeal-filled spoon over and over, licking it, and to grin back at my sister. That's how it started.

She stood near me, washing the supper dishes. She was a beautiful girl, but she had a stubborn streak. And what a temper! I was in my highchair, eating oatmeal from an aluminum pot with my middle finger wedged in the handle. My sister ordered me several times to hand her the pot so she could finish the dishes and start her homework. I provoked her by pulling it back from her reach each time. My finger was still inside the handle. On about the third withdrawal, she snatched the pot away from me.

The first joint of my middle finger came with the pot. Blood poured everywhere. I couldn't breathe for how much it hurt and how scared I was. Mother immediately called the coal company doctor. He came within a few minutes and reattached my finger to the remaining joint. Did I scream! They said I screamed from pain for hours. Later in the evening an older man in our community came to visit me. He gave me a shiny blue Boy Scout pocketknife, which stopped my tears and quieted my broken heart. I was still in my highchair because I wouldn't let anyone touch me.

The company doctor, Dr. Collins, saved my finger. He was a dedicated doctor, and I believe my faith in doctors is strong because of him. Collins delivered over four thousand babies in the area, including three of my brothers and sisters. Each time he drove his black Model A Ford truck up our road, I thought to myself, *A new baby is coming somewhere*. We kids always ran behind his truck to see if we could find out what had happened. I still laugh when I think of my aunt. When she was a little girl, she thought the doctor brought new babies in his black leather bag.

Shots for childhood diseases didn't exist in those days. Diseases took many young children, especially smallpox and diphtheria. My family and I were all lucky that we survived. Usually, when one of us caught something, everyone got sick.

My first experience with death involved an animal, but I can still see the sights and hear the sounds. A friendly older couple lived next door to us. The man had a retired mine horse that he put to work, plowing gardens in the community. When the weather was pleasant, we rode old Soap Stick

Bob and his coal company house in Grays Flats, West Virginia, 1998. His family lived in the right half from 1929 to 1941. Renovations since then include a garage door, removing the Armsteads' front door, and siding. Photograph by S. L. Gardner.

on Sundays. The worn-out horse became sick, extremely skinny, and finally died in the stable on the hill behind our house.

The next day my mother went to Fairmont, a city ten miles away, on the streetcar to pay a few bills and to buy groceries. Since I was only three, my older sisters were in charge of me. Soon after our mother left, we heard loud, strange noises next to our house. A large tow truck, with a long steel cable wrapped around a drum, made horrible grinding and screeching noises. The men pulled the cable about one hundred yards up the hill, attached it to Soap Stick, and prepared to drag the dead horse down to be loaded.

We watched from the window. Every time they cranked that horse farther down the hill, I let out a scream! My sisters tried to control my fears and coaxed me, "Bobby, come away from that window." I wouldn't listen, and I couldn't move. I tried to squeeze my eyes shut, but the wrenching noise popped them open every time. As long as the men didn't pull on the horse, I was all right. When they wound that screeching steel cable around the drum and yanked Soap Stick a few more feet, I screamed in terror.

That was the first time that I saw anything dead, and the first time I saw anything dead or alive being dragged. The shivers and shudders of the sight stayed with me. After they drove away with the dead horse dangling from the cable and hook, I screamed until my mother arrived several hours later. She held me and petted my fears away. Someone had to remove the dead horse, but what a horrible sight for a young child!

Mom had to use the streetcar when she shopped in Fairmont because we had no automobile. The streetcar was expensive, but it was our only transportation. The streetcar tracks ran alongside the railroad from Fairmont to Fairview, a town about three miles up the valley. The early morning run began at 7:30 A.M., and the last run from Fairmont was at 11:00 P.M. Any time my mother or father arrived at the stop during daylight hours, my brother Bill ran down to meet them to help carry bags home. Of course, he also wanted to be the first one to find out what they bought.

One evening each week Mom rode the streetcar to church in Fairmont and returned on the last car, arriving at 11:30 P.M. I watched from my bedroom window and would not go to bed until I saw the lights and the sparks from the trolley pole, bringing her safely home.

My mother's religious beliefs took her away from us, and I missed her. Then the coal company gave blacks a tiny building near the mine for services. Our mother made us go with her twice on Sundays. She always had me in Sunday school or church. I was mostly a good and obedient boy, and she had high hopes that I would enter the ministry. I walked and walked, carrying a little satchel with a Bible in it, going to church. I heard my friends out playing football while I was in church. The elderly women with their bad breath kissed me and said, "Little Bobby's going to be a preacher." When they did that, I'd turn away to wipe my face and gasp for fresh air.

My mother became deeply involved in the Christian way of life. Though my father and a few of my sisters and brothers complained about Mom's strict beliefs, she insisted on raising us in a biblical home. She said a blessing for each meal we ate together. After all the family went to bed, she sat downstairs by gaslight to read and study the Bible. Once or twice a year she read the whole Bible and often quoted scriptures during any argument or discussion. My father had his own version of religion, and he knew the Bible well enough to come back at her. I'm not saying Mom was right because she read the Bible. Everyone had their own opinions.

The church members held prayer services in our home two or three times a month. Those days were filled with fuss and bother, and as kids, we dreaded the work. My sisters had to scrub the floors and dust everything in the house. My brothers and I shoved the furniture out of the living room and set up chairs. We all had to get cleaned up with shiny faces and our best clothes. Sometimes the show was comical.

The church women read the Bible, sang, banged on tambourines, and shouted "Hallelujah!" My mom played her upright Baldwin player-piano, or she put sacred music rolls in to play while everyone clapped and sang. The house rocked and the floors shook. The only thing missing from these joyous celebrations was my dad. He disappeared on prayer service nights.

My mom's favorite song was "The Old Rugged Cross." She kept that roll in the piano slot between meetings. Since I was too small for my feet to reach the pump pedals, I pushed them by hand when I wanted to hear music. She didn't permit me to touch her beautiful piano, and I received a spanking each time I tried. "The Old Rugged Cross" is a beloved Christian song, but when I hear it, I look over my shoulder for my mother.

I believe her religion helped Mom be content through all our hard times. She loved God, and she loved her family. Her life and certainly my father's life were difficult because we were so poor, but they took care of us, disciplined us, protected us, and raised us with strict values of right and wrong.

Born a black boy into poverty, my origins, race, family, and circumstances made me who I am. I would not want to change that. If I had the power, however, I would change some of the hardships that my mother and father had to endure. ■

CHAPTER TWO

Growing Up in Coal Camps

My father, James Henry Armstead, was the undisputed "king" of our household. He directed the family to his way of thinking. He was staunch—not mean, but strict with a heavy and demanding voice. My father disregarded the opinions of his wife and older children most of the time. His word on a subject was, like the law, final and just. When he said "No," he meant "No. End of discussion." Although he was not an educated man, he read newspapers and kept up with national events. All these things made him appear wise and confident to his family.

My father was five feet eight inches and weighed about 180 pounds. He had a thick, muscular build and barely knew his own strength. I favor his build. I always loved and admired my father. Any time he entered a room, he had a presence that commanded respect and attention. As a young boy, I studied him closely so I could learn everything about

James Henry Armstead at their Fairmont, West Virginia, home at age sixty, 1960.
Courtesy of William Armstead.

him. He taught me about life and what to expect when disappointments
come. Dad was born in 1900 near Bessemer, Alabama. He and his brother
Clifford worked in coal mines with their father, William.

My mother, Queen Esther Gardner, was born in Birmingham, Alabama, in 1893. Mother was a small and fragile woman, and she was beautiful. Before she married my father, she taught elementary school. She also
had her beauty certificate and did hair on the side for many years. Her own
hair always looked styled and flattered her delicate face.

With the promise of better working conditions and higher wages in
the coal industry, the whole family relocated to Watson, West Virginia, a

little community outside Fairmont, in 1925. The extended family included my great-grandmother, my grandfather William and grandmother Isabelle, and my uncle Clifford. Conditions were not much better in West Virginia, but all the men gained immediate employment at the Fairmont Coal Company, one of the many coal companies in Marion County. The Watsons, Flemings, Hutchinsons, and others owned a huge mining operation in Watson. As the mine grew and profited, the owners became very wealthy. Trains and river barges transported coal from the Watson mine down the Monongahela River Valley to Pittsburgh. Their coal was then shipped by rail to Ohio and to all the northeastern states.

My brother Bill and I were born in Watson. I was born at 3:00 A.M. on December 8, 1927. I am told it was a frigid night. Watson was a sturdy coal camp of duplex houses with four rooms on each side. A house might have ten to fifteen children living in it. No house had a white family on one side and a black family on the other. It was either all black or all white.

My grandfather's house sat on River Row, where all the black coal miners and their families eventually moved. Though we left Watson when I was two, I visited my grandfather each summer. His home became my second home. After his shift in the mine, we often walked down to the company store, next to the West Fork River, and bought lunch meat, cheese, cinnamon rolls, and bananas for his lunch. On the way back, we sat in the cool shade of a huge oak tree and ate ice cream to pass the time and relax by the river.

My grandfather Armstead had light-colored skin. Very light. He could have passed for white, but he never did. Sometimes when I walked with my grandfather, kids that saw us teased me later, "What were you doing out walking with that old white man?" I would get fighting mad and shout, "That was no white man, that was my grandfather!"

After working in the Watson mine for nearly five years, my father took a job in the Grant Town mine in 1929. We moved to one of the four company houses at Inktom Hill outside Grant Town. My third brother was born there. They named him Clifford, after our uncle. Grant Town had three places where blacks could live: Inktom Hill, Black Bottom, and Grays Flats. Like most black communities in coal camps, they were either a long walk from the mine or were right next to the mine and the railroad tracks, where it was noisy and dirty.

We lived through the Great Depression in the Grant Town area. Throughout the country, people who lost their jobs and their money stood in long lines, many wearing tattered clothes, looking for work. In winter they fought frostbite. If they couldn't find work, they stood in soup lines for a cup of soup or a hot cup of coffee supplied by the Salvation Army. None of these desperate scenes existed in Grant Town. Joblessness was not tolerated in a mining company town. Everyone who needed to work had a job in the mine or in a company-owned business that supported the mine. Some enterprising private businessmen and women had little stores, restaurants, or beer joints that thrived, but if a man lost his job or business, he moved on.

Even before the Depression, a coal miner's wages could barely support a wife and one child. I'm sure my dad read about the Depression, and the news reports influenced him to stay put, where he at least had a job. After living a short time on Inktom Hill, my struggling parents, now with nine children, moved over the ridge to Grays Flats, one mile above Grant Town.

Throughout the coalfields miners lived in look-alike houses built and rented out by the local coal company. Rows and rows of these single and duplex houses, called coal camps, dotted the hillsides and valleys surrounding the mine. Beneath the startling, shrill train whistles and clanging bells, we heard the constant rumble of "skips," or railroad cars, bumping into each other. At the mine, workers filled a car with coal and then moved the train, or "skipped" it, to bring the next car into place for loading. Metal coal-car couplings clanked all day and all night, except Sundays. Sunday was a quiet day.

Anytime I went outside, even in the winter, I inhaled the foul smells of Grays Flats and Grant Town. Every yard had an outdoor toilet, and in the hot summer, they smelled horrible. Each spring the coal company paid Luke Anderson, a black man, to clean all the outside toilets. The heavy odor of human waste gagged us and clung to our clothes for days after he "honey-dipped" the toilets.

I lived my entire childhood breathing in smoke and the stench of burning coal. The smell resembled scorched linen. Day and night we smelled the slate dump, or "gob pile," near our home. The company moved coal-mine waste and slate to the dump all day long. As slate accumulates with coal, methane gas builds up. Spontaneous combustion often ignites the gas, and coal fires smolder for months. Unless the wind blew burning coal smoke away from the slate dump, gray smoke hung in the sky all the time. We breathed the poisoned air outside and inside our home and never thought about it.

In Grays Flats one street went to a dead end, with six houses on the right side and four on the left. Our house, first on the right, set back against a steep hill. We had a back porch but no back yard. From the front our basement crawlspace looked like a first floor until you noticed the high wooden porch with many, many steep steps up to the main floor. The outside was never painted, but the house was strong and sturdy. Cold air seeped in around the windows, so Mom lined the window frames with rags.

The road by our house adopted the name Frazier Street after a black couple who were among the original settlers in Grays Flats. They were childless and the first couple to own an automobile. The first time Mr. Frazier drove up our road, the deafening roar scared me to death. I ran into the house and climbed into the crawlspace to hide. I cried and cried until my sister heard me and coaxed me out. Once or twice a month my father asked Mr. Frazier to drive us to Fairmont for groceries. If this gentleman was too busy, my father took us on the streetcar so we could help carry bags. I preferred the streetcar ride to the rutted and bumpy, narrow road.

Standing on our front porch I could see the road to Grant Town. Across the road and through the tree line, I could see both banks of Paw Paw Creek with its narrow foot bridge. On the other side of Paw Paw Creek lay the streetcar tracks and railroad tracks. Sometimes I watched the trains moving out and wished I could hop on and ride the coal to the end of the line. My world was comfortable, but I wondered what lay beyond it.

Most of the houses held two families, like in Watson. Each family had four rooms: a living room and kitchen downstairs and two bedrooms upstairs. Though the outside of the house was strong, the walls between families were like cardboard. One could overhear conversations of anyone next door. For instance, when Jimmy up the street broke his mom's good reading lamp, he got a whipping for punishment. The kids in his adjoining house blabbed it all over the neighborhood, and we teased him without mercy when he came out to play. If parents fought with each other or yelled at their children, the news traveled. There were no secrets in Grays Flats.

Most women in coal camps had at least three to five children, and many had eight to ten. Ours wasn't the only big family crowded into four rooms. My dad eventually moved my mom's kitchen to the basement to gain a third bedroom. We had very little furniture other than a kitchen table and benches, beds, and, of course, my mom's beloved piano.

Our house number was 109. Each coal miner's payroll number matched the house he rented. The miner attached a brass tag with this number on it to every coal car he loaded for payroll credit. In the big book at the company store, we were 109. No names, just numbers.

The Grays Flats coal company houses had no inside toilets or running water. We didn't get electricity until 1935. We did have a telephone in our house so we could call the company store. They had a daily delivery service that helped my mom because we lived far from the store. In winter, it was a godsend. Kerosene lamps provided light until the company furnished natural gas. After that, pipes that hung below the ceilings pumped in raw gas. Open-flame mantles, attached to the pipes, controlled the spray of light in each of the downstairs rooms. In the two upstairs rooms, we used kerosene lamps. Small coal or gas stoves provided heat in winter. In the kitchen the oversized, smoldering coal stove, used for cooking and heating water, kept the downstairs toasty warm in the winter but steaming hot in the summertime.

One outside hand-operated pump provided all the water for twenty families. Anytime I looked out the window, someone was banging up and down on that old red pump. Every boy big enough to carry a one-gallon pail full of water had to tote water for his family. Our house stood fifty yards from the pump, and I carried water on the hottest day in summer and on the coldest, iciest day in winter. If any boy, including myself, spotted another boy headed toward the pump, the race was on! Carrying water definitely built up my arm and leg muscles. As an unwritten rule, we had to give adults first chance at the water pump, even if we arrived there first. To be polite, I pumped water for women and elderly men, whether I liked them or not.

Since our house full of people needed so much water for cooking, drinking, washing clothes, and bathing, carrying water was an endless and aggravating chore. Bucket after bucket after boring bucket. Even the wives with no children kept lots of water on hand. Some of them had extra money to pay a kid in the neighborhood by the week to carry water. I took advantage of this and stashed the money in my sock drawer.

Saturday nights that old pump got a workout. All the families needed extra water for baths and enough left over for Sunday morning. In the wintertime fights occurred at the pump. Rushing to avoid the icy winds made us very impatient. "I was here first!" followed by "No, I was here first!" followed by pushing and shoving with arms and hips. After a snowstorm, pails often vanished. "I put my bucket right here! I take one sled ride, and somebody steals my bucket! My mom is gonna kill me! You stole it, didn't you?" Shouts and accusations swelled up into fist fights. To avoid fights, many pails got bent or smashed as we held on to them while sled riding so they wouldn't get stolen. The company store sold lots of water pails, especially in winter, for we used and abused them without mercy.

In my home hot water simmered on the cookstove most of the time. Without fail, the pans boiled during the late afternoon in anticipation of my father's arrival from work. The Grant Town mine didn't provide any bathing facilities in the 1930s. A daily fill-up of a number 3 zinc tub was absolutely necessary, for Dad came home covered with coal dust from head to toe.

Coal miners' work clothes were something to behold. Usually torn at the sleeves and knees, they were shabby and often greasy. I believe my father had two sets of work clothes. Dad had a Sunday ritual after we got electricity. He had his own sewing box with thread and needles. Early in the evening he turned on the radio for news of the Depression and listened while patching his torn work clothes. My mother had already scrubbed and washed them with a scrub brush. Trying to get Dad's work clothes clean was just as hard on them as him wearing them.

Laundering was the most time-consuming chore any woman had to endure. Mother put our dirty clothes into large washtubs overnight with soap and water to soak. The next day she, or my older sisters, scrubbed them on rub boards, rinsed them, wrung them out by hand, and hung them outside to dry. During the winter months, the clothes froze. The solid clothes looked like people leaning away from the wind. Too heavy for the pins, they flipped off the line and lay on the ground like sticks of wood. Then my mother had to drag them inside and lay them across racks behind our Burnside coal heater to thaw. Sometimes it took another day before she could iron the clothes with a smoothing iron that she heated on the kitchen cookstove. She ironed every piece of clothing so none of us looked wrinkled or messy. Laundry and ironing went on day after day.

Each night my mother made dough for my father's biscuits. He ate them every morning for breakfast and carried some in his lunch pail. She must have made thousands of biscuits in her lifetime. She was up before daybreak every work day to fix my father's breakfast and start him off to work at the mine. He stoked the coal fires and packed his own lunch bucket. Since our only refrigeration was a small icebox, Mother had to call the company store almost daily to order milk, eggs, or some other cooking essential. Every afternoon around 4:00 the delivery truck brought the groceries around to homes with "order" signs in the window. "Come and get it!" rang out through the neighborhood.

Sunday mornings my mother cooked a huge breakfast and started preparing for an outstanding evening meal. Early Sunday mornings the kitchen swarmed with activity and laughter. Mouth-watering aromas of breads baking, meats simmering in rich onion gravies and sauces, and vegetables steaming brought me downstairs to get into trouble. I tried to pick and snatch what I could until one of my sisters shooed me away with "Kitchens are for women. Get out!"

Though the girls had to work to help Mom and we boys mostly played, Sunday was still the family day of the week. Delicious meals, church, games, and family activities filled our Sundays. That day of the week seemed to give everyone enough refueling of energy to start over with work and chores on Monday. I know it was the day Mom smiled the most, though she worked in the kitchen for hours.

My mother never worked outside the home because she always had family to care for and household chores to face. I loved and appreciated the things my mother did for us. I especially admired the devoted love she had for each one of us. She nursed and comforted when any of us had a cold, earache, toothache, or just didn't feel well. She was always on the spot. My mother was the greatest woman who ever lived. I called her "my miracle mom."

My father was a hardworking man and a good family provider. For fifty years he worked seven to fourteen hours in the mines every day he was able to work. The Grant Town mine workday was twelve to fourteen hours in the early 1930s.

Even with both men and women working so hard, no one had an abundance of anything during these hard times. Neighbors were friendly and borrowed from one another to make ends meet. Mothers borrowed salt, sugar, flour, onions, potatoes, or whatever they needed. Fathers shared tools for household repairs and gardening. The men banded together at harvest time.

Every spring in Grays Flats my father planted a large garden to keep food on the table for our growing family. We actually had three vegetable gardens. Two were in a level area near the house. A nearby mountain spring made watering them easy. The corn did better up the hill behind the house. Some folks planted their cornfields nearly a mile back in the hills. During the summer months children worked in the gardens and the cornfields, weeding and hoeing. I swatted flies and sweated hours of my childhood away battling every kind of weed known to man.

Boys also got up early to go pick berries and apples for mothers to can for winter. No one told us to do these chores. We watched the bushes and trees until the fruits ripened to sweetness and then gathered them home to help feed the family. Besides these tasks, boys fed hogs and chickens, cut wood, and piled coal up for winter. Girls made beds, washed dishes, and helped with laundry. They also cleaned the kerosene lamp globes and trimmed the wicks. As soon as my sisters were old enough, they learned to wash dishes and bake cookies. They learned to bake cakes and fruit pies and, later, to cook a full meal. Also, my sisters ironed shirts as good as any professional laundry.

Dad kept four or five large hogs for butchering in the fall. Hogs have a strong manure smell one doesn't forget. The hog pens stood fairly close to the house because the farther away from the house they were, the farther you had to carry slop and corn to them. Butchering time, a few days before Thanksgiving, was exciting to us kids. Most of the boys played hooky from school to watch.

When the piglets were born, we brothers each adopted one as our own and named it. Each summer I enjoyed watching mine grow and put on weight. We poured buckets and buckets of corn to fatten them up. Watching our father bring "Sunny" or "Pokey" down to slaughter made me sad. The sight of the hogs going to their death made me think of the Bible's sacrificial lambs.

Three or four miners got together and butchered five or six hogs at a time. The blood and mess made my stomach turn over, but I marveled at how fast and skillfully they worked. The men gave fresh meat to the widows and elderly and the retired miners in the community. That kind of giving and sharing helped to make the residents of Grays Flats a close-knit group of people who genuinely cared about one another. To me, it was a great place to grow up. Scrabbling to survive during hard times played a major part in growing up there.

Most miners raised chickens for meat and eggs. Some even had cows for milk and butter. Nature provided additional meat and fish. During hunting season coal miners who could afford guns hunted wild game. The men in our family fished year round, and all species of freshwater fish came to our table. I saw men and boys standing next to Paw Paw Creek in all kinds of weather, some with just a stick and a string, trying to hook a few fish for dinner.

Living off the land and the fruits of our own labor saved us from the destitution that lay just around the corner. My father took charge of our daily survival in two important ways. He delegated all the chores that he didn't have time for to us children. And he went down into that mine every day. I admired him so much for taking care of us. Though he and I weren't affectionate (he left that to my loving mother), one way I stayed close to him was meeting him after work at the mine and walking him home. Those trips were never boring. ■

CHAPTER THREE

Grant Town in the 1930s

When I was nine years old, I could walk fast enough to get into the heart of Grant Town within fifteen minutes. The tremendous hill climb near my house slowed me down a bit. I never got tired of the bustling sights and sounds of horses, wagons, and automobiles. I enjoyed watching the people hurrying about their business. From the summer I turned five, my mom trusted me to go straight to the mine to meet my dad. She didn't have to warn me to stay out of trouble.

A lone, skinny little black boy didn't attract any attention, except from one group of contrary white boys.

"Hey, where you going, boy?"

Ignore them. Keep moving.

"Hey, I asked, 'where you going, boy?'"

"None of your business," I grunted, glaring at the big mouth. Keep moving. Look ahead.

"None of my business, huh? Then you'd better just take your business to the other side of my street.

You hear me, boy?"

"Not today." I left that promise open, that someday I might do what he demanded and cross over to the far side. I never did. I kept walking, looking straight ahead. For some reason, I felt fearless when I was alone. No bully-boy got inside that armor and stung me. My sights were on the road ahead and seeing my dad.

If I had a nickel, I'd stop at the pop factory for a chocolate soda, a delicious new invention. The guy that ran the pop factory had a barn on his property where the local undertaker kept his hearse carriage. They stabled the coal-black horses that pulled the hearse in that barn, too. When I was older and more ornery, I scared my little brothers by saying, "I'll take you to see the horses." They knew what I meant. Death rode behind those horses, and they didn't want any part of that.

Next to the Grant Town mine, tiny one-family company houses crowded the long road we called Black Bottom. The tracks ran behind the houses on one side. With the railroad and the mine close by, the area was coal-dust covered and noisy. Seventy to eighty black children, my friends from school, played in the yards and on the street.

"Hey, Bobby, how you doin'?"

"Great! How you doin'?"

"Going to meet your daddy again?"

"Yeah. Going to meet my daddy. Come over to the playground Saturday, if you can."

"We'll try. If not, see you Sunday at the baseball game."

Seeing my friends, even for a minute, put me in a great mood. Because their parents had no big yards for gardens and no place to plant corn, these kids had a more carefree summer than I did. I envied them for that, but those poor kids had to walk a mile to school out my way through the cold winter. I considered myself lucky that our school was right across from my house.

Next stop, the mine! The rickety wire cage and elevator shaft stood across from the Koppers Coal Company store. I crossed the single-lane iron bridge to the mine, parked myself on the steps to the store, and watched for my father to come up on the cage. I always recognized him. Even though everybody was black from head to toe, I knew my dad.

Sometimes he didn't come up at 5:00 and I'd worry myself. *Is Dad hurt inside that mine?* Then I'd walk home alone and wait and worry. Later in the evening, between 7:00 and 8:30, Dad would come home, cold and hungry.

After he took a bath, I'd rub his back with liniment if he was achy. When he did get off work on time, we'd play a game. I'd pry his lunch bucket from his hand and carry it as my own, dying to know if there was anything left. After a few steps, he'd eye me sideways and say, "Bobby, you don't fool me. Go on, look inside." I'd pop the top off the cold, dusty box to peer inside. Occasionally a biscuit hid in a corner, but usually the box was empty. When it was, I'd flash him a big grin, and he'd throw his head back with a loud laugh. Then he'd wipe his smile away and say seriously, "Bobby, would you want to stop at the Grille for a cookie?" My answer was always a resounding "Yes!"

I pictured that delicious cookie waiting for me as we strolled toward Grant Town's busy Main Street. The road spilled over with work-worn coal miners and horses. I always took notice of the activities surrounding three special buildings. Two were large boardinghouses for single men and the other was the company-owned Grille. Vi's boardinghouse stood close to the mine entrance. She earned extra money on Sundays by selling barbecue and sandwiches from her front door. People rumored that the coal-company police tolerated the gambling den in her basement as long as no one spilled blood.

The Grille and the larger boardinghouse sat on top of the hill in the middle of town. The Grille was a favorite gathering place for everyone and gave me a window to a different world. What a place! The sweet odor of stale beer and tobacco seeped out from the ceilings, walls, and floors and took my breath away each time I stepped inside. On the main floor were the soda fountain and snack place, where friendly clerks sold candy, ice cream, and other tasty delights. My cookie heaven. In the dim, smoky light beyond the soda fountain, I could see the bar and pool tables for whites. I knew blacks had a separate bar in the back room, but the only clue was music and laughter coming through a doorway.

This was the only stop my dad made on our walks home. He'd wait outside until I appeared, sucking on a cookie. Then we'd go on home after he'd checked to see if the Red Cross Distribution Center had a sign posted. The arrival date for a government-issue shipment caught every miner's attention.

The Red Cross Center occupied one end of the larger boardinghouse across the street from the Grille. Many men lived in this fine two-story white house which had a picket fence guarding the yard. The federal government issued food supplies four times a year to miners with families. When I passed by the center, I imagined all that free food stacked to the ceiling. At the announced times I went to the center with my father and two older brothers to pick up flour, prunes, cornmeal, dried beans, rice, and lard. Never any meat—too precious to give away. The other food helped stretch meals for our big family.

For several years in a row, we received putrid-looking green canvas shoes with black soles. We grumbled under our breath when we saw them in the doorway. We had to save them for Sunday school. For weeks of Sundays, we looked as if we wore green bags on our feet. They were dog-ugly, and none of us liked them. I hid mine under our bed every chance I got to avoid wearing them.

We put the free food and supplies in gunny sacks or used our home-made sleds or wagons to pull them home. If somebody in the crowd dropped a package, a cry went up. "It's mine! I dropped it!" Then a heated reply. "Oh yeah? How can you tell? Besides, you dropped it, you lost it!" Inevitably, someone threw a punch. A free-for-all was not unusual. To avoid this nonsense, we guarded our haul carefully. My brothers and I pulled, and Dad walked behind to scoop up any bags that slid to the road. No one argued with him.

Since we were a big family, we got two twenty-five-pound bags of flour. The flour came packaged in calico feed sacks. Mom saved every one of these muslin flour bags and gathered them from friends, neighbors, and church women. Then she washed and bleached them out to make dresses, petticoats, and shirts. She also made nightshirts and gowns for all of us. My brothers and I felt ashamed to wear the flowered, girlie prints to bed, but we did. We preferred long underwear, but each of us only had one set.

When Mom had enough extras, she got two or three friends together and had quilting parties, usually during the winter months. Bill and I, her furniture movers, cleared out the living room and helped set up those splintered old wooden quilting frames. Did those women ever quilt and gossip! We put our ears to the door to hear the news. Occasionally, they whispered that some young girl in the neighborhood got "spoiled." I didn't understand what spoiled had to do with the girl's stomach growing. My brother told me they meant the girl was pregnant. After that, the word spoiled seemed so silly that I had to laugh any time I heard it. Sacks that once held flour and beans became quilts, bedspreads, and clothing. Nothing got thrown away. We used and reused everything from the government issue.

As my dad checked for the distribution sign on our walks through town, I looked to see what movie was playing upstairs at the Grille. Movies gave us an escape into the fantastic world outside the coal camp. In the theater whites sat on one side and blacks sat on the other.

Black and white. White and black. The only thing I was aware of as a very young child was that some people had white skin and some people had black skin. Mine was black. I began to sense other physical differences at about four years of age. I noticed my white friends had blue eyes with brown or blond hair, and I had dark eyes and black, kinky hair.

Growing up, I knew I would go to the black school near my house, following my older brothers and sisters. When I was finally old enough to go, I began to realize that I *had* to go to the black school. Why could black kids play with white kids after school or on weekends, but we couldn't go to school together? Why was there a black school and a white school? None of it made any sense to me.

When we went to the company store, or church, or to the Grille, we passed by the white kids' school in town. Theirs was a big two-story brick structure, built solidly with many pieces of playground equipment. Inside, they had radiator heat, water fountains and sinks, and electric lights. Our school had neither electricity nor running water. We had coal stoves, one outside toilet, and gravel for a playground. We did have one see-saw and one swing. Black kids always played on the black playground. We were forbidden to play with white kids on the white school playground, after school or in the summer.

"Their playground is much better than ours. And their school is, too. It isn't fair!" That was the first open expression of the injustice I felt.

"Coloreds and whites are kept separated."

"Why?"

No answer but a murmured "Just because that's the way it is. You accept it, young man, or it will eat you up."

That's what our parents taught us to do—accept racial prejudice as normal and the segregation of blacks and whites as "the way it is." My mother, with her religious beliefs, worked hard to keep the word "hate" from our hearts and minds. She taught the Golden Rule every day. She taught us that we were each very special—loved by family and loved by God.

With me, she succeeded. "Hate" is not in my vocabulary. I can honestly say that I never hated anyone. I sometimes felt resentment for things said or done to me, but I never let anyone see my resentment, and I rarely spoke of it. I'm not a racist. As a child, and later as a man, if anyone treated me badly because of my skin color, I either ignored it or faced it down—boy to boy or man to man. I knew from a young age that life was too precious to carry around the burden of hatred and bitterness, so I chose not to do it.

Armed with the love of my family, I accepted segregation. We all did. Black children hiked back and forth from Black Bottom past the white school each day. That was in the 1930s, twenty years before the Supreme Court ruled that all public schools had to integrate. Students at our school brought their lunches in brown paper bags. Very few kids had fruit. Many unfortunates never had any lunch at all. They stood around and begged at lunch time.

I could see our two black schools from my upstairs bedroom window. A small, unpainted one-room school housed the first three grades, plus pre-primer grade, later called kindergarten. Another long building housed fourth through sixth grades on one end. Across a thin partition were seventh and eight grades. The teachers had their hands full, but they dedicated themselves to us. Gas mantel lamps provided light, and coal stoves kept us warm. The school board hired janitors to sweep and dust each evening, but during the class day teachers had to appoint one of the older boys to bring in coal.

After finishing the eighth grade, we could ride the school bus to the new Dunbar School in Fairmont, the only black pre-primer through twelfth grade school in the whole county. The Marion County school buses brought black students to Dunbar School from all the surrounding camps: Grant Town, Idamay, Carolina, Barrackville, Monongah, and Rivesville. Most mornings I heard the older kids scrambling down from Inktom Hill through our yard to meet the bus.

The arrangement for high school was very easy for our family because the bus stopped on the road near our house. Some high school students had to walk long distances from small coal camps because the bus wouldn't stop unless there were lots of kids. If a kid, black or white, lived in a company house, he walked to a central stop, often miles away. If the parents owned the home, the bus stopped right in front. Some coal miners' kids had to quit after eighth grade because they couldn't possibly walk so far to get a bus to their high school.

All black children in our area attending pre-primer through eighth grade had to walk to the Grays Flats' school. There were no buses for them. These rules and policies forced black people with children to live very close to the mining towns or else give up their children's education.

"They're dumping slate!" was a great call to action in our neighborhood. To keep the narrow roads in shape for cars to travel during the winter months, the coal company spread slate along the berms. Good lump coal got tangled up in the truck loads being dumped. Boys of all ages and sizes, black and white, piled coal in personal stockpiles to haul in gunny sacks to their own coal bins. I guarded our stockpile from other boys' sticky fingers while my brother Bill gathered coal. If we found lots of coal, we used our wagon or homemade sled to haul the load home.

Dumping slate along the road may appear to be a gift of free coal, but it was strictly business. Miners with automobiles couldn't get to work to dig coal if a road washed out. Furthermore, it was a good way to get rid of waste. The company didn't do anything unless it benefited the company.

Getting the load of coal out of the ground was the top priority of any coal company. From day one, all they cared about was a car of coal. They didn't care how it came out of the ground as long as it kept coming faster and faster. After a car of coal, their main concern was for the horses in the mine. Companies cared more about the horses than the men. Many men, with a house full of children, got fired because a horse broke its leg and had to be shot. If a company lost a horse to injury or death, it had to buy and train a new one. If a man got hurt or killed, there was always another man to take his place.

My father was one of those men treated little better than a slave. The Grant Town mine was neither better nor worse than any other mine in the West Virginia coalfields. I'm glad he lived through it, but I don't know how he did. ■

CHAPTER FOUR

Grant Town Mine, Company Power, and the UMW

The Grant Town mine was a huge coal mining operation. At one time, a ten-foot-high electric fence, topped with barbed wire, surrounded the Grant Town mine and parts of Grant Town. Men seeking work registered for temporary permits to see the mine superintendent. Armed guards, carrying loaded shotguns, made visitors to the coal camp sign up for thirty-day permits. Visitors whose permits expired faced arrest or a brusque escort to the gate.

By the late 1920s, the company had removed the fence, but "yellow dogs," the mine guards, roamed the area on horseback for years after that. Yellow dogs were mean-spirited policemen with the absolute power of judge, jury, and executioner. Their presence commanded respect, fear, and contempt. They also operated a brilliant spotlight that lit up the skies and swept a circle from dusk to dawn to guard the mine and search out the enemy.

The enemy was the United Mine Workers of America, the UMW. Coal miners became the enemy, too. Many men, who worked for almost nothing, wanted to learn about the union and join the UMW. The coal company used the yellow-dog bullies to keep the union down as long as possible. The term "yellow dog," meaning a worthless or mongrel thing, comes from the yellow-dog contract that companies forced miners to sign, saying they wouldn't join the union. Yellow dogs were the enforcers of that contract. In the cemetery at Grant Town, one tombstone reads "Killed by mine guard—1924." The man was likely in the wrong place at the wrong time.

The white camp had a cement wall around part of it that was off limits. My friend sat on the wall, watching his white friends play marbles. A yellow dog rode up and demanded he get off the wall. Being fearless, my friend argued. He received a smack across the face with a billy club to knock him off. The terror tactic worked. My friend didn't make that mistake again, and he carried the scar for as long as he lived.

At the mine office the yellow dogs guarded the grass as if it was a seam of prime coal. If anyone stepped on the grass, the "grass police" grabbed him and shoved him away with a stern warning. Everyone knew that mine foremen verbally and physically abused their employees. These company men, also called yellow dogs, were specially trained to drive the miners to the edge, almost like slaves.

I watched my dad go to work day after day and come home night after night, thoroughly exhausted. He did it for me, for us. He rarely discussed his work with me, but I overheard conversations about the grueling hard work, danger, and fast pace the men endured. "Get the coal out. Move it! Move it! Safety be damned! Get the coal out!" Because he couldn't afford an automobile, my father walked to work at 5:00 A.M. in good weather and bad. He came home soaked with sweat year round, and in winter his boots were often packed with ice.

When Paw Paw Creek overflowed its banks after a heavy rain or snow melt, my dad had to wade the bitter cold river of water before he climbed the hill into Grant Town. Going underground five hundred feet to begin a twelve to sixteen hour workday with wet shoes and pants would make any man want to give up, but Dad didn't. Many times he was too exhausted to eat supper. I watched him collapse behind our coal stove, still dressed in his work clothes. It hurt to see him suffer.

In the morning I heard the yellow dogs outside banging on the front door with their billy clubs, yelling, "Hey, Jim! Time to go to work!" My mom had to yell back "He's up!" to make them stop. I can still hear the black horses snorting. They were blowing steam, snorting, and neighing at 4:30 every morning.

Ninety-five percent of all coal miners rented company houses, like ours, so they had to work or lose everything. If a miner didn't go to work, the yellow dogs put his family out of their home. They threw the furniture and all the family's personal belongings onto the street. I saw it many times and felt pity, and the underlying fear that we could be next.

There were twenty-two hundred men on the company payroll: eighteen hundred underground and four hundred above ground. In those days, miners handled the coal over and over to get it out of the ground and onto the coal cars. All the young boys at Grant Town knew exactly what their fathers did in the mine and had pride that their dad was a fearless coal miner.

Those underground worked as timbermen, trackmen, coal loaders, drivers, or hoist operators. Their job titles tell exactly what task they performed. Timbermen installed four-by-eight wooden posts to hold up the ceiling or roof. Trackmen dug level paths and laid metal tracks in the mine tunnels, called "headings." Loaders loaded coal and got paid by the ton. Drivers used horses to haul coal cars along the tracks to the underground dumping point. Other men shoveled the coal onto the elevators, or hoists. Hoist operators brought it up to the surface. Of all these jobs, I thought my dad's sounded the most interesting because he got to work with horses.

Above ground the coal cleaners, slate pickers, and sorters washed, separated coal from slate, and sorted it by size. The men worked on the coal as it rumbled past them on conveyor belts that eventually climbed high above the ground and dumped the coal into the tipple, a huge storage bin. From the tipple the coal tumbled down to fill railroad coal cars.

The whole operation had one main boss, the superintendent. The Grant Town mine superintendent was a tall, raw-boned German man with little or no college education. Dad said he had the memory of a thousand elephants. He was "the Man" who did all the hiring and firing. After a few days he could call a new employee by his first name, or his check number, most often by both. The superintendent also knew each horse by name. Since there were as many as 250 horses owned by the company at one time, this was remarkable. Horses were indispensable, and they received more attention and recognition than any of the miners. Under the superintendent were one or two assistant superintendents, a general mine foreman, two to twelve section foremen, and day-, evening-, and night-shift foremen.

About five hundred of the twenty-two hundred miners were black men. Blacks did the meager-paying, backbreaking jobs, often getting paid less wages than their white fellow employees doing the same job. The hardest jobs were timbering, laying railroad track on the "bottom," a mining term for the floor, and shoveling mud and water out of ditches. I could always spot men with these jobs because their clothes were stiff with sweat and dried mud. Black miners often worked in the worst areas of the mine. These included headings with low ceilings or water and areas with bad air that needed cleared and ventilated often, causing dead time, or time without pay.

Miners made the most money loading coal if nature didn't interfere. When the roof fell or water seeped into his work area, a loader had to work two to four days clearing out tons of rock or draining water. Since the loader wasn't loading coal, he was on dead time until he cleared his area. Then he had to wait until the timbermen supported the roof with posts and the shift boss inspected the work area and declared it safe. Mom got real quiet any time Dad mentioned a roof fall. Roof falls were common, and they maimed and killed.

The most dangerous mining process was blasting, or "shooting the coal." Many men who used explosives were inexperienced. No one could be in that part of the mine when they blasted, and Dad had to keep the horses calm. Every miner who loaded coal had to shoot it down first. He had to "undercut" the coal face, or dig out a wide cut next to the bottom with a pick. Then, with a chest auger, he drilled a long hole into the coal face. He put just the right amount of explosive powder into the hole and tamped it in. Next, he poked a hole in the powder and stuck a blasting cap inside. The cap was an explosive that looked like a rifle cartridge attached to a long cord. Then the miner came back from the wall, yelled, "Fire in the hole!" and lit the cord. The blast shook the earth and spewed coal dust as it loosened and brought down a ton or so of coal.

After chipping down chunks from the wall and smashing up the huge shelves of coal that fell, the loader shoveled the coal into a two-ton car. When he finished loading the car, the miner hung his numbered tag on its side to get credit on his paycheck. A horse and driver pulled in an empty car. Then they pulled the full car to the coal dump, where miners shoveled the coal onto the cage to be hoisted to the surface. The weighman, a company man, marked down the miner's tag number and the weight of the coal. My dad had to be careful those tags didn't get lost as he drove the horses to the dump.

Loaders normally worked twelve hours, but they had to clear any amount of coal shot down before leaving for the day. This rule forced loaders into extra hours if they shot down a big load. Disregarding the clock, they finished or faced dismissal. If there was no dead time, a good miner could shoot down and load six to ten tons of coal in a day. "Sixteen Tons" (from the song) is a myth, unless he "double-backed," or worked two shifts.

In the 1920s loaders earned only 19 cents a ton, or between $1.00 and $2.00 a day. During the mid-1930s the rate went up to 40 cents a ton, paying a loader $2.40 to $4.00 a day. Some mines paid more to discourage union organization. Although loaders made the most money, few miners in other jobs received even $30.00, before deductions, for two weeks' pay. That's less than $30.00 for twelve days, or 130 to 190 hours of backbreaking work. My father earned a straight amount each day as a driver, starting around $2.00. Slowly his pay increased a dollar or two to $5.00 a day in the late 1930s. Occasionally he loaded coal.

Since Grant Town was a deep-shaft mine that used an elevator with a steel cage, the horses lived underground. Even with electricity in the mine, the lighting was poor and the animals went slowly blind. If they survived this hard life and came up for retirement, the exposure to daylight permanently blinded them.

Most people believed mine horses were merely dumb animals. Dad disagreed, claiming he knew that horses could count. When rushed, a driver might try to add a fourth car to the normal three-car load (six tons). The driver declared his horse heard the fourth coupling pin drop, and it refused to move. The horse stood absolutely motionless until it heard the fourth car being uncoupled. Only then would the animal begin to pull his load along the track. My dad coaxed and clicked at his horses constantly, straining his voice. He said as long as he kept them safe and treated them with respect, they worked hard for him.

In mines with horses or mules living underground, the rodent population grew until it was out of control. Nests of mice and rats came in with hay and grain. They soon multiplied until there were thousands trying to find food. Rats were a big problem at the Grant Town mine. I heard that some rats there were so big they could open a lunch bucket with their tails. Miners tolerated rats for one reason. They predicted danger. When rats scurried away from an area of the mine, the men knew they were in bad air or a roof fall was coming.

While loaders blasted and shoveled coal, my father harnessed his horses and lined up empty cars to replace the full ones. He was good at his job. On payday several loaders gave him tips, sometimes a whole dollar, for keeping them supplied with empty cars. One loader from Grant Town told me, "Your dad is quite a driver. He never makes me wait for an empty. Yes, sir. He is fast!"

After a long day of driving the horses, my dad still had to clean up after them, bed them down, and feed them. That's why his day was so long. His job security depended on the surefootedness of his horses and his skill to keep them safe. If a horse got hurt during a shift, the driver received a severe reprimand and three or four days' suspension without pay. If the horse was killed or broke its leg and had to be killed, the driver got fired. Dad had to watch every step the animals took in the mine, and the mental stress and strain of the job, though different from loading coal, was exhausting.

Drivers had one big advantage over coal loaders: no work expenses. Loaders had to buy the auger drill, picks, axes, shovels, powder, and blasting caps. I don't know what a stick of powder cost, but they had to buy ten to twelve sticks of powder at a time. For a beginning loader, the tool costs were deducted at five dollars a payday until paid for, but the company still owned the tools. If a miner quit or got fired, he had to return the tools. Materials and supply costs, like auger bits, powder, and caps, went on and on.

Miners had other expenses besides tools and supplies. Any man who used tools paid a blacksmith's fee of fifty cents every payday for sharpening and repairs. The company also deducted one dollar each month from every employee for the doctor's services. In our big family someone was often sick or injured, so one dollar was a bargain for our medical care.

Prior to the invention of battery lamps and hard hats supplied by mining companies, the men underground used old-fashioned carbide lamps. Miners wore canvas caps and attached the carbide lamps to a metal clip on the front. They had to buy their own lamp and, every two weeks, underground miners had to buy a pound of carbide from the company to light their lamps. After work, some evenings, I stood in line with my dad while he bought carbide, the only work item besides clothes that he had to get at the company store.

Deductions for work items cut some miners' pay in half. Policies forcing men to buy items the company should have supplied plus poor wages were only two ways the company took advantage. Other ways involved unmasked theft. So much was stolen from the poor coal miner.

One example of stealing was weighing. The weighman, who checked off each tagged car as it left the mine, was always a company man until the unions forced a change. If the weighman was dishonest, he could say the load was short or he'd simply give the credit to a buddy. My dad knew of these abuses but had to keep his mouth shut.

If the weighman, or the section boss, found small bits of rock or slate in the car, it was "red checked" or "red tagged." The weighman hung one red tag on the coal car and one on the loader's cap to humiliate him. The company took the car away, which meant no pay for shooting down and loading two tons of coal. The next day that miner had to go into the office and get a tongue lashing from either the general mine foreman or superintendent. Even though my dad was not a loader, he fought hard, along with the union, to get rid of the company weighman and replace him with a more fair-minded union man. He said red tagging was a disgrace and out and out theft.

Another way all coal companies stole from the miner was through the company store. Once hired, a miner had to buy work clothes, tools, and supplies at the company store so he started his job already in debt. The store also sold everything a family needed to maintain a household. The products sold were high quality and expensive. After a few months of buying essentials, especially for a large family, he spiraled deeply into debt. The convenient delivery system was free, but groceries and household items were so high priced, the company got the money anyway.

For me, the company store was a wonderful place to explore. Merchandise was spread out everywhere, displayed to entice me to buy. Everything was shiny and new and stacked high and wide. I loved to browse and wish, especially in the toy department.

Miners dealt in scrip. They were paid in cash, but to buy at the store, scrip was the preferred exchange. Because of this system, few employees spent their paycheck anywhere else but with the company. It was like bondage, really, because no one had much choice with such low wages. Company-made scrip was often fake coins and paper that looked like play money. We also had a card with numbers around the outside that clerks crossed out when we bought items or services from the store. The office issued metal scrip coins to deal at the store.

We called scrip "clacker." One day my pockets jingled with that tinny clacking sound, and my buddy teased me, saying, "You have a pocketful of clacker, don't you?"

"Yeah, no money. Just clacker."

"What do you mean? It's money. You can buy stuff with it at the store or the Grille. It's money."

"Nah, it isn't money," I said. "Not real money like nickels and dimes."

"Then give it to me, Bobby. I'll see if it spends like real money."

I said, "I'll just keep it" and walked away jingling the clacker in my deep pockets. I liked the sound and feel of having money, even though it wasn't real.

A miner with a large family often got a "snake" for pay instead of scrip. A snake was a squiggly line across the paycheck stub that told him he was in debt to the company. Besides the snake, the words "bal due," for balance due, and his debt amount appeared on the paycheck.

Enterprising persons set up exchanges where they traded scrip for cash at a 25 percent profit. Mary Coalbucket had an exchange next to the Grille. The miner gave her $10.00 in scrip and received $7.50 in cash. Miners did that just to get the cash because the company store made change in scrip only. The exchange was a racket, netting huge profits. The scrip system was a no-win deal for miners.

When they could get a little ahead of this system of payment, a few miners bought cigarettes at the store by the cartons, as many as they could get on the next payroll. Then they sold them for cash money to buy else-where or just to have a few real dollars, but those schemers still owed for the cigarettes. No one bettered the company on any deal.

I loved the company at Christmas time. In the spirit of the season, they gave each coal miner's child a gift. We received a box of hard candy, an apple, an orange, a bag of nuts, and maybe some chocolate drops. Most kids did not see those items all year long, so the Christmas treats caused great excitement. Hundreds of black and white children, including me, stood in a long line at the Grille for a few tidbits of food that disappeared in less than an hour. Many had their toes exposed to the cold, were unkempt, and wore barely enough clothing to keep warm. As I got older, I realized how pathetic this ritual was.

My mother pulled us through the bleak Christmas season with her enthusiasm over celebrating Christ's birthday. Every one of us kids had to participate in the church's special choirs and Christmas programs.

During the Depression people didn't waste money on frivolous things like toys and decorations. The tree and pine branches were our only decorations. We went to the woods and cut our tree and made our own ornaments for it out of paper or cloth. The ornaments had to be handled with great care and kept from year to year. We strung popcorn and hard berries for the tree also. Everything came from the company store, so my parents controlled the gift spending. At that time of the year, keeping eight to ten children clothed in sweaters and warm clothes was the top priority. Most kids in our community, regardless of age, received one toy. Pleased and grateful for that one toy, we didn't know how little we had. In our family, we shared our toys.

The climax of Christmas in Grays Flats was the big holiday meal on Christmas Day. As with most families, our thrill of the season was that greatly anticipated feast. Preparations went on for days. Though our parents saw that we never went hungry, that was one of the few days a year that we could eat and eat and eat. Mom made sure we felt blessed to have all that meat and bread on the table.

Coal miners continued struggling to make a decent living, but the company stayed one step ahead. A small raise? Prices went up at the store. Many believed the United Mine Workers union held the answer to a better life. My father believed this.

John L. Lewis, the president of the UMW, and his followers struggled to get miners across the country to unionize. The union worked to get better wages and insurance and better working conditions in the mines. At one time, the UMW had over 460,000 members. We learned about the UMW from the radio and from listening to Dad and his friends talk.

The Grant Town mine had voted in the union in 1918, but it grew very slowly. With every attempt to join, employees faced threats of losing their jobs. No matter how large or small the coal company, miners had to endure insults and physical threats. Strikes occurred as coal miners in the area slowly joined the UMW. By 1935 the union was strong enough to stand up for miners' rights. The union stopped the yellow dogs from banging on our houses early in the mornings. The pay rate per ton for loaders, and per day for other jobs, increased. Still, miners remained indebted to the company store.

During this time we started hearing "Mr. Roosevelt this" and "Mr. Roosevelt that." The new president, Franklin D. Roosevelt, came into office with what he called the New Deal. Our teachers taught us about the New Deal, which put many able-bodied men back to work. The president became hero and savior to the working man as his policies started to pull the country out of the Depression. His picture hung on the wall in my classroom. Along with the New Deal, Roosevelt started the Works Progress Administration, the WPA. They built roads, dams, buildings, sidewalks, walls, and so on. Even in my limited travels, I saw crews of men working in our own county. Radio newsmen talked on and on about eight million men getting back to work.

A New Deal law limited all workers to a forty-four-hour week and said workers had to be paid at least twelve dollars a week. Designed to force employers to hire whole new shifts of workers and help "put America back to work," it had the opposite effect in the coalfields. This law slashed miners' work hours by more than half and cut everyone's pay. Coal companies, including the one in Grant Town, knew they faced production losses if they obeyed the forty-four-hour week rule, so they encouraged miners to keep working long hours. Smaller, remote coal companies simply ignored the law. Large coal companies had already started bringing machines into their mines. Miners knew they would soon face massive layoffs. Those miners were willing to ignore the new laws, working long and hard to postpone the inevitable. Dad's union met more frequently, trying to find ways to save jobs. When the groups met at my house, they usually talked in low, secretive voices.

Grant Town's Local Union 4047 elected my father to two offices, recording secretary and financial secretary. They paid him thirty dollars a month. My dad was a strong advocate for miners' rights and worked hard for the UMW. He wrote letters to the national office, keeping them informed on local conditions. He also wrote letters for men who couldn't write. As the financial secretary, he collected the union dues, but I never saw any money.

My sisters taught my dad how to type on the old Underwood typewriter the UMW gave him. When I was ten, I stayed up late at night and helped my father. He paid me one dollar each time. While he typed letters to John L. Lewis, to the district, and to the national union headquarters in Washington, D.C., I placed each letter into the proper envelope. After imprinting the Local 4047 mechanical seal on the envelope, I closed and stamped each one. I loved helping my father and earning my own big money. Some might consider this work a chore, but to me, it was fun.

My family and I found other opportunities to have fun and to get into a little trouble. ■

CHAPTER FIVE

Family Stories

Those born to a large family know what growing up in a full house is like. Though noisy and busy, it can be great fun when everyone cares about each other. We did.

Our grandparents grew older and couldn't live alone, so they came to live with us. When the grandparents lived in, they had their own room. Children slept everywhere. Four in a bed was normal to us, two at the head and two at the bottom. We lived on top of one another, but we were happy.

All my brothers and sisters had unique personalities. Some were gentle. Others were feisty. Those close in age worked and played together. Most of the time I stuck with my next oldest brother, Bill. Thoughts of Bill and my wild sister Homerzella are crystal clear because their middle names were "Trouble." Also, since Barbara Jean was the youngest child, and a big surprise, we spoiled her and protected her the most.

Homerzella was the bombshell of all my sisters. She arrived in 1924, three years before me. Set in her ways, Homerzella was stubborn as hell and had a temper when riled. She was a chubby teenager. This gave her an inferiority complex tangled with a chip on her shoulder. Nevertheless, she treated all of us well, with a good-hearted and comical nature.

Every neighborhood had a bully who whipped all the boys his age or size. Our neighborhood had two in one family, my brother Bill and my sister Homerzella. She even took on older and bigger boys. She was a tomboy and totally fearless. Whatever we dared her to do, for our own entertainment, she succeeded in doing it with style and, usually, with injuries.

Homerzella destroyed a pair of girls' shoes every two or three weeks, running or skating on ice. This problem cost my dad too much money, so one year he found a solution. He used to buy my brothers and I sturdy leather brogan shoes to wear to school and to do chores around the house. They had a metal tip across the front, a metal horseshoe cleat on the heel, and they covered the ankles. One day Bill came home with a pair of brogans in a box. Homerzella asked, "Are they for you or Bobby?"

Bill took great delight in saying, "They're not for us. They're for you."

She howled, "I'm not wearing ugly old boys' shoes!" Then she cried and cried and swore she would never wear them outside the house. She did have to wear them, however, and it took her several months to destroy them. After she wore out that one pair of brogans, Homerzella tried to take better care of her shoes.

Homerzella wore a bull's-eye for trouble. Our mother warned her not to ride the brand-new bicycle my parents finally managed to buy for Bill and me. One day while Mom shopped and Bill and I worked in the cornfield, Homerzella slipped away from her chores and rode the bike. Bill found it, tucked away behind the house, with the left pedal snapped off and gone. Who did it? Homerzella.

She had to be where the action was and usually created it. During one snowy winter we boys built a homemade bobsled out of an old fourteen-foot ladder. We sawed the front prongs off to make it slide smoothly down the nearby sled run. The biggest and best slope was a steep three-hundred-foot grade with a small bridge to cross at the bottom. The bridge, made from old railroad ties, had no guardrails on either side. A gas line ran parallel with the bridge. This sled run was dangerous and off limits to the girls.

One night Homerzella schemed a way to ride our bobsled. She insisted on going for a fresh pail of water. Mother told her there was plenty of water inside for the night and that she was not to go to the pump. She went anyway. Homerzella filled the water pail, placed it on the back porch, and took off for the sled run. She charmed her way to the front of that sled with eight boys riding behind. Down the icy hill they sped, screaming and laughing. I watched as the sled missed the bridge, skidded across the gas pipe sideways, and upset into the stream. Who ended up with a large cut across the chest, requiring fourteen stitches? Homerzella.

Fearless to danger, she tested her limits often. Three miles from our home, between Rivesville and Grays Flats, a friendly black fellow had rented a place with a pond. In the dead of winter, for a small fee, this man let the black kids rent ice skates he'd accumulated over the years. We enjoyed starting out early in the evenings for the long walk to the ice pond. One night the older boys skated crack the whip. All players held hands, and the last person to join the fun got on the end of the whip. We laughed as we saw Homerzella scramble to take the last boy's hand. The group circled the pond up and down, back and forth, slinging the end of the whip. They threw Homerzella into one of the wooden booths sitting along the sides. Who ended up with a broken arm? Homerzella.

We kids all loved Homerzella and thoroughly enjoyed her shameless antics. We didn't, however, like to see her get hurt or to get blamed for everything that happened in the neighborhood. Whether she involved herself or not, fingers often pointed at Homerzella. To defend herself, or to hide the truth, she became an accomplished storyteller.

One Halloween night an event in the neighborhood caused quite a stir. The suspicion fell on Homerzella. Our neighbor had built a huge haystack across the street from our house. Whoever owned the vacant lot didn't care, but the neighbors didn't like the looks of it. We played in the hay and dragged it into the house so our mom hated it. That Halloween we boys got carried away with our pranks, as usual. We spread tar on the schoolhouse windows, strung toilet paper from the outside toilets, and let some air from automobile tires. We never slashed them or made them totally flat. Like every Halloween prank night, we went home and sat by our warm stove, laughing and telling the girls about our evil deeds. None of us would ever think to tell on each other. Then we settled down, listened to our favorite radio programs, and went to bed.

Someone noticed a bright light flickering in the windows. Before long, tall flames leaped from the haystack across the street. What a sight! The whole neighborhood turned out to watch it burn. No one ever admitted setting the fire, but our family and all the neighbors believed Homerzella did it. She denied having anything to do with it and got angry when the subject came around to her.

Forty years after that fire, I visited her in her beautiful home in Los Angeles. As we sat around the kitchen table one evening, I said, "Homerzella, I've been wondering about something for a long time, and I want you to tell me the truth. Did you set that haystack on fire?" After teasing me for awhile, she looked me straight in the eye to answer my question. "Of course I did. Who else had the guts to do something like that?" She amazed me, being so wild and free and courageous. Homerzella stood up to my dad, amazing in itself, and got away with incredible mischief. But like all of us, she grew up.

Brother Bill was born in 1926, two years before me. From the very beginning we were great pals, but being older and much larger than me, he had the upper hand. During my first summer as a toddler, I followed Bill wherever he went. In one way that turned out to be a good thing. Mom said that when I started walking, I was very bow-legged. Some of the women neighbors nagged her that a doctor should operate on my legs to straighten them. That summer Bill walked from house to house to find playmates, and I followed close behind. The boys left me to go and play on the hill near our house. I struggled to follow Bill and the boys up the hill, calling out his name. After a few weeks of climbing the hill to be with Bill, my leg muscles developed and began to straighten.

I admired my brother Bill. He was big and strong for his age and always protected me from bigger boys. He loved to fight. Since Bill was much stronger than I, he took control of all our chores in and around the home. He totally dominated my every move, whether it was working in the garden, planting or weeding, feeding the pigs, or getting in wood and coal during the cold winter months. Bill and I shared what few toys we had. Also, our father rewarded us for a job well done with fruit or candy, which we shared. Naturally, Bill demanded and received all the credit for the work.

He also enjoyed grabbing credit from me with the local women. In the Grays Flats mining camp, wives sat on their porches during warm spring and summer days, waiting for their husbands to return from work. Often Bill and I went out early mornings with some of the neighborhood boys to pick blackberries, apples, peaches, or anything edible for our moms to cook or preserve in jars. Mom made a delicious apple or blackberry cobbler every day for supper from the fresh or canned fruit. On our way home, as soon as we got close to the neighbors sitting on their porches, Bill emptied my goodies into his bucket. All the women congratulated him with claps or kisses. He told them that I ate mine in the woods. The first time he did this, I protested. Bill put his size between me and the women and shot me a glare that shut me up. I never spoke up after that. He did the same thing with fish. We fished in Paw Paw Creek for sunfish, or "sunnies," and catfish. Some days each of us had fifteen to twenty fish on a string. Bill took most of my fish off my string and added them to his so the women would praise him for all the fish he caught. Claps and kisses for Bill.

Since Bill was my protector, I rarely argued with him about the tricks he played at my expense. No matter what the situation, he topped me every time. Wrestling with me was his favorite sport. Being heavier, he always came out the winner and held that over me. He never tried to really hurt me, but my brother Bill bossed me in everything. His stubbornness and dominance over me cost me one terrible whipping.

Regardless of what plans we had, like going to a movie, my dad told us, "You boys make sure you feed those hogs before you leave." One week, Bill got fed up with this routine. We got about halfway to the pens, carrying a big bucket of corn, and he said, "We're not going up there and feed them hogs."

I said, "Man, Dad is going to get us."

He stopped and shook his head no.

"What are we going to do, Bill? We have to feed them!" I knew I shouldn't be arguing because he had set his jaw with determination.

Bill was firm about not feeding the hogs. "I'm tired from being in the cornfields and the gardens all day. We slopped them this morning so I'm not gonna give 'em this. We'll pour it out." And we did. We did that morning and evening four days in a row. I was scared of what might happen, but I kept my mouth shut. I knew not to cross him.

That Saturday evening I overhead my dad talking to my mom. "Esther, those pigs have been up there squealing for two or three nights. Are those boys feeding them like they should be?"

She answered, "They're supposed to be."

He came right back with, "Not supposed to be. Are they feeding them?"

Since he was getting hot about it, she told him, "Yes."

The next morning my dad went up and found our three pigs dead. They were good-sized, and Bill and I starved them to death. We killed our pigs.

My dad worked on me for an hour. Through it all, I heard my mom telling him over and over, "It's not Bobby's fault. You know he can't carry that bucket by himself."

Since Bill was too big and strong to whip, I got it all. I understood why my dad was so angry. I felt terrible about the pigs dying, and I'm sure Bill did too, but I was smack in the middle. I knew I had to take the punishment because my dad favored Bill, and that was okay with me. Bill was bigger than any boys we ran with, and he worked hard. When our mother prepared to punish Bill, my dad stopped her, saying, "Don't worry about it. Bill will be all right." They knew he'd never strike back. It wasn't that.

Bill's size and his high-spiritedness caused my dad to allow him to make mistakes. Everyone knew Bill wasn't evil. He was fun loving, ornery, stubborn, and bossy, but not evil. In the pig incident, if I'd told on Bill, he might have stopped protecting me. Since I couldn't help being feisty and scrappy with the boys, that would have been a punishment worse than a whipping. We stayed loyal to one another.

In any big family the youngest child usually holds a special place in the hearts of all. That is certainly true of my "baby" sister. The sixth girl and last child, Barbara Jean, came into the family in 1937. What a big shock to all of us! The timing was rough on my mom.

We took care of grandparents at home until they died because nursing homes were rare and expensive. During the years Mom raised us kids, she cared for my dad's grandmother and my dad's father, who was blind. She also cared for her own mother.

Christmas 1936 was a bad time for my mom. She lost her mother on December 16, and she was four months pregnant with Barbara Jean. I had just turned nine, and no one could explain to me why my mom stayed in her room day after day. She was grieving for her mother and about to have a brand-new baby, with eight children still at home. Mom just stayed in her room, grieving and worrying and praying.

The arrival of Barbara Jean the following spring was like a celebration of life. Mom pulled out of her depression and came back to her old self, much to everyone's relief. My parents were proud and happy with a new baby girl. Naturally we spoiled her from day one, showering her with lots of love, hugs, and kisses. She was the apple of my father's eye. After all, the last girl born to our family, Homerzella, was sixteen years old. All the family catered to Barbara Jean's slightest whims and wants, but she remained a lovable child.

When I was twelve and doing my own thing, hustling, a Christmas incident turned the house upside down. Barbara Jean was three at the time and loved dolls. Some company produced a nationally advertised black doll baby. Since it was a wonderful idea, and new to us, my mother wanted Barbara Jean to be one of the first little girls to have one. She went to all the department stores in Fairmont to find one, but most stores didn't know anything about this black doll. Mom worried herself to a frazzle looking for that doll.

On her last desperate day, she stopped at a prominent furniture store that carried toys during the Christmas season. After telling my mom that he didn't carry black dolls, the white male clerk made an outrageous suggestion. "Why not purchase a white doll and have it painted black?" Mom left in a huff, infuriated by his remark. When she got home, she described the episode to my father. I listened from the top of the stairs, waiting for the explosion sure to come. It did.

Dad was furious. "I'll tell you what I'm going to do! I'm going down there and demand an apology from the manager! They can't talk to you like that!"

She pleaded with him. "No! You can't! Please don't do that! You go down there and cause trouble, they might take away our credit. You worked so hard to get that. Let's just forget it. Besides, I don't think he had any idea he was insulting me. He didn't look mean or anything."

"Paint a white doll black! Of all the . . . Esther, you really think he thought it was a good idea?"

She was done. I could barely hear her final words, but I could hear and feel the pain in her voice. "I don't know. All I do know is I'm exhausted, and we have to go get that little girl a doll. And we have to do it today."

Barbara Jean didn't get a black doll that Christmas, but she received a "beautiful white one," as we all referred to it, to let our mom know we sympathized with her difficulty. My baby sister loved her doll and was too young to be aware of the storm that brewed behind our mom's frustration.

The doll incident was not the only time insensitive people affected our lives. When one of us suffered from a hurtful remark or a racial problem, we all supported that person. Since we grew up in a house full of love and respect, we helped each other whenever we could. As a family, we shared the hard times and miseries, but we took great pleasure in the good times.

One highlight of the good times is the lively picture of everyone crowded around the radio, our main source of entertainment. Before settling down to listen, we filled the room with laughter, then "Shhhh! Shhhh!"

All of us kids learned to tune the radio to our favorite shows. We always listened to *Amos 'n' Andy*. They were white men who imitated black people and black families. One man from the show, "Kingfish," was outrageous. I was almost a grown man before I knew he, too, was a white man. That amazed me. We listened to scary shows, *The Inner Sanctum* and *The Shadow*. Our favorite cowboy story was *The Lone Ranger*. Cowboy shows, comedies, and boxing were my personal favorites. Just like early television, everything that came over the radio was broadcast live in a studio or live as it happened.

One event left a lasting impression on me. On April 3, 1936, I listened to the execution of Bruno Hauptmann for the kidnapping and murder of the Lindbergh baby. We had to sit very close to the old radio. I thought I heard the current sparking. In a minute they pronounced him dead. Our mother didn't believe in capital punishment. After it was over, she said, "I don't know if they put the right man to death." The doubt she planted stayed in my mind. Was he the right man and, if so, was it right to kill him? Live broadcasts like that were exciting, but they stirred me up and made me uncomfortable.

Thoughts of listening to radio programs and events conjure up delicious smells. Our mother cut the skins off the hog fat and baked them in the oven. And sweet potatoes. She roasted sweet potatoes for our evening snacks. The warmth of the house and spicy aromas filling every corner of the kitchen and living room intensified our excitement. Anyone who had a leftover chore to do brought it into the living room, hoping to share the work. We helped each other with sewing, mending, laundry sorting, vegetable cleaning, and corn shelling while listening to the radio. It was an incredible time of sharing.

Some programs made us laugh so hard we couldn't hear the next joke. Others scared us so badly we didn't want to go to bed, but the boys hid their fears with brave denials. "No, it didn't scare me. Maybe you, baby, but not me."

Most other good times I shared with my family and friends involved sports, games, hustling, or an effort to make our endless chores more fun. ■

CHAPTER SIX

The Fun Side of Life

Summertime cloudbursts got my attention. I pressed my forehead against the living room window, uttered a deep miserable sigh, and moaned, "There goes the swimming hole again."

A voice in the room, usually Bill's, answered my misery. "Yeah. I guess we'll just have to make it deeper, won't we?"

That comment broke the gloom. We'd burst out laughing, get in a huddle, and start making plans. Even if we had to work at having fun, Paw Paw Creek was the place to be on a hot summer's day.

Hard rains washed everything down from Fairview and swept away our dam and makeshift diving board, a railroad-tie contraption. To bring back the swimming hole, the first thing we had to do was pull out all the big rocks, branches, and anything foreign in the pool. Then, without any thought to time, we replaced our diving board and dammed up the lower part with discarded railroad ties that lay along the tracks. I tried to help with this heavy work, but I was too small. Brother Bill was our commander-in-chief. Most of the fun came in designing a better diving board and scheming to make our pool ever deeper and deeper. Sometimes we got it to five feet. Definitely over my head. Then the next storm swept it away.

Most of us boys swam naked until the girls came by to steal a peek. Then we all exploded in dares and jeers and endless laughter. During their surprise visits we stooped down in the water until one boy, who never swam naked, went to gather our cut-off pants and bring them back. The girls screamed at us and tormented us, but no one bared his all!

When the water receded below our dam, my friends and I walked the creek banks with rolled-up pant legs searching for pieces of junk. Metal buckets, lids, and pans washed down from homes upstream all the time. We also found children's toys, balls, scraps of metal, and the best treasure, automobile wheel covers. I dragged my junk home, stored it in my yard, and waited for Saturday morning.

An old Italian fellow named Tony came through Grays Flats every Saturday morning with his horse and junk wagon. He looked at least seventy years old, and his ways tickled me. How that old horse and wagon stunk! Tony always stopped at our house first because my fine junk pile intrigued him. I anticipated a big payoff each week, but we had to bargain. The deal started the same every time we met. Tony climbed down from his old beat-up wagon and carefully evaluated my junk. He kicked or picked up every piece to examine it. Trying to read his face for a reaction, I spoke in a serious tone, "Tony, it's worth at least seventy-five cents."

He never met my price. Never. His reply was always the same: "No, no, Bobby. I'll give you thirty-five cents, and you load it while I eat my sandwich." I learned that thirty-five cents was generally his top price, regardless of what I had for sale. I think Tony enjoyed our arrangement because it was so predictable and went on summer after summer. Also I kept my eye out for aluminum and copper because he snatched that stuff right away. After he paid me, Tony climbed back on his wagon and actually ate in the midst of all that stench. As my stomach turned over, I tried to save back a few pieces for the next week. He knew me. Though he was at the front of the wagon and couldn't see me, he always hollered back, "I mean load all of it, Bobby!" He must have had a mirror on that old horse.

I accepted the thirty-five cents with gratitude. A movie cost ten cents. Bottles of pop and all candy bars cost a nickel. The candy bars were gigantic then. I'm sure the Baby Ruth was a quarter-pounder. Each week I stashed at least ten cents in a sock.

Tony never dealt in clothes. People didn't discard clothes during hard times, especially in big families. We handed them down until they were rags and then used the rags for cleaning until they disintegrated. We recycled everything out of necessity.

Our dad's old worn-out work boots gave us great protection from snakes. While picking fruit and blackberries, we stirred up many snakes, especially blacksnakes. One hot summer day Bill and I were almost home after picking our pails full of blackberries. Bill spotted an old decayed tree stump about two feet high and two feet wide. As he wrestled it up to his shoulder, he said, "This is perfect for the wood stove." We continued walking out of the woods and into Grays Flats. Near our back porch Bill threw the tree stump to the ground to break it apart. To our horror, a five-foot blacksnake slithered out from the broken pieces. I got the shivers thinking about Bill having that huge snake next to his face. We cornered it so it couldn't get away. Our yelling and jumping around drew a big crowd of neighbors to our yard. Everyone marveled at how big it was. Some men said it was the largest blacksnake they'd ever seen.

An old wives' tale circulated around the group that if a person built a fire around a snake, its legs came out, and it walked. Bill and I had heard that tale before and, with encouragement from the others, decided to put our snake to the test. We gathered wood and built a ring of fire, placing the snake in the middle. Our blacksnake did not sprout legs and walk. As we watched with hope for a genuine miracle, that poor snake burned to a crisp right before our eyes. What a horrible sight! It stayed with me. More important, I never again put my faith in old wives' tales that promised miracles. After that day, if anyone mentioned the word snake, we had to tell about the experiment and our crispy blacksnake.

Some days a snake story helped get us through the work. Once a month over the summer our father insisted we hoe the cornfield. For at least a week, he awakened us at 5:00 A.M., just before he left for work. Each day we had to hoe weeds until noon. In cool, cloudy weather, we worked all day. We goofed off and played in the cornfield quite a bit, but we also got a lot of work done.

At harvest time this cornfield gave us six wagonloads of feed for the hogs. Night after night in front of the radio we shucked and shelled the dried corn until blisters came. We could quit for a few nights until they healed, and then we had to shell again. The word cornfield makes me weary, thinking about that brutal work. The only thing worse than hoeing weeds was shelling corn.

During our tiresome hoeing chores, we took our breaks sitting at the edge of the field. From there we could watch the coal-mine waste buckets come up to the slate dump. The buckets carried about a ton each and ran on long cables for a quarter of a mile from the mine, up across the ball field, to the dump. All day and all night the screeching cable brought full buckets of waste up, dumped them, and carried the empty buckets back. I watched the smoke from the smoldering coal as it hung in the valleys or drifted on the breezes. The company sent water cars up to keep the fires down and contain the methane so it didn't explode. Sometimes the coal exploded anyway. Fascinated by the smoke and fires, some days I spent more time watching the dump than I did hoeing corn.

We were never bored. There was always something happening. The highlight of the summer was a fun-filled day in July. The black churches in Marion County sponsored a picnic at Morris Park in Fairmont. Every black kid in the county looked forward to that day, and some years over six hundred kids showed up at the park. Mothers packed lunches and hurried us along on the streetcar to get to the picnic before 9:00 A.M. to get good tables. Out-of-town relatives planned their visits around that special event. After every family fed their kids, the churches treated all of us to ice cream and pop. We looked forward to getting into Fairmont for the church picnic every summer.

Mostly we just stayed around home, but still, we weren't bored. In the afternoons we played in the creek or at the black school playground near our house. We climbed up and down the one seesaw and took turns on the one swing. Pitching horseshoes was popular, but we couldn't play that unless some boy who owned the horseshoes showed up to play. My favorites were hide and seek, kick the can, and mushball, a game similar to softball.

In the evenings we played "soakie." The name referred to the water-soaked ball we used. Even the girls played with us. If you got a hit, whoever got the ball tried to smack you with it as you ran the bases. Sort of like dodge ball with water. Some of the older boys threw the ball too hard at the girls to make them quit and go away, but we protected our sisters whenever we could. Homerzella had a good arm and stung the boys at every opportunity.

Another sport was stilt walking. We built our own stilts out of scrap wood. I wasn't very good at it, but I loved watching the other boys try to walk with stilts. The fun didn't stop until somebody broke a leg. That wasn't our goal, but it usually happened.

My brothers and the neighborhood boys taught me how to shoot marbles. What a great pastime! I always had marbles rattling around in my pockets. That game was a big deal to us, but I believe marble shooting is now a lost art. Any time I think of marbles, I can smell and taste Mom's buttery biscuits.

On Saturdays, before I ran down to the playground to shoot marbles with my friends, I sneaked into the kitchen and buttered and jellied several biscuits. Then I stuck them into my pocket with a piece of salt bacon. I took advantage of my mom's habit of setting a pan of biscuits next to the cookstove to keep them warm after breakfast. At the playground when I got hungry, I pretended to go to the outside toilet. Then I sneaked behind it to eat a biscuit so my friends didn't know I had them. When I came back, they said, "Bobby, where did you go?"

I acted disgusted and said, "Where do you think? I went to the bathroom."

"No, no. You have grease around your mouth. You have biscuits!" With that, they threw me down, dug the biscuits out of my pocket, and helped themselves. I always forgot to wipe the butter off my mouth.

Sometimes my mom said, "Take the boys this tin of biscuits." She knew some of my friends never got a biscuit except from her. I do believe it's strange she never "caught" me sneaking them out of the house. She knew.

My friends, black and white, shared biscuits and double Popsicles. We took it for granted that we were the same, except for school, and we just accepted that part. We didn't have any racial problems.

One of my good buddies, Sam Jones, was an outstanding marble shooter. I lost more marbles to him than anyone else, but I kept trying to beat the best. I'd think, *This time I'll do it.* I never did. When I ran out of my own marbles, I stole Bill's from his secret hiding place under the porch. Sam won Bill's marbles away from me, too. This happened several times until Bill put a stop to it.

Bill threatened me. "You stole them. You lost them. Now you'd better get them back!"

I had to go into action. My plan was simple. I waited behind the schoolhouse door for Sam to come outside. Then I jumped on his shoulders and thumped him until he fell to the ground. He was a big guy. I wrestled with him until his pocketful of marbles rolled out and scattered all over the porch. Finally, I grabbed him by the collar and said, "If you don't give me Bill's marbles, I'll tell Bill, and he'll whip you tomorrow." I definitely used Bill's protection to my advantage.

Sam got very angry with me. "I won them fair, and now you take them back." He knew if he didn't give them up, he'd have to fight Bill and lose them anyway, so he gave me a handful to shut me up. He complained bitterly about this unfair practice of mine.

Sam Jones won the West Virginia Marble Championship in Charleston in 1937. They gave him fifty dollars and a brand-new bicycle. To us poor young black boys, Sam's victory was incredible. We couldn't believe one of our own could achieve anything so great. His determination and skill made him an even greater celebrity twenty years later.

My friend Sam grew up in Black Bottom. He never knew his real father, but he looked just like his mother. I remember her well. She hung around the beer gardens with different men. None of them was a family man like my father. Occasionally in the evenings, my dad went out and threw baseballs with Sam. I had no idea those hours with my father would make such an impression on his life. Years later Sam told me something I never knew. "Your dad used to take me out and show me how to throw a knuckler and a curve ball." The reason this fascinated me was that, when Sam Jones told me that story, he was a major league baseball pitcher. His career story had a slow start, but he rose to the top.

When we were young, Sam and I went to school together, but he was two years older. He left school and later got drafted into the service. Sam never played on any organized ball team in Grant Town or Fairmont. The first I knew of his connection with baseball, he was in Ebensburg, Pennsylvania, with a service team. Then it came out in the local paper that he was with the Cleveland Buckeyes, a Negro League baseball team. We'd lost touch, as childhood friends do, and this news came as a great surprise.

When the Cleveland Buckeyes came to Fairmont in the early 1950s, they promoted the game on the radio and with posters announcing that Sad Sam "Toothpick" Jones from Grant Town was their star pitcher. A white retired major league pitcher had the name Sad Sam Jones, so someone added "Toothpick" to our Sam's name. A tremendous crowd cheered him on at that exhibition game in the East-West Stadium. I was there and couldn't believe my eyes how good a pitcher he was.

Sam Jones joined the Chicago Cubs in 1955 at the age of 30. On May 12, 1955, he pitched a shutout against the Pittsburgh Pirates. In the ninth inning he struck out Dick Groat, Roberto Clemente, and Frank Thomas. He was the first black man to pitch a no-hitter in the major leagues. We were so proud of him. From 1951, when he went to the Cleveland Buckeyes, until 1964, when he ended his career with the Baltimore Orioles, he struck out 1,376 batters and pitched seventeen shutouts. Besides Chicago and Baltimore, he played for St. Louis, San Francisco, and Detroit.

Sam came back to visit when he could. He always drove a flashy, big Cadillac so we could see his car and know where he was "holding court." Every time I saw Sam, he gave me a big hug and bought me a drink. Sam was very generous with his money. Too generous sometimes.

One week when the Cubs were in Pittsburgh, Sam borrowed Ernie Banks's car and drove down to Fairmont Saturday evening before the big game on Sunday. After an evening of baseball stories and reminiscing over the bar, he wanted me to drive him to Pittsburgh and come back home. Then on Sunday I was to come to Pittsburgh and pick him up. I told him, "No, no. I don't want that responsibility." Ernie Banks's car? No way!

Sam left very late that night. The next day he pitched another winning game. The announcer kept saying, "Jones is hot today. I wonder what he did to get so hot?" I didn't understand how he did it.

Sam died of cancer in 1971 in Morgantown, West Virginia. He was only forty-six. Though I didn't see him in his later years, I enjoy thinking about our long friendship. He was my good friend, a famous and admired friend. For everyone in our area, especially blacks, he was our hero. He made it to the big time.

Hero worship of black athletes came slowly to us as kids because blacks were banned from all national team sports, with one exception. The Negro League baseball teams filled the gap, and were they ever popular! When I was between nine and eleven years old, the Negro League teams came into Grant Town on Sundays to play the black coal miners' teams. My dad played for Grant Town then. He loved baseball, followed the national leagues in the newspapers, and attended every exhibition game in the area. He had a great time playing against the Negro League teams.

Next to the road, near the present location of the Grant Town Power Plant, there was a huge ball field. Tall wooden bleachers, with a canopy, curved behind home plate. Low, uncovered bleachers extended out along both base lines. The Pittsburgh Crawfords, the Philadelphia Stars, the

Birmingham Black Barons, and the Baltimore Elite Giants came there to play. Some Sundays three thousand people watched the games.

Cars lined both sides of the road out of Grant Town when the Negro Leagues came in. The slate dump was located at the top of the hill, so layers of smoke hung over the ball field at times, and the cables screeched overhead, but that never stopped the game. Just like in the major leagues, the smell of hot dogs and the cheers and jeers of the fans filled the air. The clamor of the roaring crowds echoed through my mind for days.

During one game I watched Josh Gibson hit three consecutive home runs over the fence up the hill. What a thrill! He was a famous Negro League catcher and a heavy hitter. In 1936 he hit *eighty-four* home runs. And he was quite a showman. In the last innings of our games, he caught while sitting in a rocking chair. When a player in the field held up his arm, Josh fired that ball straight to him. Then somebody else held up his arm, and Josh hit the mark. From a rocking chair behind the plate. He was a tremendous crowd-pleaser and kept tongues wagging about his antics for weeks afterward.

A group of us boys started out the games in Willow Creek behind the bleachers. We waited until a pop foul flew back over the bleachers and landed in the creek. After we fished out enough baseballs to each have one, we went to the gate and got in free. The ticket taker always said, "Good job! You boys go sit anywhere you want to." We selected the best possible seats we could find.

Satchel Paige came to Grant Town. In the 1930s he was a "barnstormer," playing exhibition games with different teams each week. Satchel was an outstanding pitcher but didn't fit the image the owners wanted for the first black man to enter the major leagues. He was openly self-assured and a little too cocky, but also a great showman. He eventually settled in with the Kansas City Monarchs, hoping to get into the majors. Jackie Robinson, a young teammate of Satchel's on the Monarchs, went to the Brooklyn Dodgers in 1947 as the first black to break into all-white national sports. The next year, Satchel received an offer from the Cleveland Indians and joined the majors at the age of forty-six. He did very well, but it's possible he could have been one of the best all-time pitchers in major league baseball if race hadn't prevented him from being drafted in his younger years. Though I never saw Jackie Robinson play, I felt privileged to watch some of the other greats in the Negro League play baseball in Grant Town.

When my father returned from an exhibition game at Rosier Field in Fairmont one Saturday in 1938, he told me about one outstanding player. He said, "Bob, there's a young boy who came with that Black All-Stars' team today. He's going to be one heck of a catcher. The kid's only sixteen years old, but he sat back on his haunches and threw men out at second base. His name is Roy Campanella. They put him in the last couple innings. He is going to be a great catcher some day." When Campanella joined the Brooklyn Dodgers ten years later, one year after Jackie Robinson, my dad reminded me of that day. Dad was right. He was a great catcher!

Each time a black player joined a major league team, we celebrated the barriers of segregation coming down. If it happened in organized sports, the rest would follow in time. That was in the late 1940s and the early 1950s. Before that time, most black people, and especially young black men, had little interest in national sports, except for boxing. Baseball, basketball, and football didn't want black players. The only thing young men could do was team up with brothers and friends to play softball or basketball on vacant lots or playgrounds designated for blacks only.

The efforts of two outstanding black athletes excited our interest in national sports. The sports they excelled in were not popular at first, but those men paved the way for our enthusiasm, long before Jackie Robinson. ■

CHAPTER SEVEN

Our First Black Heroes

Until I knew about track star Jesse Owens, I wanted to be a cowboy or a policeman. Fascinated by guns and the authority that went with them, I didn't know that black cowboys and black policemen were rare. We went to the movies and saw only white cowboys doing heroic deeds. Still, I aspired to be a cowboy. Jesse Owens blasted open the door to a world of possibilities of what I could become. He made me believe anything was possible.

In 1936 Jesse Owens, a black athlete from Ohio State University, shocked the entire sports world by winning four gold medals and setting three new track records at the Olympic Games in Berlin, Germany. He was the first American to win that many medals at the Olympics. We were so proud that those honors, symbols of excellence for a whole world of athletes, went to a black man.

The news media labeled Jesse the world's fastest human. After the gold medal ceremony, Adolph Hitler refused to shake his hand simply because he was black.

Owens defeated Germans to win these prestigious awards, proving a black man was superior to men from Hitler's "master race." Since I was only eight, I was too young to understand what was going on in Germany.

Before the Olympics, during Owens's training period, word spread that "this black boy" was so fast he actually had a chance to win at least one gold medal. Every young black boy, including me, started looking up to Jesse Owens as his personal idol. He was my first true hero. In my quest to become the fastest runner and best high jumper in my neighborhood, I ran hard and jumped over anything high off the ground: backyard fences, garbage cans, and homemade hurdles. My brothers and I joined in contests daily. Our parents began scolding us for the abuse to our brogans or tennis shoes.

Around the same time, the sports world started buzzing about a six-foot two-inch, two-hundred-pound black heavyweight boxer out of Detroit named Joe Louis. We could identify with this man because he grew up poor. His father passed away when he was quite young in Alabama, and his mother moved her large family to Detroit.

Joe Louis started his boxing training at the Brewster Center in Detroit. After finishing his amateur wars, winning all his fights in early knockouts, he had turned professional in 1934. He earned the nicknames "Brown Bomber" and "Detroit Destroyer." My father followed Louis's rise in the newspapers and often said, "Let's listen to the Joe Louis fight on the radio." As boxing promoters and gamblers pounced on this young black man, who practically destroyed all his opponents, including ex-champions Primo Carnera and Max Baer, the call went out to the whole world. Was there someone, somewhere, who could defeat this boxing phenomenon? My dad predicted, "You just watch! Joe Louis will make it to the top!"

Boxing buffs, promoters, and sportsmen searched the four corners of the earth to find a suitable opponent for this unbeatable warrior. We heard about this search over the radio and waited anxiously for each new bout. They came from every major city in the world. From countries in South America and Europe, and especially boxing-crazed Cuba. Louis demolished every one in a few blistering rounds. The boxing world started to compare Louis to such outstanding former fighters as Jack Dempsey, Gene Tunney, Luis Firpo, and the great Jack Johnson, the only former black champion of the world. On several occasions during his reign as champion, white promoters had denied Johnson the right to fight white men, but that time was in the past.

In boxing circles rumors started that an outstanding German fighter named Max Schmeling was the logical contender to defeat this highly touted young black boxer from Detroit. The promoters made Schmeling a symbol of Nazi Germany, fighting against the American black man to avenge Jesse Owens's victory in Berlin. We knew our Joe could take care of Max, the German.

The publicity was tremendous. In his worst defeat, Joe Louis lost to Max Schmeling. We were heartbroken. I was so hooked on boxing by then that I felt as if his loss was mine. The newspapers said Joe was overconfident from winning so many fights. After that loss, the Brown Bomber trained carefully and didn't underestimate another opponent.

The heavyweight champion of the world, Jimmy Braddock, sat on his title for two years, not defending it even once, until he accepted the challenge from Joe Louis. The scheduled fight date in Chicago was June 22, 1937. I was nine.

I'll never forget that day. We worked in the cornfield until about 5:00 in the evening. As we walked home, dripping with sweat and carrying our hoes over our shoulders, we looked down the hill toward our house. Bill shouted, "Bobby! Look! The company store truck is backing into our yard. It's not Christmas. What is this?"

We scrambled down the hill. The delivery men unloaded a tall, padded, floor-model Zenith radio from the Koppers Company store. We had a small, weak radio that didn't work well at all. My dad stood there with a big grin. "I got you boys a present. You know, Joe Louis is fighting tonight." We danced around and hooped and hollered. I felt like jumping out of my skin, watching the delivery men haul that fantastic radio up the steps and into our living room.

After we got our chores done that evening and got cleaned up, we all gathered around the radio. My dad plugged it in. When those lights came on, a whole new world opened up. Voices came in sharp and clear and loud. Joe went down in the first round. We held our breath, hung on every word, and wondered if he could actually lose. We didn't have long to wait. Joe came back like a fierce lion. Braddock's manager wanted to stop the punishment, but the champion stayed in the ring. Finally Braddock fell on his face, bleeding, and took the full count. The champ lost the title but gained everyone's respect for not giving up.

Joe Louis was the heavyweight champion of the world. We heard the screaming cheers on the radio and piled outside to beat on tin cans and holler at cars. Our second black hero! After Jesse Owens. Though Jack Johnson was the heavyweight boxing champion back in the early 1900s, he was a flamboyant man with women and flashy cars. He wasn't a good role model like Joe Louis.

As soon as Louis earned the title, nearly every black boy in the country received a pair of boxing gloves and learned to box and to defend himself. My father bought Bill and me one pair of gloves. That meant each of us had only one glove. Since Bill was left-handed, I did well, boxing him, until he hit me with his left. I couldn't defend myself. Claiming to be just like Joe Louis, he always won.

Joe Louis defended his title twenty-five times over a period of eleven years, eight months, and seven days. No one ever beat that record. In a rematch with Schmeling, Louis knocked Max out in the first round and almost killed him. Eighty thousand charged-up people watched the fight of the century, which was over in less than three minutes. Louis became the first boxing idol of black people all over the world, a symbol of excellence in the modern day. He retired undefeated on March 1, 1949. To earn money for back taxes, Louis had to fight again, but it was never the same because he was over the hill. He finally lost to Rocky Marciano in 1951 and retired for good. That was a sad day in the boxing world.

Other great black fighters earned worldwide recognition: Sugar Ray Robinson, Henry "Hammering Hank" Armstrong, Archie Moore, Ezzard Charles, Kid Gavilan, Floyd Patterson, and Cassius Clay, who changed his name to Muhammad Ali. I followed these fighters careers closely, but my enthusiasm for boxing started with the Louis-Braddock fight on our brand-new Zenith radio.

Unfortunately, like with the Hauptmann execution, the radio also brought disturbing news. The rumor mill at the Grant Town mine forecasted that machines were coming to do the work of men. The radio news confirmed it. There was nothing any miner, black or white, or any union, no matter how strong, could do to stop this progress. Machines moved coal out faster than men. Machines didn't need wages, benefits, or housing.

At the Grant Town mine twenty-two hundred men, including my father, wondered whether the next work day would be their last. ∎

CHAPTER EIGHT

Machines Change Everything

Coal loaders were the first to go.

By 1938 the Grant Town mine had installed two major machines. I overheard my dad and his friends discuss them. One, the coal-cutting machine with a chainsaw-type blade, could undercut six feet deep into the coal face. The men could shoot down thirty tons of coal instead of one or two. Then the other new machine moved into place. With giant, crablike arms, the coal-loading machine, or loader, scooped the coal up onto its belt-type surface. The belt tumbled it back out of the way, usually onto the bottom or into empty cars. Before long, electric locomotives on tracks, called motors, came into the mine. They pulled in empty cars and pulled out full cars of coal. Horses and drivers worked a little while after that, but motors soon replaced them. Eventually, shuttle cars, mounted on rubber wheels that didn't need tracks, moved the coal from the loader to the dump.

Some timbermen, trackmen, and loaders kept their jobs, but the mining machines created massive layoffs. Every two or three months, three hundred or more men got laid off at the Grant Town mine. Strikes came from these layoffs. My dad continued to work steadily, even after they retired the horses. I don't know how he did it. During that time, I often heard my parents whispering in their bedroom late into the night. Every day I wondered, *Is this his last day? If it is, where will we go? What will we do?* Dad tried to get the men to vote in "plant seniority." With this union policy, the last man hired was the first man fired or laid off. The miners didn't listen and kept their "classification seniority." If the job was still there, miners in that job class continued to work.

When men got laid off, the company gave them only a few days to move their families and all their personal belongings out of their company house. Yellow dogs forced the move if the laid off miner didn't move fast enough. The town was in turmoil. Friends and neighbors were anxious with worry, and sometimes hostile to one another. Families that had to leave were angry and resentful that others got to stay. No one knew anything until the miner's name appeared on a layoff list. I said "Good-bye and good luck" to many friends I never saw again. Several families left for the city that seemed to offer great promise: Detroit.

As machines replaced men in the coalfields, steel plants and factories in Detroit, Cleveland, Pittsburgh, and Chicago benefited. The newspapers wrote of thousands of strong, able-bodied men, young and old, leaving West Virginia to search for work elsewhere. Rumors filtered back that plant managers in the northern industrial cities hired coal miners without hesitating. These managers knew they could capitalize on miners' willingness to do backbreaking labor without complaining.

Seeing so many friends leaving Grant Town was difficult, but this revolution in the industry brought other problems. My dad began to grumble. "It's more dangerous down there than ever before. So and so got hurt today." Miners had no prior training on these new machines. Though they were good, hard workers, most of them were illiterate. Uneducated men now had to run complicated machinery. Mine supervisors would not consider using Italian, Polish, or Slovak miners, who had difficulty with English, for machine jobs. Supervisors also discriminated against Irish and black miners as they hand-picked their favorite employees from local white men. All men who weren't white, native West Virginians faced losing their jobs. The once-friendly competition between the groups of loaders turned to resentment as the layoffs continued and hand-loading jobs disappeared.

My dad often came home with horror stories. "The machines are so loud, we can't hear the roof 'working.' The roof fell in near me yesterday with no warning. It's so loud all day long, I can barely hear what the foreman is telling me to do. And when those loaded cars are ready to go, you'd better have your hands down at your sides!" Hearing of severed or mashed hands and fingers frightened me. Every day that my dad came home from work without getting hurt was a relief. Good miners who had worked at their own pace found they had to work much harder to keep up with the fast-paced machines. Cutting machines kicked up so much coal dust that visibility decreased and breathing problems increased.

The change was good for profits, but bad for the men. And the layoffs continued. The company transferred outspoken union men into one crew and then dismissed them as a unit no longer needed. A gathering of men assembled every evening to complain, argue, or to discuss the possibility of or need for a strike. Despite his union ties, my father kept working until February 1941. I was thirteen years old and eager to finish eighth grade in Grays Flats and begin the high adventure of riding the bus to Dunbar School in Fairmont. My sisters and brothers talked about how great their school was. Though I looked forward to the new school experience in the fall, I was content in my home and the close-knit community of Grays Flats. I felt things were good and hoped that my place in the world was secure and unchanging.

Then one day my dad brought home the bad news. "Start packing. They gave me one week to get us out of this house. We're moving to Fairmont."

My world turned upside down. ■

CHAPTER NINE

Fairmont, 1941

Moving away from Grant Town was the first real disappointment of my young life. With the help of a neighbor and his truck, ten of us moved to a very small rental house in Jackson Addition, one area where blacks lived in Fairmont. In that house we were even more crowded than in Grays Flats. Many of us were growing up and getting bigger, so space for us to simply eat and sleep was a problem. Indoor plumbing helped. We didn't have to go outside for water or to use the bathroom.

Luckily, the mine at Dakota needed drivers. Within two weeks my father got a job there. He walked a mile and a half up the tracks to go to work. Sometimes on Saturdays I walked partway with him. Even if it was cold enough to see steam rising off the Monongahela River down below, we talked until I had to turn back toward home. On these quiet and peaceful walks, I enjoyed listening to my dad talk about work.

"Son, do you know what a 'dog hole' or 'scab hole' is?"

"No, sir."

"Well, you need to know. That's what they call a mine that has no use for a labor union. They're small, you see, and so they can keep the union out if they want to."

"Did you ever work in one of those mines?"

"No, and I wouldn't unless I had to. Dakota has a good union. They got us a nine-hour work day. And showers. Separate, of course. Dakota is also a captive mine. Do you know what that is?"

"No, sir." I didn't know much about mining, but I found myself wanting to know more and more.

"A captive mine has a contract to deliver coal to big businesses, factories, and hospitals. Even if the whole UMW has a nationwide strike, I'll still be working. The coal to heat those places and run production lines is critical, so the union has to let the captive mines stay open. I'm glad I'm in a captive mine. This is a good job, and they have no machines. They still need horses, and that's good for me."

I hesitated, then asked, "Will the machines come?"

"Don't know. Could be the coal will run out first. You never know until they tell you."

Since I knew my dad was content with his job, I learned that day that we were staying for good. At least until the coal ran out or the machines came. That conversation helped me to see my new home differently. Since I had no hope of returning to Grays Flats, I had to accept the move to Fairmont.

I enrolled in the eighth grade at Dunbar School. Walking into that three-story brick city school with electricity, radiator heat, and indoor bathrooms was like entering a new world. The change from a two-room school in the country to one with hundreds of students and different teachers for each subject overwhelmed me. Getting acquainted and adjusted was a slow process because I had to move to a different class every hour. The teachers were pleasant, but I thought they were all too strict, like my parents. Classroom discipline was number one on every teacher's agenda. Most of them had attended Dunbar and gone to the all-black West Virginia State College in Charleston.

Like any young man of thirteen, I started to notice girls, but I also became keenly aware of my opportunities and limitations in school and in town. Moving into Fairmont in 1941, I experienced a kind of culture shock. Exciting new things to see and do surrounded me.

The school provided hot lunches, or we could carry our own. Many of us, however, chose to walk to Mr. Saul's, where he welcomed us with a wave and a smile. Saul Robinson, a black man, owned a small family store a few blocks from Dunbar School. He sold pepperoni rolls, a local favorite, for five cents. For seven cents he split one and added sauce. At Mr. Saul's I could buy a bottle of cold pop and half a delicious sandwich for eight cents. Even if it was only pennies at a time, that man had a knack for making money. Mr. Saul developed the first snow cones in Marion County. He shaved a block of ice and poured a choice of flavors over it: three cents for a small paper cone and five cents for a larger one. He bought a truck and made a good living traveling the neighborhoods, selling snow cones and candy. I admired his sense for business. Often we walked downtown to G. C. Murphy's to buy day-old cookies. For five or ten cents, we could buy a big scoop of assorted cookies, usually broken. Some days that was lunch.

Going to Dunbar had one big drawback. Six of us had to walk almost a mile into town past the all-white Miller School, located just a few blocks from our house. Blacks and whites lived separate lives in Fairmont. Segregation affected where I could go and where I could eat. Most Dunbar students who had extra lunch money walked to Frank's Hot Dog Stand at the corner of Jefferson and Jackson Streets. They could buy a hot dog for ten cents or a hamburger for fifteen cents. Frank's Hot Dog Stand was the only place in Fairmont that a black person, young or old, had the privilege of sitting down to eat. Two counters faced each other. Whites sat on one side and "colored" sat on the other side. Though a white man and a black man had worked together the night before, the two could only wave to each other across the counters. Frank's had two entrances, one for white people and one for Negroes.

An ice cream parlor on Adams Street was Jim Crowed along with the other restaurants. I could go inside and purchase ice cream cones or take-out pints and quarts, but I could not sit at the counter or tables there to eat. On hot summer days a familiar sight was blacks strolling along the street with melting ice cream running down their hands and arms.

St. Regis, the Palace, and the dining rooms of the Fairmont and Watson Hotels were four fine restaurants in downtown Fairmont. St. Regis was the best. Slacks' Bar and Grill, Lupo's, and Union Lunch were also popular and said to have great food. I don't know much about the insides of any of these restaurants. They didn't serve colored, except for take-out orders, and then only sandwiches. We had to go to the back door and get the attention of the busy chef or cook so he'd finally ask, "What do you want, boy?" Long waiting periods followed any order. We learned to go on nights when business was the slowest, but they still made us wait.

At the famous and elegant Fairmont Hotel, the entire staff, except for waitresses, was black; however, blacks couldn't stay there as guests until the Civil Rights Act of 1964 guaranteed equal accommodations for all citizens in public hotels and restaurants. The only black employees permitted to eat in the kitchen were a few cooks and waiters. They ate the food that remained after the white guests had been served. The only black employees permitted near the front entrance were the doorman, the bell captain, his two bellhops, and the elevator operator. All other black employees, maids and kitchen help, had to enter and leave by the back entrance.

With few exceptions blacks experienced humiliating separation and limited opportunities to work. Besides mining and service or maintenance work at the hotels, the only jobs available to black men were as janitors at the department stores and retail shops. Though blacks spent thousands of dollars in G. C. Murphy's, McCrory's Five and Ten, and Hartley's, all the clerks and salespersons were white. No good-paying jobs existed for black students either. The retail stores refused to hire young black women. Service stations and delivery truck services refused to hire young black men. Boys had to resort to shining shoes, racking balls in Slack's Pool Room, or hope to get on as a bellhop at the Fairmont. I did all these jobs. During my early teens I had three or four "arrangements" going on all the time to keep money in my pockets.

I also did odd jobs and errands for elderly people, mostly old widows, in Jackson Addition. I carried in coal, mopped floors, and fed chickens and hogs. I gathered coal for one lady every day. She gave me a crisp dollar bill each Sunday evening. For years I had a paper route. The day of the week I dreaded most was Sunday. Throughout my early teenage years, I had to get up at 5:00 on Sunday morning, walk downtown to get my papers, and deliver them to my customers. Even on the coldest, most blustery winter's day, I stood on a street corner and sold what I could of the remaining heavy papers. After that, I had to rush home to get to Sunday school, or I'd hear from my mom. On Sunday afternoons she sent me to Baptist Youth group. Then I went back over my paper route that evening to collect my money. I often heard, "You'll have to wait until next week when my husband gets paid at the mine." Though disappointed, I always replied, "Okay, see you next week." I knew their word was good. Many slipped a week or more behind, but I got paid eventually.

Since only a few miners owned cars or lawn mowers, I didn't do much car washing or mowing. Very few of us found opportunities to earn even a small amount of spending money to help ourselves or to help supplement the family income. Fathers generally supported the whole family, whether there were two kids or twelve.

Modern appliances that existed were expensive. Mothers had too much to do at home with child care, cooking, canning, washing and ironing, and cleaning chores that it didn't pay them to go out and "scrub white folks' floors" for two dollars a day. The big department stores began to hire colored women to operate their elevators, if they were good-looking and near "high yellow" in their complexion. High yellow women, those with light complexions, definitely had more job opportunities. Women of darker complexion had to compete for work at the Fairmont and Watson Hotels. They were either chambermaids for the many guests in the hotels or house maids for well-to-do white families. Both jobs involved changing beds and washing out commodes. They had no other choices.

Segregation not only restricted work opportunities, it also limited the fun we could have. Many theaters competed for business in Fairmont, but only two allowed Negroes: the Fairmont and the Virginia. For two years before closing, the Lee Theater on Main Street opened its doors to blacks. In these theaters, as soon as I bought my ticket, I knew I had to go upstairs to the balcony. Some black kids delighted in pitching popcorn and ice cubes out over the balcony so food or ice rained down on the whites sitting underneath. My upbringing taught me to stay away from these kinds of shenanigans.

When I was a child growing up, my parents taught me certain things to remember when out in the white world. "Avoid trouble. Look for signs. Obey the rules, written and unwritten. Not knowing all the rules is never an excuse." I remembered those teachings and stayed inside the boundaries.

One learns quickly by listening and watching. The white community assumed that I knew not to go into Hagen's Ice Cream Parlor and sit down to eat. The same unwritten rules applied to all restaurants except Frank's. Whites assumed I knew that if I went to the movies, I couldn't just go in and sit down. I had to go upstairs immediately. No one could make me like it, but I accepted those things. I had to. We all had to in those days. Discrimination and prejudice were the going practices in Fairmont and Marion County. Blacks were always considered second- or third-class citizens. We all knew our place and limits in society.

Access to public recreational facilities didn't exist for blacks in the 1940s. I couldn't skate in the two public skating rinks. I couldn't swim in the city swimming pool until the late 1950s. Black men helped to build it, and the East-West Stadium, under Roosevelt's New Deal program. By the time I could swim there, it was old and dilapidated. Between jobs I joined my friends to swim in Buffalo Creek or the much wider and deeper Monongahela River. After a heavy rain, the water ran deep and currents were swift. Definitely more fun, but also more dangerous. Every now and then some young people took chances and drowned.

On the opposite side of the Monongahela River in East Fairmont, two streets had a local reputation for trouble and danger. I heard about this "den of iniquity" as soon as I moved to Fairmont. We talked and joked and teased about going "across the pond." One street even had a nationwide reputation. At one time an unofficial national survey claimed Merchant Street had more drinking bars per block than any other street in the United States. Compared to gambling cities like Las Vegas, that's a lot. Frequent brawls erupted in the brothels and bars on Merchant Street. Drunks put out of one bar could stumble next door or across the street and easily find someone to serve them. These bars, like the restaurants and the Eastland Theater, were off limits to blacks. Nearby Water Street was not. What a place that was!

Down the hill from Merchant, Water Street ran along the Monongahela River for only a few blocks. In the "red light district," black and white bums, prostitutes, and lowlife types lived and seemed to thrive on this deplorable street. Illegal gambling was commonplace. Fights and murders occurred often. During an evening religious service in a little back room, screams and gunfire might be heard in the same building. The activities on Water Street kept the city patrol busy, breaking up and investigating brawls, stabbings, and shootings. Saturday night was the worst. Robberies and murders went unsolved because the dangers of investigating them overruled the desire to solve crimes among the lowlifes.

The only way to get to Water Street was to walk or drive over the Monongahela on the toll bridge from Fairmont. The toll charge for automobiles was five cents. To get down to Water Street from Merchant Street, visitors usually parked on Merchant and took one of two equally dangerous paths. One way was to walk across several sets of railroad tracks and go down a long, steep cement stairway. Another was through a long tunnel that ran underneath the B&O Railroad tracks between the two streets. Residents of Water Street had to walk through this tunnel for food supplies, beer, and liquor. Lowlifes stopped in the tunnel to drink, urinate, and defecate. Broken wine and whiskey bottles and human waste fouled this horrible place. Often, it was nearly pitch dark in the long tunnel.

The people eventually died off or moved away from the Water Street slum district. Some of the abandoned homes and business buildings fell down, and the city demolished the rest when they developed Palatine Park in the 1950s. They even changed the name of the roadway through the park to Everest Drive. Water Street ceased to exist. Merchant Street survived as a crowded business area. Two bridges connect the area to Fairmont: the newer Third Street Bridge, built on a curve, and the High Level Bridge.

The attention that the national survey brought to East Fairmont was a source of shame, but another mention of Fairmont was a source of pride. We had the fastest interurban streetcar line in the country, and I rode on it. The streetcar, which had an overhead cable, ran seventeen miles on narrow tracks from Fairmont to Clarksburg. The year I was thirteen, my friends and I went to Clarksburg every Sunday night to meet some girls and go to the movies. A round-trip train ticket cost 25 cents. We had to leave the movie theater early to catch the last train home. It pulled into Fairmont about 11:30. That train really rocked on Sunday nights, traveling seventy miles per hour. What a thrill ride!

Every time I rode along Fairmont Avenue toward Clarksburg, High Gate captured my full attention. Between Eighth and Nine Streets, behind a tall iron fence and massive gates, stood High Gate, a mansion like no other. Coal baron James E. Watson, owner of the Watson coal mine where my dad had worked, built this twenty-five-room house and estate around 1910. High Gate cost over $1 million and took three years to build. Today, $50 million couldn't build this "most handsome mansion in West Virginia," as tour books call it.

High Gate is luxurious, with Vermont, Tennessee, and Italian marble floors and mantelpieces, hand-carved oak railings and walls, and mahogany and oak parquet floors. I'd seen it as a kid when I visited my grandfather in Watson, but the reality of High Gate didn't hit me until I was a teenager. Watson built this stupendous showplace from profits gained by the sweat and blood of coal miners like my father. I couldn't look at the mansion with its servants' quarters, tennis courts, huge carriage house, and perfectly terraced landscaping without thinking about how we lived, jammed into a couple of rooms. I learned that when the Watsons lived at High Gate, they kept a staff of nearly twenty-five black men and women to serve the family and maintain the house, grounds, and horses, then automobiles. They worked as maids, butlers, cooks, gardeners, chauffeurs, stablemen, and caretakers. Among the rich and important guests who enjoyed this service, and the Watsons' hospitality, were Presidents Taft and Wilson.

Even though J. E. Watson built High Gate before my family moved to the Fairmont area, I believe it stands as a symbol of the overwhelming inequality between mine owners and miners. Instead of using profit money to reward his employees with increased wages, he built himself a palace to show off his tremendous wealth. Even at the young age of thirteen, seeing that grand estate, and knowing the selfish greed that it stood for, was a bitter lesson in life. More important lessons lay ahead for me. The last day of my thirteenth year, December 7, 1941, started out like any other Sunday, delivering papers and going to church. It turned out to be "a date which will live in infamy." If a boy can leave his childhood behind in one day, that Sunday was my day. ■

CHAPTER TEN

War, Life, and Work

I was out in the street, playing football with my friends, and had just come inside. Sunday afternoon dinner preparations were underway. The sweet aroma of breads baking filled every room. My mouth watered as I washed up for the meal that promised to be outstanding.

Suddenly, I heard my father shouting. "Come here! Listen! There's a flash bulletin on the radio! Pearl Harbor's been attacked! The Japanese bombed Pearl Harbor!"

We rushed into the living room from all directions. My family began to wail and scream around the radio. Somebody shushed us. The room quieted as quickly as it had exploded. The radio announcer told about the loss of ships and about American soldiers and sailors. He spoke of hundreds, maybe thousands, of Americans killed. He spoke of battleships and planes destroyed and on fire at our naval base at Pearl Harbor. Cries and muffled whimpers filled our living room. I was astonished, frightened, bewildered, and speechless, all at the same time. I didn't know what to do or say. Soon, we all began to cry because we knew our country was going to war.

Geographically, I had no idea where Pearl Harbor was. I didn't understand military strategy or know anything about the locations of our navy or air force bases. My mother, father, and sisters knew about a huge naval base on a Hawaiian island in the Pacific and explained to the rest of us. A small comfort came from knowing it was far away, but that didn't calm our fears. The tears turned back into angry words and shouts. At some point in the excitement and confusion, I heard my father calling me. "Bob! There's got to be an Extra. I want to read it. Run downtown and get us some papers."

I took off for Bobets' News Store. They had stacks and stacks of *Fairmont Times* newspapers, ready to deliver. There were dozens of black and white boys grabbing armloads of papers and stuffing them into bags. They scattered to run all over Fairmont to deliver them. I grabbed a bundle for myself. After I ran home to give my dad some copies, I rushed door to door selling the Extra. Then I ran back for more. I received a penny for each copy I sold. The front-page headline read "US AT WAR" in tall, bold capital letters and beneath that, "Pearl Harbor and Manila Attacked by Jap Bombers." I was nervous and scared. What did this all mean? How was it going to affect my family and me? What about my dad, my older brothers?

The next day, December 8, was my fourteenth birthday. There was no celebration, but I didn't care. A national radio broadcast connected our school and nearly every building throughout the nation to the president. I listened as Franklin D. Roosevelt asked Congress to declare war on Japan. He reported the terrible loss of life and damage done. We later learned the Japanese had sunk or badly damaged seven battleships, including our own state battleship, the *West Virginia*. Nearly four hundred airplanes, lined up in rows, had been demolished or damaged. And the worst tragedy of all: this treacherous sneak attack killed more than twenty-three hundred Americans and wounded over one thousand.

After Congress voted, the president announced that the United States had declared war on Japan. We sat quietly in our classroom. Numb, actually. No one wanted to talk about it with the teachers. I knew that this would probably be the outcome, but when it was said, out loud, by the president, the words still shocked me. I imagined every man in my family marching off to war and never coming back. Three days later, December 11, Japan's partners in war, Germany and Italy, officially declared war on the United States. Not surprisingly, Congress declared war on Germany and on

Italy. Of course, we had no choice, but this news terrified me. My vivid imagination had me on a battlefield in Europe before it was over and done.

People bought every newspaper that I could carry for weeks. Worry lines creased everyone's faces. The radio spoke war news to us every waking hour. During the early months, many people feared that this war would come to our own country. The newspapers were full of the buildup for war. We feared that bombs would fall and we'd have to fight for our land. Thoughts of enemy soldiers prowling my neighborhood cost me sleepless nights.

Whether from a sense of patriotic duty or for a chance to make good money, many older men moved away from Fairmont to work in the war plants. Some of the neighbor men left their families at home, only to return on long weekends every few months. Many coal miners who didn't get drafted left their jobs to go to the industrial cities. They grabbed the opportunity to earn a better wage for a day's work. This outpouring of miners created vacancies in the mines. The increasing demand for coal to run the war factories around the clock meant that coal companies had to produce as much coal as possible.

My father was one year over the draft age. Besides, he still had eight children living at home. He stayed in the Dakota mine. Like many miners left in the coalfields, he began to work many overtime hours. None of my immediate family had to go to war. Thank God. James had a couple of kids by 1941, so he was exempt. During the war he worked in a factory that made railroad car wheels. At sixteen Bill was too young for the draft.

Ironically, World War II ended the Great Depression. During the war, anyone able to work could find a job. Factories, plants, and coal mines increased their wages. Some of our friends at school began to prosper. They showed this by wearing better clothes and shoes, and getting increases in their allowances for lunches and personal things like movies, carnivals, circuses, and dances. I took time to enjoy these entertainments whenever possible, but those times were rare with all my jobs. I paid my own way because I didn't want an allowance. I did what I could to help at home but knew my parents needed money for food and clothes for the entire family.

Though we were doing better, some folks continued living on the edge of poverty: young widows with children, single-parent families, and disabled miners. Those families who couldn't afford to buy coal to heat their homes resorted to stealing. In fact, they often had their children steal for them. Long lines of full coal cars snaked back from the mines into the wooded countryside. The busiest operation was Barnesville No. 38 mine in Bellview, not far from our home. Every couple of minutes as the loading continued at the tipple, the train skipped a car's length. Skip. Clank. Stop. Over and over. During the stops young boys climbed onto the cars and pitched clumps of coal into piles on the ground. They rode the skip and made another pile of coal. This went on until they had stockpiled what they needed. After the train pulled out, the boys returned to gather up the coal into gunny sacks and pack it home. Occasionally an angry conductor caught sight of this thievery, jumped off the train and ran them off, shouting curses and swinging a billy club. I watched, but I never stole coal for my family. I did help other boys cart it home sometimes, so I guess I was an "accessory after the fact."

The Fairmont Coal and Coke Company left eight or ten coke ovens sit idle and abandoned along the railroad tracks. These coke ovens were about six feet tall, ten feet wide, and twenty feet deep. With the back end partially buried into a dirt bank, each oven looked like a firebrick igloo with a rounded top and small doorway. The company had used them to burn coal into coke for use in the steel plants. Soon after the company ceased operations, street derelicts, recluses, and "winos" cleaned them out, moved in, and set up housekeeping. They pulled bricks away to widen the doorways and knocked out holes for windows. Naturally they got their coal for heating and cooking from the loaded coal cars. Very handy indeed.

When I was fourteen or so, my friends and I enjoyed going down and talking to these people. We often stopped by to visit on our way to fishing or swimming in the Buffalo Creek. They gave us food, and we helped them carry their coal from the train. We learned each individual's name and which coke oven he called home. Most huts had dirt-covered floors, but the residents made them livable and homey. Some even had portable radios. Three or four of these fellows soon had girlfriends living with them or coming in as regular visitors.

In this little community the living conditions weren't my idea of a comfortable home, but for some, the situation was ideal. They had no utilities or rent to pay, only to live their lives by the railroad tracks and hope no one bothered them. As a kid, I found it exciting to know and visit these people. Our parents didn't know we hung out with them. They would have been horrified, thinking we were in danger. But we weren't. Sometimes we teased and made jokes about how the coke-hut people lived, but their way of life taught me an important lesson. I came to realize that as long as a man has a place to live, regardless of what it is or where it is, he has a right to complete privacy and contentment.

During the early war years, with things looking up economically for most families, my mother received a gift that changed our lives for the better. Her father passed away and left her money. Before he died, he said, "I want you to build a house for my grandkids." My parents bought a lot in Jackson Addition and began building a six-room house with a full basement underneath. Though I was very busy with school and all my jobs, I enjoyed all the activity and the excitement my parents felt at owning their own home. I couldn't wait to get more space for myself. When we moved in, the extra, larger rooms made us feel as if we had built ourselves a mansion. My mother said it was her dream come true.

She had dreams for all her children, too. Mom had tried her best to motivate me with an inspiring speech. "Bobby, you can be anything you want to be. You could go to medical school or law school. I'd like that. You can do well and go on to college and be a doctor. Just think of it! A doctor! You could do it, Bobby!" The trouble was that it was her dream. I didn't see myself as a future doctor, or a lawyer. I wanted to follow her directions and make her proud of me, but her hopes didn't match my character. For instance, she thought I should play the piano. She sent away for a course with books and all. Learning and practicing the piano was slow and tedious. Just not me. I'd sit there doing scales and wish I was outside with my friends. To make her happy, I tried, but I finally told her I couldn't do it.

I did average in school. My favorite class was art. I loved to draw. I drew cowboys and cars, Popeye, Mickey Mouse, or anything that took my eye as having interesting lines. During the Christmas season my sophomore year, my history teacher asked another boy and me to do an art project. She wanted a three-by-five-foot picture of the three wise men for her classroom wall. She definitely appreciated our efforts because she hung it in a prominent place in her classroom. And she gave us each an A for the six weeks' grading period.

About ten years ago I saw my retired history teacher on the street. With a fond sparkle in her eyes, she said, "Robert, I still have that picture of the three wise men." I couldn't believe it! She took my art work into her home when she retired. Though I had done the work nearly fifty years before our chance meeting, her appreciation of it made me feel very special.

Drawing gave me great pleasure, but it didn't put money in my pocket. As I said, I had several arrangements for earning money going on all the time. I continued delivering papers and shining shoes. I also worked as a pin boy at the Fairmont Bowling Alley in the old Opera House. I earned a nickel every time I placed the bowling pins on the spots and sent the ball back. Blacks couldn't bowl there, but they hired us to set pins. A local tailor paid me to sweep and mop his shop and wash the outside windows each day after school. On Saturdays he gave me $2.50.

On Tuesdays and Thursdays I mopped the front showroom floor at Select Bakery. Saturdays after closing time around noon, I started a job that kept me in constant motion (and bent over) until 11:00 at night. The bakery had an enormous work room in the back. I started by scraping up all the dough ground into the floor during the week. Then I scrubbed that whole floor several times until it was "clean enough to eat off of"—my instructions. Finally, I waxed it to a brilliant shine. Exhausted, I still had to walk a mile home. My pay for that job was ten dollars a week.

Even during school months, I suspect I worked nearly fifty hours a week. Including money earned in the neighborhood, I made about twenty dollars. I must admit, having twenty dollars in my pocket most of the time made me feel like a grown man.

In 1943 and 1944 I got to leave these menial jobs and spend the summers at the shore with my dad. Sounds like fun, but it was pure work. ∎

CHAPTER ELEVEN

My First Real Job

The opportunity to work at the shore, and be with my dad, happened so fast. There was no time to think. Lack of mechanization had become a problem at the Dakota mine. The company couldn't compete with other mines' production, and my dad had gotten laid off. Rumor spread that work was available in southern Maryland, so Dad and some other men drove down to check on it.

The federal government had begun building Patuxent River Naval Air Station in a very strategic area forty miles south of Annapolis, Maryland. Folks living there got a couple thousand dollars for their property. Then, whether they resented it or not, the government demolished their homes and cleared a huge area for the base. A big hospital for ten thousand navy men and women was already in place. My dad got a job firing the boilers at the hospital for twelve hours a day, six days a week. He ate in a gigantic cafeteria that served three meals a day to all the construction workers and navy personnel. The cafeteria also served as a short-order restaurant in the evenings.

My dad wrote Mom a letter. "If Bobby comes down here, I can get him a job in the kitchen. Put him on the bus if he wants a summer job." Mom followed his directions. In the short span of forty-eight hours, I quit all my jobs and found myself on a bus heading toward our nation's capitol. Thrilled by my dad's confidence in me, I went to downtown Washington, D.C. Dad had scheduled an interview for me with Golden Commissary, the company that ran the cafeteria services. I had to lie about my age because I was only fifteen. They sent me down to Patuxent to interview with the manager of the cafeteria. He hired me right away.

I started out busing tables. They noticed that I knew how to work and soon put me in charge of the busboys. Keeping all those tables clean was a big job, but I had fun. And I had the run of the whole place. The manager gave me more responsibilities within a short time. Three times a week a guy drove down from D.C. to bring in meat to the cafeteria. Before it arrived, I lined up my dad and five or six other black guys to unload it. Then I had to check off the beef, pork, and chicken from the order list and help transfer the meat from the truck to the freezers. I gave the men free meal tickets as pay for their work.

Another surprising job responsibility came my way. One day the manager stopped me and said, "Robert, go to the payroll clerk. Tell him you are going to start delivering weekly paychecks to the employees. You'll have to learn everyone's names. Take the checks to all the cooks, bakers, salad makers, and busboys. I'm counting on you." Though it was a huge place, I came to know everybody who worked there. That wasn't an easy task because the turnover was continuous. Many people got fired for sloppy work.

Another of my jobs was to take inventory in the warehouse every week. I had to count bags of sugar and flour, and cartons and cartons of canned goods. I stayed up until 1:00 in the morning taking inventory. When I turned the sheets into the manager, he always said, "Good job, Robert." He trusted me with a lot, and that made me feel great.

I got up between 6:00 and 7:00 in the morning. First thing, I headed for the bake shop. I loved just sitting around with the bakers each morning. They gave me free coffee and a hot bun. All the men on the base were older, so I didn't get to hang out with guys my age. The younger busboys all lived at home.

The base set up a big room, with seating for four hundred, to show movies. Some nights I helped by taking tickets, and they let me watch the movie for free. People were friendly, and I enjoyed that. After a movie, around midnight, I'd walk back through the cafeteria to get some comic books or something I needed, like toothpaste. Often the chef stopped me and asked, "Hey. Bobby. You going home?" Some people there called me Bobby.

I replied, "Yes. Why?" I knew what he wanted because I saw tables full of people.

He'd shake his head and say, "I need you."

I smiled, being needed, and went back behind the counter and grabbed an apron. Then I worked an hour or so fast-frying burgers and hot sandwiches on the grill for people who were eating late. I enjoyed that, too. Though it was kitchen work, I considered it important work.

Pilots, flight crews, construction guys, and hospital workers came in and out all the time. The government-contracted construction companies worked on building airplane hangars and other buildings. The new runways were right outside the cafeteria. We could hear planes taking off for Europe. After work sometimes, I sat out and watched the planes come in. Somehow it brought me closer to the war. That job made me feel as if I was doing something for the war effort.

I made sixty dollars a week. Two hundred forty dollars a month was *big* money. I slept in a barracks next to my dad and ate all my meals at the cafeteria. In some respects, it was like being in the service. For extra money, I shined shoes for some of the fellows in the barracks. Since we got free room and board, I sent most of my money home. Mom saved it for me. I worked all summer, enjoying every minute. Of course, I had to come home and go to school in the fall. My dad stayed on at the hospital.

In the spring of 1944, near the end of my junior year in high school, an unplanned development changed the course of my life. Showering attention on one special girl resulted in us getting married, with a baby on the way. My responsibility to support my new family took precedence over finishing my education. I left high school to find work, but I had to settle for odd jobs. Two months later, I got a letter saying I had done such a splendid job at Patuxent River that I could come back to work for the summer. That's what I did, eventually getting assigned all the jobs I'd done the year before. My wife stayed with her family while I lived on the naval base in Maryland.

The second summer, the manager gave me an important responsibility. Secretary of War Stinson, the Joint Chiefs of Staff for the Armed Services, and other Washington dignitaries came down for a big dinner meeting. The manager put me in charge of waiting the tables in a special dining room off the cafeteria. They came into the room with their brass

Bob at age
sixteen, 1943.
Courtesy of
William Armstead.

shining. I was very nervous, but I served their dinners and cleaned up the tables. Afterward the manager said simply, "Robert, well done." I never received any bonuses, but sometimes, like that night, there were big tips.

I had several responsible jobs at Patuxent. If they knew how much responsibility had been given to a young man of fifteen and sixteen, I suspect somebody would have been in deep trouble. I enjoyed proving that I could handle all that. At the end of the second summer, I had to return home and try to find another real job, one with a future to support my family. Relocating to another city wasn't an option to me at that time. Even though jobs were scarce, I preferred to stay in Fairmont.

Reading about the war in Europe and in the Pacific kept me agitated. The United States and the Allies held their own with Japan and Germany. I wanted to go and fight for my beloved country, but at sixteen I was too young. The newspapers reported the deaths of our soldiers by the hundreds every day. Some close friends died in the war. It was heartbreaking to have these friends and other acquaintances come home in boxes. We mourned for their grieving families as we struggled to keep our household going.

I applied for a job as a bellhop at the Fairmont Hotel. The bell captain, a black man who supervised the full-time and part-time bellhops, reviewed boys' applications. If he didn't like a boy's parents or family, he refused to hire him. He said he'd let me know when an opening occurred. When they called for me to report to work, I was pleased because it was a select little group. I guess I passed his inspection. The pay was low. On a busy day, however, I made seven to eight dollars in tips.

The Fairmont was an older, but elegant hotel, six stories high with two elevators. It had polished marble floors and a grand staircase that led to a beautiful dining room, banquet halls, and a huge ballroom. Below the entry level, the ground floor had fancy little stores, a barber shop, and a game room. It was a center of activity, and I enjoyed working there. I had to be neat and pressed, watch my every move, and learn to be extremely polite. The money was all right, and I was fairly content.

Before long, unfortunately, things changed drastically. Less than a year after I started, the hotel suffered a business slowdown, and I was laid off. Another once-elegant hotel in Fairmont, the Watson Hotel, needed someone to do heavy cleaning, like windows and walls. Desperate for work, I took the job, but it was difficult. The building, almost fifty years old, was run down. The whole inside needed extensive remodeling. From the outside, it still looked like a grand hotel, but not inside. The Watson had twenty-foot ceilings with dirty and chipping paint. The mosaic marble floors were worn and dingy. The suites, once light and airy, now smelled old and stale. The elevators creaked and moaned, announcing their age to the whole building.

About eight regular tenants lived there permanently. The overnight guests and these tenants were unhappy about the hotel's condition and complained to anyone who would listen. I became an unwilling target of these complaints. The atmosphere was dreary and discouraging. Occasionally, I got a call from the Fairmont Hotel to substitute as an extra waiter for conventions or to work a party. Nothing reliable came from that, and the contrast between the Fairmont, where I wanted to be, and the Watson, where I had to be, was like night and day.

The Watson Hotel only paid me forty-two dollars a month. Horrible, humiliating pay. I searched for other work, but any place that hired young black men had no openings. By the time I was eighteen, I was trying to support my wife and now two children on this meager income. Because money was tight, we had to live with my family. I was miserable, hated my job, and saw no way to change things.

The war ended in Europe on May 8, 1945, and in the Pacific on September 2, 1945. Though my situation troubled me, I rejoiced for the end of the fighting and the return of my friends, and especially my father. Dad came home from Maryland when the smaller mines in our area started into production again. He found work at No. 93 Jordan mine between Grant Town and Rivesville, but not for long. Besides having his only "lost time for injury" (three days for broken ribs) at Jordan, they had a big layoff within a few months.

Sometime in the fall of 1946, my father got a job at Barnesville Shaft, Consolidation Coal Company's No. 38 mine, not far from our home. Two hundred yards from the north end of the Bellview Bridge, the No. 38 tipple towered over Buffalo Creek as it pointed toward Barrackville, a thriving coal camp upstream. The lamphouse, where miners picked up their lamps, sat to the east of the bridge. The mine operation was practically in town, huge and impressive.

The B&O Railroad served many mines in this valley. Diesel locomotives, one in front and one in back, pulled long coal trains of fifty-ton coal cars through there daily. That's where the ongoing coal theft took place from young boys and the coke-hut people. Barnesville Shaft had installed machinery and was in full production. My father was glad to be home and back in the mines. With him home and working steadily, somehow I felt things would improve for me. They did. I got my "greetings" notice from the draft board.

The war was over. My friends who survived were home, and now I was leaving. After the initial shock, I looked forward to the new adventure. I saw the army as an opportunity to change my direction, get some financial stability started, and perhaps learn a new trade. I traveled to boot camp at Ft. Hays, near Columbus, Ohio. For three days I got probed and punctured, and I learned to drill and march. No picnic, but I was ready to work toward changing my life.

Then I got the bad news. "Soldier, we have to turn you down. You have heart palpitations, and you have flat feet. Two strikes. We're going to send you home." Very discouraged and disappointed, I went back to Fairmont and back to the Watson Hotel cleaning job. A dark, dark time. I was a lost soul.

The next summer, still searching for something better, I enrolled in an art class at Fairmont State College. I thoroughly enjoyed the class, but the practical side of me knew this was just a fun thing. I could never make a living at it without years of struggle. My financial situation, and personal misery, made me open and ready for an important question from my dad. ∎

Part 2

1947–1998

CHAPTER TWELVE

Into the Mines: Barnesville Shaft

Son, do you want to go in the coal mine? Would you like to?"

In those seconds of silence as we stared at one another, I reviewed my situation. I was nineteen and working for thirty-six dollars a month take-home pay at the hotel. That was a meager wage in 1947. The army had turned me down, so that was out. I lived at home with my parents and had my own family to support. Helping my parents with our expenses was important to me.

"Yes. Well, I wouldn't really like to, but I need to go somewhere where I can make some money." I knew that in the mines I could make the same money in four days that took a whole month to earn at the hotel.

"Are you sure? You must be absolutely sure."

"Yes, sir. I'm sure."

"Good!" He nodded his head with approval. "I'll speak to the superintendent as soon as I can and ask him about it." As he walked away, I heard him mumble, "This is good."

And that's all he said about it for several days. I kept my eye on him every time he came home, but he never said a word. I knew not to ask. The uncertainty gave me time to think it through. What if the superintendent said he didn't need anyone? What if I got the job and couldn't cope with the work?

As a young boy, I did not want to become a coal miner. Now here I was, on the edge, ready to jump into it with absolutely no confidence. Finally, I figured out why it troubled me. Tall men, black or white, who looked strong and healthy, didn't have trouble getting work in the mines. Men of smaller stature had to be very persistent or get a recommendation for a chance to prove themselves. Some mines controlled how many blacks they hired to keep peace with their white employees. Also, many men simply didn't have what it took to be a miner. I was medium height, black, and unsure of my abilities.

A few of my friends had gotten jobs at Grant Town or in other mines. Their dads arranged it. One thing provoked me about that whole situation. White guys knew, when they graduated from high school, or even quit school, that their daddy could get them a job in the coal mine the next Monday morning. It happened all the time and gave the white guys confidence and an edge over us. Black guys couldn't count on that because their fathers rarely had that "pull." I wasn't sure whether my dad had it or not, but he was willing to try, for me.

Waiting to hear the word, I pumped myself up. If my dad got me this opportunity, I would make it work. I would not let him down. Besides, I needed a good-paying job with a future. I had no choice. Though I only weighed 130 pounds, I enjoyed boxing as a pastime. My arms and shoulders were strong, and I was quick on my feet. Boxing gave me stamina and a fearless attitude. By the time my dad came home with the news, I was ready. I was sure. I wanted to be a coal miner.

Finally, Dad said matter-of-factly with no sign of his feelings, "The superintendent wants to talk to you. Go see him tomorrow." He did it! I had a chance! Then the fearless attitude started to crumble. I couldn't help thinking over and over, *What will he say? What will I say?*

Superintendents have varied reputations, most of them tough. I was scared, but I went to see him. He looked me over, apparently noting my size. Then he got right down to business. "Son, your dad's a good worker here. You think you can carry one end of a fourteen foot, six-by-eight bar?" He called it a bar, but I knew he referred to a wooden post, thinner but longer than a railroad tie.

"I'll do my damnedest to carry my end." I knew he wanted confidence, and the rest just popped out of my mouth.

"Good! You come to work Monday morning." He turned away to shuffle papers. I knew the meeting was over, so I mumbled my thanks and left the office.

I nearly ran home, spurred on by this new happening in my life. I couldn't contain my excitement and couldn't wait for Monday morning. My mom smiled and praised me, but her eyes held a note of sadness. I knew this wasn't her dream for me, but my dad was proud. I could tell. Through the weekend work of cleaning at the Watson Hotel, all I could think of was my new job. Ten dollars a day was big money. I was happy to quit the hotel with only a few days' notice. I couldn't wait to go into a coal mine and work with real men. A new word meaning masculine power and strength described my feelings exactly: I felt macho!

My dad had been working at the Barnesville Shaft as a driller for a year. The following Monday morning he and I walked to the mine, carrying our lunch buckets. I would be twenty years old in four months. For the first time in my life, I felt like a man.

We arrived half an hour early. After signing up at the payroll office, I also had to sign to buy my own work gear: hard hat, safety boots, and mining belt. Then they sent me to the lamphouse. Someone gave me a battery lamp to place on my hard hat and a round piece of metal with a number on it. I immediately thought of my dad at Grant Town, being a number with no name, but it wasn't like that at all. My instructions were to always take this tag off the checkboard before entering the mine and to be sure to place it back on the board after coming out. They said this was the only way the timekeeper could tell if I worked that day or if I was absent. On the dark side of this procedure was a well-known fact told to me later. If there was an explosion or fire, there would be no question of who didn't get out.

Barnesville Shaft was a slope mine with an opening to the outside, called a drift mouth, or pit mouth. The colliery, the above-ground mine complex, including the tipple, sat at the bottom of a hill. The miners entered there, but the coal seam was farther down inside. The section foreman had me follow him down 102 steps into the mine. He told me mine horses used to pull loads up this steep slope before the company installed railroad tracks to haul the coal.

Mining terms weren't new to me. I grew up hearing them. I thought I knew what to expect, but entering a mine for the first time made my heart pound. Once inside, I was overwhelmed by the lights suspended from the roof, the seam of coal, and rows of countless timbers supporting the roof. Men stood in groups, waiting for their ride. The section foreman led me to a platform where we climbed into an empty two-ton coal car. Inside three of these cars, eighteen of us sat on empty rock-dust bags or on an eight inch square cement cap block. We sped along to the section in this mantrip, the name used for our cars and the motor that pulled us.

The foreman checked the headings for methane gas while all the miners on his section gathered in the "dinner hole," a cleared place where we could sit down to eat. He gave us a ten-minute safety speech about accidents that had occurred, not only at this mine but at other mines throughout the coal industry. This daily ritual, designed to make us aware and more cautious, saved lives and was my first of thousands of safety lectures.

Besides machine operators, the group included men who pumped water, hung trolley wire, laid track, and those who hauled supplies like concrete blocks, posts, cement, bags of rock dust, cables, and pipes.

The foreman showed me around the section and explained what operation each machine performed. Everything, what I saw and what I heard, excited me as the men switched on the power to all the equipment. Each machine seemed to come alive like an awakening prehistoric animal. Within ten minutes, machines rumbled in every heading. He finally brought me to my crew boss on the timber gang. And that was it! I was officially a timberman. Our timber leader was a little black man, a good and religious man who was all business.

That first day he said, "Boy, now what's your name? I know Jim. You Jim's boy?"

"Yeah, my name's Robert. Everybody calls me Bob."

"If I can't think, I'll just call you Junior." That name stuck because he never did call me Bob. People see me in town from the Barnesville Shaft work years and they still call me June or Junior.

Eighteen men worked on our section. The coal mining process was conventional. Each mine section had between five and eight headings, or tunnels, about one hundred feet apart. As a timber crew, we worked behind the miners, shoring up the roof to maintain the rock above the coal where the machines did their work. Our timber leader was a hard worker. The crew consisted of four other fellows and myself. He told us how many bars, those fourteen-foot timbers the superintendent spoke of, to put up and where to put them. I did whatever he told me to do.

The bars were heavy, so the other crew members were very careful with me. I soon learned that on the average day, twenty-four sets went in: two side posts and, on top of them, a fourteen-foot crossbar. We placed these sets every four to five feet along the heading. That means that, as a crew, they expected us to handle, cut, and set seventy-two heavy wooden posts somewhere in the section. Nothing ever fit right, so we had to drive wedges in to fit the posts tight against the crossbar or the bottom, the floor of the mine. The others had experience at the job, so I watched them carefully to learn how to do it right.

Sometimes, though he was a small man, the timber leader would nudge me aside and say, "Boy, get out of the way!" Then he'd swing and swing and drive that wedge in, step back, and say, "Now it's tight." He taught me well. I tried to get the hang of it and worked hard to do a good job. After the first day, I dragged myself up those 102 steps, walked home with my dad, aching all over, and went to bed.

Once I got into condition to lift, carry, and pound in wedges, I enjoyed it. I especially liked getting to know the men and the foremen. The order of authority in a working mine can be confusing. The mine superintendent is in charge of the whole mine operation. He may have assistants to help him. The general mine foreman relays the superintendent's orders and takes care of personnel problems. Barnesville had three eight-hour shifts so we had three shift foremen who made job assignments. Then each section of the mine had a section foreman for each shift. He was responsible for the safety of his miners and for the coal production on his section. Crew bosses, like my timber leader, controlled a small group of miners doing a specific job.

The superintendents and foremen needed certification for their positions. They had to take classes and pass a test on managing miners, production, and safety procedures. Crew bosses didn't need this schooling. In 1947 only nine black foremen existed in all of West Virginia. They had to travel to the one school that certified black men: West Virginia State College near Charleston. Of course, without experience, every miner, white or black, started at the bottom of the ladder, assigned to a crew.

Naturally, I was leery of my physical surroundings at first, but not afraid. I often wondered what would happen if the top got too heavy and the bars couldn't hold up the mine roof. The darkness never bothered me.

On Saturday the mine was idle. Within a few weeks, they asked me to work on Saturdays. That paid time and a half, so I jumped at the chance.

On the first Saturday I worked, the section foreman asked two other fellows and me to pull and withdraw bars. I couldn't believe what I was hearing. We had to go in with a long rope, hook it around the posts that were supporting the crossbars, jerk them out, and then pull all the bars out and stack them. This procedure in mined-out headings saved the company from buying new ones. We didn't work with the coal at all, just the wooden timbers.

As he demonstrated the technique, the section foreman yanked a crossbar and yelled, "Watch this!" Over and over I thought to myself, *This man is going to kill us!* Above our heads the rock strata groaned as gravity took over. Chunks of coal pitched down and big cracks split open the top. Though certain that my death was only moments away, I couldn't run or hide my eyes. The roof buckled with deafening crunching and cracking. Tons of rock thundered down and spewed dust all over us.

When the smoky cloud cleared, I was still alive. We all were. I had witnessed a miracle. We didn't die. My fear, and then shock, obviously amused everyone. They started laughing and pounding me on the back. I joined in, hiding my terror with nervous laughter until the shakes went away. That first mine roof cave-in carved itself into my memory forever. Whether controlled or unplanned, the many roof falls I experienced over the years never equaled the thrill of that first one.

Any time dangerous work went on, the section foreman stood nearby, making suggestions about the safest and easiest way to do the work. I soon learned the right way to do things, and I learned to have great respect for the danger around me. After a couple of weeks, I got to know all the fellows on my crew. I was the youngest. The crew worked like a family of bees. Each individual had a job to do, but he always lent a helping hand to co-workers by pulling cables out of the way, shoveling, or helping to raise bars. Nearly half of the miners on my section were black men. Words of prejudice or discrimination never came up. We all worked and sweated together to produce coal.

Working with these fellows day by day, I learned about their families, where they lived, how many children they had, what their hobbies were, and on and on. I felt as if I was part of a new, big family. We looked forward to meeting each other at the start of the shift. We worked safely and as fast as we could. Then we came out and went home. This was a way of life. The best part was getting back to our families, without any accidents.

I became more and more enthused about coal mining four hundred feet underground. The bright lights, telephones, constant motion, noise, and supply tracks going everywhere made me feel as if I was a moving part of a miniature city, all underground. Though the machines ran on electricity, a distinctive oily motor smell hung in the air. Some of the smells of a city street floated by. Besides our lunches, we brought down and shared hot chocolate and coffee.

The air temperature was about fifty-two degrees, briskly cool, and gigantic fans on the surface kept the air moving all the time to clear out the gases. My coveralls' collar, which I wore up to keep coal dust from sifting down my back, flapped in this strong breeze. Unlike life on the surface, I found that a coal mine is void of bright colors. The coal was as black as a starless night. Occasional gray sulfur bands ran crossways or diagonally downward through the seam. The wooden posts and bars were brown. White rock dust covered all the surfaces. The men, regardless of race, were black from head to toe by the end of the shift. It didn't matter what color of coveralls we wore, they turned black with coal dust.

There's an interesting phenomenon about miners and coal dust. I picked up on this when I was young and my dad came home covered in coal dust. No one in the industry refers to it as dirt. A coal miner is covered in dust, not dirt. Soil is dirt. Above ground, people work in the dirt and get dirty. Miners consider working in soil or earth to be less prestigious than working in coal, a precious gift of nature. Coal dust is ever present in the coal mines. Its existence is matter-of-fact and part of the process of coal production. The negative qualities are totally ignored. Like wearing a badge of honor, a miner feels almost a sense of pride to wear coal dust on his body or clothes.

When I started at Barnesville, we had no facilities to bathe. I came home, stripped at the door to my thermal underwear, and took a bath or shower immediately. As shower facilities became a union issue or company courtesy, we didn't have to bring the dust home. Mothers and wives may have considered it dirt, but they only said it once. To be considerate, we men tried to keep the coal dust out of our homes.

In the summertime there was more moisture in the mines than in the winter. Water ran down through the veins of coal and pooled on the bottom. In the wintertime, the mine dried out. The blocks of coal had a dry surface, and suspended coal dust was more prevalent in the winter. Rock dusting, though a year-round necessity to keep the explosive coal dust contained, was more critical in the dry winter months.

I hadn't been at Barnesville very long when the company purchased a battery-operated timber machine. This was the first machine I used. It was strong and powerful and noisy. We picked up a bar with levers and supported it with the jacks. The machine had a saw on it. If a bar was too long, we could lay it across, measure with a tape measure, and saw it into the correct length. The same thing with the side posts. If one was too long, we could always put it on the machine, measure it, and cut it. We needed fewer wedges. The timber machine made timbering an amazingly fast operation.

Within a few months I got word that I was leaving the timber crew. I knew I'd miss working with the men I had come to know, but the new adventure excited me. I became a shuttle car driver, and I loved it! A shuttle car, nicknamed a "buggy," is only about four feet high but is twelve to fifteen feet long and about eight feet wide with a long bed to haul coal. This electric shuttle car runs on six rubber wheels and will go as fast as one can control it. Since there is no turnaround room in a heading, both ends have headlights. The seat swivels so the driver can go forward with either end of the shuttle car.

They didn't start me out hauling coal right away. They let me drive it in the crosscuts, the tunnels between one heading and another. These small passageways cut through at right angles to the main line, where the shuttle cars ran coal all day. I ran in the empty crosscuts until I knew that I could steer and control the car without cutting across my own electrical cable. If the cable caught on a corner and ended up laying slack on the bottom, the driver had to use skill to avoid running over his own cable. The shuttle car had a self-winding reel that kept the cable taut and retracted or played out as I moved from the coal face to the dumping site.

When I started hauling coal, the shift foreman said, "Bob, now take your time. There's no hurry." Each day I got faster and faster. Driving the shuttle car took me right up to the coal face with all the noise and dust. That's where the real action was, and I enjoyed being part of the action.

There was a disregard for safety rules at that time. If a light on either end was out, the section foreman might say, "You go ahead and run, and at noontime we'll replace it." At times the seat to the shuttle car was missing. Other times it was loose and swiveled wildly. I was young and strong, so I challenged myself that I could run the shuttle car just as fast without a seat. I stood up to operate it and started to prefer running that way. My muscles soon got conditioned to staying slightly stooped to avoid hitting my head. I imagine down through the years that's how I earned the reputation as a damned good shuttle car operator or a "buggy devil."

When the section foreman got on his section, he surveyed the surface where the shuttle cars ran. In the wintertime, some operators complained, "Boy, is it dusty in here!" Coal dust kicked up by the car wheels hung suspended in the air. The section foreman then ordered someone to open the valve to the four-inch water pipe and spray the surface to keep the dust down in the main line. Then the rock-dust crew came in and dusted the roof, ribs, or side walls, and the bottom.

In conventional mining there's a sequence of operations to extract the coal. Each operation requires a specialized crew with tools or a specialized mining machine. The process is very much like the one in my father's day, but instead of hundreds of men picking, loading, and hauling manually, machines do much of the heavy work.

What really amazed me was the machinery. Sometimes I found myself hypnotized as I watched the skillful operators glide through their work. For instance, the improved cutting machine weighed eight tons, ran on rubber wheels, and had a nine-foot oblong cutter bar. A thick chain, packed with sharp bits as big as a man's fist, ran around the cutter bar. The operator raised the bar up and turned it flat, like a knife. Then he started the bits running. As the bits churned into the coal, the machine advanced the cutter bar nine feet into the face near the bottom. He took his time and cut across from left to right with that huge cutting bar. After he'd cut approximately fourteen feet across, he backed up, turned the blade over, and then sliced the coal about three-quarters of the way up on the sides and in the middle. It took him less than twenty minutes to make the cuts.

After the cutting machine backed out, the drillers drilled three holes nine feet deep, one to the left side of the middle slice, one to the right, and one below. Their job took about twenty minutes also. Then they moved out. Just like in hand loading, but on a much bigger scale, a miner called a shot fireman went in with his powder and caps. With a tamping stick, he shoved four or five sticks of powder deep into the holes and put clay dummies behind them. He hooked up his cable and walked back about one hundred feet to detonate, and then hollered, "Fire! Fire! Fire!" Regardless of where I was in the mine, I heard and felt the blast. After the smoke cleared, a huge pile of coal lay on the bottom, filling up the end of the heading.

After the blast, the loading machine moved in. Now twenty feet in length, it still resembled the original, smaller loader with monster, crab-like digging arms. I never got tired of watching the five-ton loading machine burrow into the coal, working its hinged arms that flexed like a human's arms. Chunks of coal moved down the loading machine conveyor belt and simultaneously dropped off the back end into shuttle cars. When it backed out, the timber crew moved in to set timbers, and the process started over again.

Electric shuttle cars carried eight to ten tons of coal, and I took on a load in less than three minutes. As I pulled out full, the next shuttle car pulled in empty. Timing was everything or there would be coal all over the place. That was an all-day-long process from one heading to another. One shuttle car was always going loaded to dump into the rail cars or onto a huge conveyor belt to the outside. Empty ones were either returning to the loading machine or waiting to move in for a load. Shuttle car operators looked out for each other but ran as fast as conditions allowed to move out as much coal as possible.

All the employees on day, afternoon, and midnight shift worked hard to beat the loading of the previous crew and to get recognition. Our mine had long cars on tracks to the outside. There was an operator at the dumping point. It took between two and three shuttle car loads to fill one car. As we dumped and filled each car, the operator pushed a button to signal the motorman to skip to the next empty car. On an average smooth-running shift, we could load 300 cars. We always loaded at least 275. At times we'd go over the 300 mark. The company appreciated this.

When we didn't reach our shift goal, the problem was usually cable trouble. The cutting machines and the loading machines ran on electricity and their thick cables stretched anywhere from 150 to 300 feet to the power source. The cable could break anywhere, near the machines or along the way. Then the mechanic on the shift had to stop production, cut the power, and splice the cables so the machines could resume operations. Sometimes when production stopped, I helped the mechanic skin the cables with a sharp knife, put the splice rings on it, or tape them up. The section foreman appeared if there was any trouble or breakdown, and he called the mechanic. Right or wrong, the section foreman was the man in control. If something needed doing, employees talked to him, and he made the decision.

All the experienced miners operating those machines impressed me. Naturally, I aspired that someday, if I worked long enough in the coal mines, I could attain one of those positions with a higher hourly rate. But I had a lot of patience. *I'm in no hurry*, I thought. *I'll wait my turn.* I got unexpected opportunities to learn other mining jobs at Barnesville Shaft. My dad's helper quit, and since it paid more, I worked with him as a bore-hole driller for awhile. That was hard work, carrying around and holding up a ninety-pound drill. Keeping it steady to drill the holes in the face was a challenge for two men of medium stature, but we were strong and got the job done. When the company brought in pneumatic drills, helpers' jobs disappeared.

Before long, one of the loading-machine operator positions opened up. I applied for it and got the job. Since I had made it my practice to watch the operators closely, I knew that learning to run a loader wouldn't be too difficult. My teacher on the loading machine in Barnesville Shaft was only five feet six inches, 150 pounds. I found his words of advice applied to all mining machine jobs. "Bob, I'm going to tell you something. You let that machine do the work. You be the master. Don't let it work you." I learned a lot from him. Because of their striving to be equal to big men, smaller men were some of the best workers. Older guys with years of experience were also some of the best. They didn't take as many risks. I noticed that big six-feet-five-inch men stood around and complained about lifting too much or doing too much. That may be an unfair generalization, but I found it to be true.

For three years at Barnesville I moved around among several job positions, filling in at different places whenever I could, even the cutting machine. I learned a great deal in a short time. Some events from my first three years of coal mining made a lifetime impression, like that first roof fall. I liked the variety, but driving a shuttle car was my favorite job because there was more of a challenge to it. I also enjoyed driving fast through the headings.

During these years miners could do well if they worked five days a week, but some mines, including Barnesville Shaft, only operated three or four days a week because the coal market was so unstable. We enjoyed a five-day week occasionally, but that was rare. For months Barnesville Shaft only produced and loaded coal into large railroad hoppers three days a week, usually Mondays, Wednesdays, and Fridays. The mine also operated first shift on Saturdays, but the company had to load this coal into ten or twelve huge dump trucks near the tracks because the B&O Railroad didn't operate on Saturdays.

The UMW halted Saturday work. The contract stated no miners could start two shifts within twenty-four hours. If a crew worked on the Friday afternoon shift, finishing at midnight, and then returned the next morning at 8:00, they were in violation of the UMW contract. Since it was unfair to give some men three days and other men four days, we went back to working just three days a week.

The company paid with cash. The ritual of their payroll delivery looked like a scene from a 1930s gangster movie. The payroll truck carried a black man as an armed guard. He got out first, holding a shotgun or rifle.

Cautiously, he surveyed the parking area and covered a second man, who quickly carried the money into the office. Then they climbed back into the truck and drove to the next Consol mine.

Some of the miners could not read or write. Each pay envelope contained an itemized statement. I found it comical to watch them study the paper and then complain that they forgot their reading glasses. Several asked me to explain how much their total deductions were and how much money they had received. I felt sorry for these men and considered myself lucky that I could read and write and understand the statement and my own paycheck.

Most of us only averaged six days every two weeks. That didn't leave much to take home after taxes, union dues, and other deductions. For me, the pay was still more than twice what I had earned at the Watson Hotel. Like most families, we planted a large garden, and my dad and I hunted wild game.

To earn extra money on the side, I did some sign painting. Lettering doesn't require much creativity, but I welcomed the work. One company had four new trucks and needed them lettered. This opportunity came during a turn I did on midnight shift. After getting off work at 7:00 A.M., I walked to the company garage and painted one side of a truck each morning. For the first few days of the assignment, a mouthy black man hung around trying to get my job, saying he could do it better and faster. My boss stuck by me with praise and honored our agreement. At the end he told me, "Well done! If I need you again, I'll call you." I got a kick out of seeing those trucks on the road, knowing I had painted the sides.

To relax outside the mine, I began traveling at night with my friends. Water Street became a draw to us. As young men in our early twenties, we wanted to go where the action was on a Saturday night. None of us had a car, so we walked across the toll bridge. We had a blast, and I saw a lot of stuff going on there, but I never got arrested. It was not unusual to drop into a beer joint on Water Street and see a prominent white "city father" sitting and enjoying himself with a good-looking black woman.

I didn't do too much of this carousing. It didn't sit well at home. Besides, I had to stay in shape for the sport that had captured my mind and body—amateur boxing. ■

CHAPTER THIRTEEN

Boxing on the Side

Not for me!"

That was my final declaration when I had quit playing high school football. Weighing only 120 pounds was a definite disadvantage. I was fast, but my size made me a target to get banged around and run over. Since I wanted to be active in sports, I decided to go to the boxing gym. Boxing was very popular then because Joe Louis was still the undefeated heavyweight champion of the world. I had never lost my enthusiasm for boxing. A local fighter, Joe Testa, and the older guys at the gym let kids put gloves on to spar and mess around. Competing one-on-one with someone my own size sounded good, but it rarely turned out that way.

When I was younger, I enjoyed boxing matches with boys my age. Nobody kept time. We just boxed for ten or fifteen minutes, and when one boxer got tired, the fight was over. One of the boys grabbed the opposite one's arm, yanked it up in the air, and called out, "The winner and new champeeeen!" Like we heard over the radio.

One childhood fighting incident made a lasting impression on me. A boy from Cleveland, Ohio, came to stay with his grandparents in Grays Flats. They let him enter school there. We were both in the sixth grade, but this kid and I didn't get along. We ran our mouths at each other, insulting remarks that led to poking and finally to fighting. Walking home from school one day, we started into each other. Within seconds we pitched to the ground, wrestling in a pile of ashes. This kid was a real tough guy and bigger than me, but I held my own. My brother Bill came around a corner, instantly broke up the fight, and got down into my face. "Whoa, Bobby. This guy is too much for you. Back off!"

I didn't want to admit what Bill saw as obvious. I was embarrassed because this kid and I were the same age, and I thought I could take him. Because Bill was the "king" and in charge of me, I listened to him. I never forgot that. I'd think time and again, *What if I had beat that kid? Then he'd fear me or at least leave me alone.* I believe I brought the same fearlessness to boxing. The attitude served me well, to a point.

In the 1940s boxers in Fairmont trained upstairs in an old building behind the Fairmont Theater. We didn't have much equipment, except for big bags and jump ropes. We didn't know much about weight training. I ran half a mile a day and did calisthenics like bends and pushups. Except for running, we did all our training in the gym. I spent many hours sparring and learning the finesse of boxing and self-defense. We used thick, sixteen-ounce gloves so no one got hurt. After sparring and messing around for several years, I got better and better. The manager of the gym started encouraging me to agree to an amateur match. I was twenty-one when I joined the local stable of boxers.

My first fight was in Fairmont. Archie Evans was my opponent. He had already had at least five amateur fights and outweighed me by nine pounds. After the three-round match, the judges awarded me the decision. That gave me the incentive to keep boxing, and I got serious.

There were many fights in the area. I fought at Fairmont State College and at the old National Guard armory. We also traveled to Morgantown and Wheeling, West Virginia, and to Uniontown, Pennsylvania. Once or twice a month, the manager said, "Bobby, we got a fight coming up. Do you want to fight?" I always said, "Oh, yeah!" My first job in the mine, lifting timbers and bars, had made me stronger. I'd finish a hard day's work, dash up those steps out of the mine, run home, take a shower, rush to the gym, and be ready to box at 7:00 that evening.

The only photo taken
during Bob's amateur
boxing years, 1949–53.
Courtesy of Bob Armstead.

My third fight was at the American Legion. My opponent was a white boy out of Pennsylvania, Walter Kois. This guy was ten pounds heavier than me, and during the first round I could see that he was also very muscular. We sparred around for a couple of seconds. All at once, we clinched. He raised his elbow to get out of the clinch, and I went flying across the ring. I thought, *Oh my God, what have I got into?* My manager kept yelling, "Box, Bob! Box him!" So I boxed him. Though I only weighed 136 pounds, I knew I was faster than he was. I kept jabbing him. He was unorthodox with no distinct style. Each time we clinched, I could feel that he was strong in each hand. I won the fight because I outran him and outboxed him.

All my opponents were heavier than I was, most outweighing me by six to ten pounds. My style appeared flashy to the fans because I moved constantly, attacking, and defending myself from bigger boys.

Walter Kois came back for a tournament at Fairmont State College about three or four months later. They matched him to fight this black guy Sam, whom I had known to be a good fighter before he went into the service. To train for the tournament, I went to the gym three times a week for my workout. Sam was never there. I saw him on the street one day and said, "Sam, you haven't been down to the gym. You'd better get in shape."

He told me, "Oh, Bob, I'm in good shape. I'll whip him." Then he asked, "What do you know about Kois? How do I fight him?"

I knew Sam was a smart boxer, but I cautioned him. "I'll tell you what. He's a strong boy. He'll hurt you with either hand."

The night of the fight I was lying on the table in the dressing room when Sam came through with his trainer. I had my robe on. With great confidence, Sam bragged, "I'm going up and knock this guy out quick, and I'll be right back." Holding his arm out, he directed me, "Bob, give me your robe." Having scrapped with Kois so recently, I wondered at his attitude, but I gave him my robe, shook my head, and said simply, "OK."

I heard them announce the bill. In what seemed like one or two seconds, I heard *thump, thump*. That was Sam hitting the floor. Before long the announcement blared over the loudspeaker, "Kois beats . . ." Just that quick, it was over. Ten minutes later, bam! the doors flew open, and two men carried Sam in on a stretcher. He was conscious, but he'd suffered a knockout.

"I told you! Don't let that boy hit you! I told you he was strong!"

All Sam had to say was, "He caught me with his left hand."

I've laughed about that often because he went down, fast. About a year later, I read in the sports page that Walter Kois had become Penn State's boxing team captain. His picture showed him to be much heavier, possibly 175 pounds.

The week of my most dramatic fight, I worked the midnight shift and slept through the day. I was twenty-two. My family and I still lived with my parents. The night of the fight Mom woke me up, saying, "Bobby, it's almost 7:00. You know you're supposed to fight." I woke up with a start, showered, and ran down to the gym.

I didn't have fancy shoes or a robe for that fight. My weight was around 135 pounds. They introduced me. Then they called out my opponent, a black kid nicknamed "Snow Ball" White. He wore a sleek black robe and black boxing slacks with a white stripe. Written across the back of his robe were the words "Pittsburgh Core Championship." Stunned, I stared at my manager and said, "What in the world did you put me into this time? You've put me against something big!" My manager, as usual, ignored my fears and said, "You just box him, Bob. You know what to do."

When the bell rang, that kid rushed to the middle of the ring to intimidate me. We sparred around for a few seconds, not connecting. All at once, I saw an opening and threw a quick face bump. His head snapped back. He failed to protect his face, so I moved in and jabbed him again. His head went back again. At the same time, I crossed him with a right. In slow motion he rolled down to the floor. Out! I'd knocked him out with three punches in the first round. Sure, he had feinted at me, but he never landed a punch on me. I looked down on the Pittsburgh champion with the fancy silk clothes, lying there, out cold, and said, "There's your 'Snow Ball' White." Unfortunately, I couldn't even celebrate and savor my victory. I ran home, took another shower, and went to work.

My fans became big supporters because I was a winner. Many times my friends and a group of coal miners sat at ringside, screaming and hollering. I became a bit of a hero in the mine. The guys teased me. "Bob, let's see you. You got any black eyes?" Often I did. I heard over and over, "I saw you fight last night. You did pretty good." But they complained about my decisions. "Why didn't you knock that guy out?"

"Why didn't you help me?" I'd ask to shut them up. The guys made lots of jokes and had fun over my boxing. They teased me about decisions and about getting hurt. A young man doesn't fight three years without an injury or two. The only facial scars I have are from a cut over one eyelid and a gash across my nose. Both came from sparring matches, not actual fights. I never got more than bruises and black eyes on my face because I protected it and pulled back from jabs. Most of the time I preferred to tape my own hands. I broke three knuckles. Each one put me out of commission to box for a few weeks. I never got them set so they healed crooked. Thank goodness I never broke either thumb. Although I got sprains and contusions in my hands and wrists, I didn't take time to have them treated.

One night I got hurt fighting a black kid out of Morgantown. Ironically, his name was Joe Lewis. In the first round I sprained my right hand, hitting him. I switched to hitting with my left hand and won the fight. My right hand swelled and hurt for days.

My parents worried about my boxing, and when I got hurt, my mom let me know how she felt about "that violent sport." She definitely didn't approve. Mom and I had the same conversation any time I got hurt.

"Bobby, did you get hurt tonight?"

"No, Mom, I'm fine."

"Let me see. Oh dear! You'd better see a doctor about this."

"It'll be all right tomorrow." That's what I told her every time she fussed over me. Then I knew I couldn't complain, and that helped me ignore the pain. The injuries never affected my work because I ran the shuttle car and could manage with one hand.

Since Bill and James had homes of their own away from Fairmont and my sisters were more prone toward religion, my family didn't go to my fights. Dad was a baseball fan, not a boxing fan, but he did come to several fights. If he didn't see me fight but knew that I'd won, he'd say, "I hear you boys are doing all right." That was his show of approval.

The closest I came to becoming a professional boxer occurred under odd circumstances. Arnold Curry was a fighter out of Cleveland, Ohio, who traveled around the tri-state region. He was good. The first I fought him was in Uniontown, Pennsylvania. We had a close fight, but I lost the decision. Our second fight was in Fairmont, and I lost again. After that fight, his father came up to me. "Son, you gave my boy a damn good fight. Why don't you let me be your manager?" With my family responsibilities, I couldn't be on the road. I knew that getting into any substantial money was a long, hard road of fights. His offer made me feel good after the second loss to his son, but I had to say, "No, I'm not interested."

Arnold Curry won the Amateur Athletic Union Championship for the state of Ohio. That's a prestigious award. I only lost three fights in my amateur boxing career. Two of those losses were to Curry, a state champion. I always felt good about that. My third loss was my last fight. I was twenty-four. We drove to Wheeling, West Virginia, ninety miles from Fairmont. The interstate, I-79, was not built yet, and it took almost four hours to get to Wheeling over the mountains. I left work at 3:00, and we barely made it to the arena on time.

I fought four fights in three straight nights. I won the first fight. The promoters told me, "To get into the finals, you must fight again." So I fought at 7:00 and again at 9:00. We had to drive all the way back home that night, and I went to work the next morning. Of course, after two fights in a row, I had a few bruises. The guys teased me, "Bob, I hope you won." I told them I did, but I don't think they could know what it took to win two in one night.

We drove back to Wheeling that evening, and I won again. Back to Fairmont and back to work the next morning. Unfortunately for me, it just happened to be a five-day work week. The third night I fought for the Tri-State Amateur Tournament Championship of Ohio, Pennsylvania, and West Virginia. My opponent was Curtis Cole, a black kid from Pittsburgh. I knew he was good because he had defeated one of the guys in our stable here. Our guy dodged him. He lost six pounds so he wouldn't have to box in Cole's class. I weighed 138 pounds.

Earlier in the week the manager had said, "Bob, if you lose three pounds, you won't have to fight Cole if you get to the finals Friday night." Since I was forever trying to *gain* weight, losing didn't interest me. Looking back, it may sound cocky, but I told him, "Hey, I wouldn't *lose* three pounds to fight King Kong." He laughed.

That Friday night Cole weighed in at 147, so he outweighed me by nine pounds. In a lightweight championship fight, nine pounds gives one man a big advantage. Plus he was good. In fact, they had built him up to be the next Sugar Ray Robinson. In his division, Sugar Ray was the best that ever set foot in the ring, so Cole was a great fighter. He'd already won ten fights in South America and had a big reputation. Of course, I had won thirty. Everybody kept asking me, "What are you going to do?" I finally said, "I'll fight him."

It was a five-rounder, and I went the full five rounds. They gave him the decision. I lost. I had fought night after night after night, and then I lost. That's when I quit. My record was thirty and three. The enthusiasm left. That night I told myself, *I think I've run my gamut. I'm twenty-four years old and trying to raise a family. I think I'd better let it go.* It wasn't just that one loss. Many things came together that evening. Trying to work and box had gotten to be too much of a hassle. I didn't have time to train properly. As I said, we didn't have good facilities or equipment to train. We didn't even have any showers.

Guys wanted to see the pros fight. The people of Fairmont didn't continue to support boxing like we thought they would. Business places didn't support it either. Sponsors never put up prize money. They might buy meals on a road trip, but that was all. Sure, I got jackets and trophies, and maybe a write-up in the paper for recognition, but I never made any money. With everything else, I couldn't help but wonder what the point was. I enjoyed it, but I had responsibilities and decided to move on.

Some professional fighters started out just like I did. They were poor and didn't have anything. Black and white fighters alike came up hard until they earned a chance at a championship fight. That could have happened to me. The major drawback was that they didn't make very much money. Thirty-five million dollars for one fight was unheard of. I can't help thinking that I came up in the boxing world in the wrong era. Under different circumstances I might have turned professional.

I believe the best part of boxing is that it develops character. Boxing gave me incentive to aspire to a higher level of excellence instead of thinking that the world "owed me something." It also kept me off the streets. Since there were no leagues, I didn't get the chance to play Little League baseball, or Babe Ruth baseball, or Pop Warner football when I was a kid. I needed something to do with my spare time besides stand on the street corner, so I boxed, at home and in the gym. My jobs kept me busy, but I still had free time. Boxing gave me the character that prevents a young man from being interested in vandalism, burglary, or other criminal activities.

The worst part of boxing is staying in shape. That and being overmatched. Everyone I fought was bigger than me. I have always felt that if I could have just weighed at least ten more pounds, I could have played football and been a powerful boxer. In the late 1940s there were only eight divisions in the World Boxing Association. When Joe Louis fought, he was champion of the world. There weren't champions in the other divisions, just heavyweight. Flyweight started at 104 pounds. The other seven divisions were bantamweight, featherweight, lightweight, welterweight, middleweight, light-heavyweight, and heavyweight. Now, besides the WBA, there's the World Boxing Commission, the National Boxing Association, and the American Boxing Commission, each with four or five champs in many more divisions. It's still a battle to get there, but the opportunities have opened up.

After I quit fighting, I refereed for six years. Most of it was routine. Joe Testa arranged a sixteen-fight tournament at Melody Manor in Fairmont. He asked if I'd help referee eight bouts, or twenty-four rounds, of boxing. Testa had organized it for a group of young kids to help keep them straight. I volunteered to do it for no pay. I thought it was a great idea and didn't want to burden Joe with referee's wages. The kids got their pictures in the paper and some nice publicity, which I helped to prepare.

For three days before the tournament I went to the gym, helped the boys get in shape, and watched them spar. This black kid came down for the first time and said, "Hey, Mr. Bob, do you think you can get a fight for me?"

I told him, "Son, I don't know anything about your potential, whether you can box or not. These boys have all been down here working. I put the sign up and a notice in the paper, and you haven't been here to work out. I don't want you to go out there and get hurt."

He was enthusiastic. "Oh, don't worry. I'm in good shape. What do you think?"

Though he had a stomach on him and didn't look in the best of shape, he was about nineteen years old, and I thought he should know his own mind. I finally said, "OK. If you're out there when the manager comes, I'll ask if he has a boy your weight."

He got a bout, and he showed up to fight. I didn't referee that night. I was just a second, helping in the corners between rounds. He got in the ring with a gutsy kid from Uniontown, whom he outweighed by *thirty* pounds. The size difference gave our boy false confidence. The smaller guy started beating him in the stomach. When he came back to the stool, I poured some water on his head and started to rub him down.

He snapped at me, "Don't do that!" Then he asked, "How'm I doin'?"

I lied, thinking he needed encouragement, "You're doing all right."

In the second round that smaller kid pounded him without breaking a sweat. When our boy came to sit down after that round, he was dripping and blowing. I pulled his trunks out to fan him some air. He said, "Ohhh, Mr. Bob! Don't do that! How about taking these gloves off? I've had enough!"

"No, no, son. You finish what you started."

"No! I want the gloves off!"

I told him straight in his face, "When that bell rings, you are going out there."

At the bell, I helped to push him out. His opponent beat the dickens out of him. When he came back, he said, "I don't want no more." Of course, the bout was over, so he meant he wanted no more boxing.

My friends teased me for twenty years about that. They said, "Bob, you're dirty!" I didn't agree. Any time someone brought it up, I repeated my reason for pushing that boy. "He came down there, telling me he was in shape, and begging me to let him fight. I let him get enough of it." The kid didn't hold a grudge against me. He knew I wasn't being mean or dirty. He learned a lesson about preparation and truth, and he didn't resent me for being the teacher.

One night that I refereed the tournament, Joe Testa's son boxed. Joe had a similar lesson in mind that night, too. His son got a match with a very strong kid from Uniontown. That kid beat Joe's son all over the ring and bloodied his nose. After the second round, I said, "I'm stopping the fight."

Joe said, "No, you don't, Bob!"

I told him the truth. "This boy's too much for your kid."

Joe was clear on his intentions. "I don't care. He wouldn't train, and I want him to go one more round."

What could I do? The boy from Uniontown knocked Joe's kid from pillar to post. He was so outmatched that it was comical in a way. But at the same time, I didn't appreciate that Joe overrode my judgment. I believe I was correct. Two judges and I had to write out separate cards as to who won each round. The results should have been a technical knockout at the end of round two but ended up being a decision. Not *my* decision. I got caught in the middle of a family lesson, which wasn't a comfortable place to be. Sometimes in sports and in life, a man's hands are tied.

My active boxing career, from the time I stepped into the gym, early years of training, amateur bouts, and refereeing, spanned the years 1944 to 1958. I enjoyed every minute, but as the local interest faded down to none, I left the sport as a participant. For the last forty years I have been content teaching my sons to box and being an avid fan of boxing on television. Any time networks or cable channels televise boxing, I watch it.

During my amateur boxing years, I realized that my chosen career, coal mining, might not be a wise choice. The industry was dependent on many outside forces. This awareness began in the summer of 1950 with a nationwide UMW strike that lasted fifty-two days. My hands were tied. Two months of strike pay sets a man back. From the strike, we got a $2.00 a day raise each year for the life of the contract. The first year my base pay rate as a shuttle car driver went from $13.05 to $15.05 a day.

Following the strike, when we went back to work at Barnesville Shaft, inspectors started sniffing around. The mine closed for three days, and we heard other area mines had closed also. The reason turned out to be almost unbelievable. Virtually all of Fairmont had been undermined! This could cause chaos on the surface. As we returned to work, we noticed inspectors and engineers milling about everywhere. Barnesville Shaft had been worked by hand-loading miners and mechanized methods for at least seventy years under Buffalo Creek and parts of Bellview. Headings branched out toward Chesapeake and toward Jackson Addition in Fairmont. The mine at Watson, where my dad started, had been mining for as many years under the West Fork River and under Fairmont's numbered streets, plus Country Club Road and Locust Avenue. Meanwhile, the Monongah mine stretched far under Fairmont, heading toward Barnesville Shaft. The state engineers had stopped all three operations while they made that three-day underground survey.

After mining resumed, my dad came home early one day, soaking wet. In his job as a driller, he often drilled twenty-foot test holes. If the drill popped through, that meant they had found water, air, or a heading from another mine. His clothes were dripping wet clear up to his shoulders. I'd never seen him like that. "Dad, what happened to you?"

"Bob, you should have been there. All the engineers were standing around watching us. We felt that drill give, and the force of the water shoved the drill back out of the hole. That twenty-foot auger came out of there and blew us backward. Water from that underground lake gushed at us like a fire hose gone wild. Driving the wooden plugs into the hole is how we got so wet." Then he grinned. "The engineers got their shoes wet. After that, they told us, 'You guys go on home. We'll pay you the shift.'"

We worked another three weeks before we got the word. "The first mine to cut into another mine will shut down." Before the mines cut into each other, they had to preserve a massive block of coal to protect the foundations under Fairmont State College and Fairmont General Hospital. Shortly thereafter, we cut into Monongah. The engineers advised a complete work stoppage for all except Monongah mine. Barnesville Shaft was scheduled to shut down within four months. The company put up a list of twenty men they planned to keep on the payroll. Those men would recover valuable equipment and maintain gas and water levels until they sealed the mine. We weren't on the list. I tried not to think about having to leave this job, which I truly enjoyed. Rumors floated every day as to what would happen to us. Both wage earners in one house, my dad and I, faced a layoff.

One month before our scheduled termination, Mother Nature dealt West Virginia a terrible blow: the "Thanksgiving Snowstorm" of 1950. The Friday after Thanksgiving my father, our friend, and I went to work around 1:00 P.M. to prepare for our 2:00–10:00 P.M. shift. By then I had bought my first car, a 1939 Buick, and I drove it to the mine. Temperatures were normal for that time of year.

What a surprise met us outside the pit mouth after work! Every car in the parking lot was totally buried under four feet of snow. And it was still coming down. We decided the snow was too deep to walk the tracks home so we walked up Pennsylvania Avenue. It took us at least an extra hour to reach home. Automobiles inched along on the highways or sat bogged down next to the roadside.

At the height of the storm, an expectant mother, about to deliver, had to be rescued by a wagon and team of horses. This was only one of many emergencies as people were caught without heat, electricity, and food.

Fortunately, our home had natural gas, and we weathered the storm safe and warm. Mom's canning cellar was full of food, so that wasn't a problem.

All around us, however, the whole state came to a standstill. The mine was idle for over a week. No work, no money. And the layoff loomed around the corner. The B&O Railroad shut down. Engines could barely move, let alone pull anything, so the company called over the radio stations for volunteer snow-shovelers. My father and I joined many other men to shovel snow for several days and nights. It took two weeks for our checks to arrive from the headquarters in Baltimore.

About five days after the snowstorm, the mine foreman called us to ask if we would come and shovel snow from the coal hoppers sitting on the tracks at the mine. We knew it had to be done to get back into production, and we needed the money, so we agreed. What a nightmare! Each night that we trekked to the job, the temperatures hung in the low twenties, freezing the melting snow underneath. And it was windy. The hoppers had four to five feet of snow lying on top of two feet of ice at the bottom. The company had bonfires burning to keep us warm.

I could only shovel for about ten minutes. Then I had to crawl back out of the hopper and try to get warm again. Being bundled in layers of clothes made this work even more awkward. We were all sweating, but our hands and feet got numb from the cold. The first night I burned up a brand-new pair of boots trying to keep my feet warm, but that didn't matter because I wore the toes out crawling in and out of the coal cars. Moving the powdered snow was almost impossible. As I'd try to heave a shovelful out over my head, it whirled about, caught a gust, and blew back in, blinding me. After climbing and heaving and sweating and freezing for what seemed like hours, the job of chipping two feet of ice did me in. I could only stand this punishment for three nights.

A few days later the temperature finally warmed up. The snow and ice began to thaw, and things started getting back to normal. Area residents continued shoveling snow from their house roofs and driveways and tried to free their cars from streets and ditches. One-story homes started taking shape as nine-foot drifts slowly shrunk away. The freezing temperatures had refrigerated my car for two weeks. A friend drove me to the mine parking lot to check on it. I cleaned most of the snow from around it, got in, and turned the switch. Nothing. We took all eight spark plugs out, dried the condensation off them, and put them back in. The car started. Buried and abandoned cars and trucks sat on streets and in ditches for weeks. That snowfall was one of the largest in West Virginia history. I hope we never have another.

With the three-day weeks, the strike, the snowstorm, and mine closing, the last half of 1950 was a dark time. Even putting our salaries together, my father and I barely made five thousand dollars for the whole year. In December, Consol shut down Barnesville Shaft, permanently laid off many men, and transferred the rest to the other mines. I was "lucky." My dad and I got notice of our transfer to the Everettville mine, a notorious hellhole. ■

CHAPTER FOURTEEN

On to Everettville

Everettville mine was a hellhole because it was "hot." A hot mine has high levels of methane gas that can ignite at any time. Other problems earned it the nickname hellhole, but methane and bad roof were the most dangerous. Every coal miner knew this mine had a dark history, and twenty-three years had not improved its reputation.

On Saturday, April 30, 1927, at 3:25 in the afternoon, the Everettville mine exploded. Ninety men died instantly. The explosion trapped seven others inside. They died later from gases or lack of air, leaving notes for their loved ones. Rescue teams worked fourteen days to recover all the bodies. Of the ninety-seven miners killed, fifty-four were black. The cause of the explosion remained a mystery. Since the mine was on strike, and strikebreakers, or "scabs," were inside, the UMW blamed it on inexperienced workers. The company accused the union of sabotage. Some said methane gas probably ignited after blasting down coal. The mine superintendent blamed the company for not providing money for rock dust to control the methane. Whatever happened, it was the second largest mine disaster in the state's history.

The worst tragedy occurred in 1907. Two Monongah mines, one after the other, exploded, killing 361 men officially, 457 unofficially. In 1907 young boys went into the mines to help their fathers. Speculation puts the death toll over 500.

When miners work in a mine where deaths have occurred, they usually avoid talking or thinking about the past. Even if bodies remain buried inside, there is no talk of ghosts or any fear of discovery. A man simply takes care of the business of the day, one day at a time, and works in the present.

Though I was glad to have a job, I had a concern in the beginning. My old 1939 Buick wasn't reliable. At Barnesville Shaft, if my car didn't start, I walked. Everettville was twelve miles from home in Monongalia County, and we traveled narrow, curvy mountain roads. My Buick required a lot of attention. Mom came out one day while I was tinkering with the motor. She said, "Son, it seems that when you start working on your car, by the time you get to the back, you have to start working on the front end again." Her words rang true.

The Buick and I didn't get off on the right foot. I bought it on a Friday. Two days later my friend, who had taught me to drive standard shift, called, "Bob, I need you to do me a favor. An old guy asked me to take a sixteen-gallon keg of beer to his place in Barrackville. Will you drive me?" Though it was a harsh winter day with ice on the road, I said, "No problem. Let's go!" I put chains on the car, but nothing helps on ice. On Crematory Hill along Route 250 between Fairmont and Barrackville, I hit the brakes on a slick spot, lost control of the car, and flipped it over. We didn't get a scratch on us. That old car lay on its top, with the wheels still spinning. Several motorists stopped to help. They pushed it back over and onto the highway. Being young and fearless, we continued up the road to Barrackville and delivered the beer. My friend reminded me often, "Bob, that drum of beer could have hit you, killed you, broke your neck, or killed both of us."

I had paid $350 for the car. Somehow I saved $200 and asked Mom and Dad to loan me the other $150 to buy it. That was big money then. The day of the accident I parked it beside my friend's house, hiding the smashed-in side so Dad couldn't see it. Finally, on Monday morning, I had to tell them what had happened. My mom spoke up first. "Bobby, you just got that car. We let you have $150 for it. There's no money to fix it. You'll have to drive it that way." I did.

The old main portal that had exploded at Everettville was in the center of town and went straight into the mountain. Actually, three portals and an air shaft existed in the original mining operation. By the time I started there in December 1950, the mine headings had spread four miles west, where the company had opened another portal. The coal seam dipped down so the new section was a shaft mine. We had to go down in a cage.

Consol owned the Everettville mine. To adapt to varying coal seams and rock strata, mining methods differed drastically from one mine to another. Everettville was wet, gassy, and contained cramped work areas. Disregarding these conditions, the company had expanded into two new sections, laying track. All the younger fellows, including me, thought we had a future there.

My start-up pay at Everettville, as general inside laborer, was $10.60 a day, a $5.00 cut. Though we had good work records, all of us from Barnesville Shaft had to start over. Classified as new employees, we worked midnight shift, the least desirable. Each night they split us up and sent us to a different menial job, such as timbering, shoveling loose coal, or carrying supplies. At first we only worked three nights a week, sometimes four. We were eager to work full time because we had been working only three and four days a week for several years. The permanent miners worked five days a week on three production shifts.

The older miners at Everettville felt the transferees from Barnesville Shaft came to take their jobs and were hostile toward us. One of the ways this hostility came about made no sense at all. The mine foreman came in and asked the men from Barnesville if we wanted to work the weekend, laying track and rock dusting. We agreed and worked the weekend. A week or so later the foreman came around asking the permanent Everettville miners about the weekend. Ten or more spoke up, saying they would like to work. Come the weekend, maybe only two showed up.

This happened over and over. We honored our weekend verbal agreement to work, and they did not. The foreman saw this and asked us more often. The permanent miners looked on our wanting to work weekends as wanting their jobs. We told them several times, "No, fellows. We just want to work. We *need* to work." Their bad attitude got under our skin until finally one of our guys told them, "You say you'll be here to work the weekend, and you don't show up. What do you expect if you don't come to work?" That shut them up for awhile, but the resentment came out in rudeness on the job.

One day my assignment was to help the black loading-machine operator and his black helper with the dumb work of shoveling loose coal. The shift foreman saw me shoveling and said, "June, I know you're a darned good shuttle car operator, but these are a little bit different."

"I noticed, but I can learn."

That pleased the foreman. He said, "Good! I like your attitude. You go ahead and work every day. That way, when I need a replacement, you'll be available."

The loader and his helper heard this and knew I had just gotten full-time work and the promise of a shuttle car with a hike in pay. I had to swallow my excitement because the look on their faces told me they didn't like it one bit.

Later that day, the hauling crew ran out of empty rail cars. During the slowdown the loader and his helper walked away from the site to get a drink at the dinner hole. I continued shoveling. Meanwhile, the empties came in, and the first shuttle car moved in for a load of coal. Since the loader and his helper had not returned from their break, the driver asked me, "Can you run that loader?" I said, "Yes, I can. I'm not the operator, but I can load your shuttle car." I turned the machine on to run the coal back into the shuttle car. Big mistake!

Within five minutes I saw the lights coming. The loader and his helper came up fast, flashing their lights back and forth as a signal to stop immediately. I thought the mine was about to blow up! I turned the loader off and yelled, "What's wrong?" Gritting his teeth and flashing his eyes, that loader got next to me and shouted, "Let me tell you something, boy! This is *my* machine! You keep your damned hands off it!" Startled at his incredible anger, I stepped back with my hands out and said, "There it is." I wasn't going to argue and make him any madder than he already was. An argument with that loader would have come to blows, and I had enough to worry about without getting fired for fighting.

Besides dealing with the hostility, we had to adapt to the substandard working conditions at Everettville. Conventional mining, with cutting machines, blasting, and loading machines, was in place, but the equipment was old and dilapidated. Breakdowns occurred frequently, slowing down production and making foremen short-tempered.

As I sloshed through water, I noticed foremen taking methane readings constantly. I knew they had to get us out if the levels rose too high, so I didn't worry too much about that. Something more dangerous held my attention. Everettville had bad roof conditions because of the "snap top." Snap coal is highly unstable and compact. When the cutting-machine operator went in to do his undercut and side cuts, he left fourteen inches or so at the top for protection. The coal was so hard that he had to go in two or three times to cut. The state standard to set posts and bars was five feet apart. Since the top was unpredictable, timbermen came in immediately and put the posts and bars three feet apart right up to the face.

Before long we heard the coal in the top start snapping and popping, like popcorn. After a short time, the coal shot out in chunks between the bars, exposing the rock. Often the roof snapped, but no coal moved as we waited and watched. This snapping might happen once an hour or once every ten minutes. The sound unnerved us because a roof fall often followed a big chunk. When the coal snapped, miners scattered. Sometimes coal chunks shot out from lack of support. The law said that if a post or bar got bumped or knocked out, production stopped until timbermen reset that post or bar. At quitting time all timber had to be in place for the next crew.

Soon after I started running a shuttle car, a fatal accident occurred ten minutes before the shift ended at 7:00 A.M. I was fairly close but didn't see it happen. A loading machine claw grabbed one of the supporting posts and pulled it down. With so little time left, the loading-machine operator and his buddy didn't want to stop to reset, so they placed it over to the side. The operator eased his machine in to get the last bit of coal from the bottom. As he moved in, the head coal fell down over the loading machine. A chunk of coal snapped out of the top and hit the loader on the head.

I was the second shuttle car in line. The man in front of me came running back with his light flashing. He yelled over and over, "Where's the section foreman? Where's the section foreman?" Since I was too far back to hear anything over the machine noise, I turned off my car and asked, "What's wrong?" Still moving, he yelled back, "Ray got covered up! We gotta get the foreman!" In a panic we sent someone else for the foreman and ran up to the accident site. We tried to pull Ray out but couldn't move him. After we finally dug him out, I helped carry him out of the mine. He was unconscious.

They called home later that day and said, "There won't be any work tonight. That loader operator died." Ray had died two hours after arriving at the hospital. As a sign of respect, a twenty-four-hour shutdown follows any miner's death.

I knew men got hurt and killed in mines all the time. Somewhere else. My first experience with the death of a fellow miner stayed with me. Someone I knew was gone, suddenly and forever. That kind of tragedy wakes a man up and leaves him heartsick at the same time. Every snap made us bolt for awhile, but since we were all in danger, we didn't discuss it. Each man lived in his own private hell.

The section foreman got in trouble. According to company policy, he was responsible. They tried to imprison him for not having that post put back in place. He had at least six headings to monitor and couldn't be everywhere. Before a section foreman shut down the shift and took the men out, he had to check the gases in all the headings to report the conditions to the next section foreman coming in. He was five hundred feet away, taking methane levels, when the accident occurred, but he suffered a long time over that death. The stigma finally went away, and he remained with the company. None of us contract miners blamed him at all.

At Barnesville Shaft I had learned to operate the electric shuttle car, with cables trailing and power steering, almost to perfection. Everettville used battery-operated shuttle cars. These shuttle cars were smaller than electric cars and could only haul about four tons of coal. The oversized steering wheel drove hard, like a bus, making them awkward to maneuver. In the learning process, my worst time was trying to get around curves. Right after I started as a full-time operator, I had a nightmare. My sister heard me screaming and hollering. "Bob! Bob! What's wrong with you?" she said.

I woke up in a sweat, startled, and asked, "Was I driving? Like turning a steering wheel?"

"No, why do you ask that?

"Just trying to get that buggy in that curve" was all I could say as I dropped off back to sleep. Until I got the knack of that car, it bothered me that I couldn't do it perfectly. Enough to invade my dreams, I guess.

Besides wrestling with the steering on these shuttle cars, we had to deal with antique batteries. Huge, two-ton batteries, one strapped to each side, needed charging at the end of each shift. Shuttle car operators stopped at the battery house, or changing station, and helped the mechanic exchange the batteries. We struggled to jack up each battery and replace it with a newly charged one. Then we had to drive the shuttle car up to the section for the next shift's operator.

Nearly every night, around 3:00 A.M., I'd hear a shuttle car battery starting to lose power. The motor powered by a dying battery is an unmistakable, sorrowful sound. Whenever this happened, to avoid a blockage in the main line, operators helped each other. A shuttle car with a strong battery would push the one with the run-down battery back to the battery house.

Besides messing with batteries, a policy involving supplies slowed down production. If the supply runner was off work, shuttle cars had to run supplies, like bars or concrete blocks, up to the crews between trips of running coal. These small, battery-operated shuttle cars wasted time and slowed production. I learned the art of handling them, but I never liked them. Most of the other operators there loved these shuttle cars. They had never seen or operated an electric one.

Because of my experience, the company involved me in their planned switch to all-electric shuttle cars. Four months after I started working at Everettville, the general mine foreman called me into his office. He was friendly. "Bob, could I interest you in operating the first electric car to be brought into this mine?"

"Yes, sir. I'd be very interested."

"That's good to know. The plan is to start bringing it in this Saturday night while the mine is idle. We'll pay you time and a half."

"I'll be here. It's too big for the cage. How's it coming in?"

"You're right about that. And this is the hard part. We have to run it underground through the old main portal in Everettville. The going will be slow through that narrow main line, but we've measured, and it will go. Probably take two full shifts to move it over here."

"How far is it?"

"Three miles, Bob. You still want the job?"

"Yes, sir. I'll be there."

"Keep it to yourself for now. That's all."

As I walked out the door, all I could think was, *Brand-new electric shuttle car! Me!*

When I arrived that Saturday night at the Everettville portal, there it sat: a big, wide, bright orange, top-of-the-line Joy Manufacturing electric shuttle car. Smiles and anticipation all around. A foreman, a motorman, and I discussed the move. I looked forward to the challenge.

A heavy-duty mine locomotive sat ready in the opening to help pull the car along the way. The tracks ran somewhat higher in the middle and the roof dripped from seepage. Water-filled ditches ran along both ribs. Though we tried to keep it between the tracks, we slipped into the ditches several times. When that happened, we had to stop and work with jacks and wedges. Wooden and steel beams and posts crammed the narrow passageway. As we inched along, we had dangerous close encounters with these posts.

We accomplished our tremendous task, which some thought should have taken two days, in five hours. And we made it without a scratch on that new orange paint job. I was squishing in my boots and soaked to the bone with water and sweat, but what a feeling of accomplishment! We parked the car near the cage. Every few days I noticed another new shuttle car had been moved in by another crew. Five in all. Several cutting machines joined this lineup of new equipment. Sad to say, they never cut or hauled coal at Everettville.

The mine had a strong union that called numerous strikes because of the dangerous working conditions. We lost at least one day every couple of weeks. On the way to work, as we drove around the curve at Arnettsville, we could see the mine lights. An older gentleman I drove with had a sixth sense. He'd say, "Bob, I don't believe we're going to work tonight. You see those four lights up there. I believe they're having a strike." He'd be right. No work, no coal, no pay.

The Everettville UMW president, we'll call him Matt, was a young college man. He knew the contract inside and out. Matt and his committeemen kept the superintendent and the company to the letter of the contract by staging sudden work stoppages. Most of the 306 coal miners were blacks or foreigners and couldn't read or write.

At the union meetings over 200 men would fill the hall. They'd stand around drinking and smoking, asking one another, "What are we going to talk about tonight?" When Matt walked in, the room would go silent. He'd pound the gavel to start the meeting. Right off he'd say something critical—the company is doing this or that—and then he'd pause, shake his head, and look like he was thinking, *It's bad, men. What more can I say?* Someone would shout, "Matt, do you think we ought to strike?" He'd keep silent for effect. Then he'd say, "Fellows, you do as you please."

That's all he said. He was that kind of leader with that kind of attitude. The miners respected him. To get what he wanted, he allowed people to believe that he agreed with what they said. The next Sunday night maybe only two men showed up for work. I found it disgusting because sometimes I was one of those men. When asked about this, Matt replied, "I didn't tell those fellows to strike." He was smart. He had a way of getting around things without getting blamed for anything.

Every time the men struck, the company lost money—big money. No company tolerates that indefinitely. Though all that new equipment was headed to the newly developed sections, none of it ever got there. Rumor says Consol chose to shut down the Everettville mine instead of fight the radical union. I got caught in the middle of this mess.

A week or two before the end, the company put up lists of employees' names, starting dates, termination dates, and classifications. That's how my dad and I found out that we had a termination date. We started in December 1950, and they closed it down in April 1951. I only worked there five months. Through no fault of my own, I got shut out of two mines in five months. I was getting very discouraged with mining.

This time Consol had no intention of placing anyone anywhere. They kept some of the older fellows for maintenance until November, when they sealed it up. The rest lost their jobs in April and, many of them, their homes. Everettville became a ghost town. The company store closed, followed by the post office. Men with families moved out to find work. Stores and homes began to fall apart. Besides Pick Handle Hill, the old black section high above the community, very few homes have survived through the years.

The mine fell to ruin. Forty-six years later, in October 1997, the Division of Environmental Protection's Abandoned Mine Lands and Reclamation hired a contractor to regrade and seed the thirty acres of slate dumps surrounding the town. They also ordered "wet seals" to close the old mine portals. Wet seals are concrete walls with a ground-level drainage pipe. This would allow the impounded acid mine water to escape into Indian Creek at the rate of forty gallons per minute (Lamarre 1994). Plans for a water-treatment facility may not materialize because of the tremendous amount of money needed to reclaim all the other abandoned mine sites in West Virginia.

After Dad and I got laid off, unemployment compensation paid each of us $120.00 a month for six months. I tried cards, pool hustling, and gambling to earn money. My father enjoyed gambling to make money on the side. My mom, my sisters, and my wife didn't approve, so Dad and I kept our winnings a secret and "just happened to have extra money" to give them. The women stopped questioning where it came from. The Fairmont Hotel put me on as a fill-in waiter, paying $2.00 in cash to serve lunch. If I was lucky, I could go back in the evening and get $2.50 to serve dinner. We survived on unemployment, my hotel money, tips, and our gambling winnings. I couldn't find work in any local mine.

About this time in Bellview, a smart restaurant owner opened an outside drive-in Parkette restaurant. Jim Crow laws still prevailed in Fairmont in the 1950s, and blacks had no place to go inside and sit down to eat. Drive-in restaurants became a fad across the country, and the Parkette became "the hot spot" in our area, especially for blacks. We drove up, used a telephone to order, and visited with friends until the food arrived. Then, just like whites, we could eat right there in the parking lot. It may sound strange, but this was a big step from waiting at back doors. Blacks spent a lot of money at the Parkette. Sometimes there'd be fifty to sixty cars waiting around to pull in and order food.

Whites could park their car and order, like us, or park in the parking lot and walk in and sit down to have dinner. Although we couldn't go in and eat, that segregated policy didn't keep us away. We could buy and enjoy restaurant food without having to take it home. That was a big deal to us. After a few highly successful years, the owner closed the Parkette and added a fancy addition to his restaurant. Like everywhere else in the South, blacks couldn't go inside for a meal until after the Civil Rights Act of 1964.

Though I had to accept segregation, it got to me. I had worked side-by-side in danger and coal dust with white fellows for nearly four years. Underground we were friendly, shared lunches and drinks, and helped each other. We came up out of the mine, said our friendly good-byes, and went our separate ways home to our families. Some said the black coal dust was a race equalizer. They said we were all black because of the coal dust, so blacks and whites blended, and there was less prejudice in a coal mine. I didn't really see it that way. Depending on each other to work safely and stay alive was a stronger bond down there than the mere presence of coal dust on a white man.

Above ground, attitudes were different. When those white fellows were out with their families or friends, they didn't know me. During my lay-off I began to notice that many of those guys ignored me on the street. I had to change my thinking that they were my "mine buddies" and reduce them to my "former co-workers." That truth bothered me for a time, but I got over it.

Around the time my unemployment ran out, a friend persuaded me to join him in Sharon, Pennsylvania, for a job in a huge steel mill. The company hired me immediately. What a hot and dangerous job! They gave me a shovel and pointed to tons and tons of sand. I had to shovel that sand into huge bins. Within the first hour, I stripped off my shirt. Compared to the cramped, dark headings in a coal mine, the building I worked in looked like a football stadium. While gigantic cranes moved constantly overhead, lifting and swaying tons of red hot steel, I shoveled sand for eight hours. I couldn't keep my attention away from that dangling steel. If one of those cables broke, I knew I'd be a flat spot on the floor.

I couldn't cut it there. I planned to finish out the week and give it up. After three days of hot, brutal work and living in a fleabag hotel, Mom called. "Your dad got you a job at Jordan mine. The superintendent called for you. You have a job there, if you want it."

"I'll be home tonight."

I jammed my stuff in a bag and hit the road, full of relief and anticipation. The year was 1951. I was twenty-four years old and going to work in my third mine in four years. My dad had done it again. Speeding down the highway, all I could think was, *Thank you, God! Thank you, Dad!* What I didn't know was that I was headed for the most dangerous job in the mines. ∎

CHAPTER FIFTEEN

Jordan, the First Time

Acouple of months after the layoff at Everettville, Dad got a job in a little antique mine
that had no machines. Hard to imagine pick-
axes and hand loading in 1951, but several private
mines in the area kept a small crew and plugged away
at the coal. Since the mine roof was less than four feet
from the bottom, miners stooped or scuffed around on
their knees all the time. It was backbreaking, knee-
busting work and took its toll on a man's body quickly.
I went with him a couple days and had to back out.
"I'm sorry, Dad. I can't work in this dog hole!"

He shook his head and said, "Son, I completely
understand. It's rough! You do what you have to do,
and I'll keep trying to get us something else." Within a
short time he got a job at Consol's No. 93 Jordan mine
and started working to get me hired. I was relieved that
the timing was right to save me from admitting failure
at the steel mill.

On my first day at Jordan, baseball gave us an
exciting distraction. Inside the lamphouse all the

fellows crowded around a radio, listening to the playoff game between the Brooklyn Dodgers and the New York Giants. The game was tied in the ninth inning. The shift foreman hollered, "Come on, men! Four o'clock! Time to go! Let's go! Get in the cage!" Reluctantly, a few of us followed him. As the radio exploded with the crowd going wild, we heard screams from the lamphouse. "The Giants win the pennant! The Giants win the pennant!" Heated discussions as to whether they could beat the powerful New York Yankees continued throughout the day. I was too busy to join in, but I enjoyed hearing the arguments.

While the foreman showed me around, I paid close attention to the techniques Jordan used. Keeping all the rules, regulations, and systems straight the first few days of a new job was a challenge.

Approximately three hundred men worked at Jordan. Some miners from Barnesville Shaft and Everettville greeted me with "Hey, June. Good to see you." After the six-month layoff and the Sharon Steel disaster, I enjoyed being back inside among friends. They helped me, and I had a good feeling about this work because none of the hostility of Everettville carried over to Jordan.

Conditions there were much better than at Everettville. Jordan didn't have snap top or heavy water seepage, and methane levels were lower. Consol bought the Everettville mine in the mid-1940s, but since it didn't produce the coal they expected and the union was radical, they didn't have their heart in keeping it going. I learned that the company decided they could mine the coal of the Everettville seam from the Jordan mine because it wasn't very far away. Some of the brand-new equipment from Everettville was already in place when I got to Jordan. I looked forward to driving one of those new Joy electric shuttle cars.

During my first couple of days, I learned something about my dad's mine accident six years earlier in 1945. His old foreman, Albert Pyle, took me aside and said, "You know your dad is a hell of a worker, but that accident was my fault. Did he tell you about it?"

I remembered Dad crunched his ribs and lost three days' work, but I said, "No, I don't think he ever told us exactly what happened."

Pyle took the full blame. "The loading machine was placed, but it wasn't running. It had those big digging arms on it. I should have rerouted the men past that machine, but I had them walk across it. The face was slick, and your dad slipped with a bar on his shoulder. He fell against one of those digging arms and broke his ribs. Jim was a heck of a strong worker, but that accident, that was my fault. I felt bad."

The foreman didn't have to tell me the story, but I was glad he did. My dad had only one lost-time injury in fifty years, and it wasn't even his fault. What a record!

Since I only filled in on the mining machines, I didn't have the classification to run one, which suited me. By the grapevine, my good reputation as a "buggy devil" always caught up with me in a new mine, and I was content to allow that to happen. Until it did, I got the feel of the mining methods and work practices and got to know the different crews before I started running the shuttle car. All classified jobs were already subscribed, or assigned, at Jordan, so I started at the bottom of the ladder again as a general inside laborer. Each day I went to work, the shift foreman had me help the timbermen carry posts, or he assigned me to shovel coal around the cutting machines and the loading machines.

Most sections of the mine had four or five headings bustling with activity and noise. Men and machines advanced, extracting coal. Two or three other sections were in retreat, working backward from the face, taking *all* the coal. As they mined it out, this process left nothing but rock and slate, called gob. At Barnesville Shaft miners had called retreat mining honeycombing. Another nickname there was to "split the block" because machines actually sliced the pillars of coal. Except for pulling posts a couple of weekends, I never got too involved in retreat mining at Barnesville.

After a few days of doing dumb work at Jordan, the foreman said, "Bob, I'm sending you to work with a post-puller operator." As was expected, I smiled and said, "Fine." The assignment was not welcome. I hid my anxiety because I knew the only place post-pullers worked was in retreat sections. All I could hope for was that it wouldn't be for too long. It was. For seven long months I did the most dangerous job in the mines. Getting out alive every day was a triumph. There's no room for error in retreat mining. One false move, and you're dead.

We took our equipment into an abandoned, worked-out heading and drilled four or five holes into what we called "stumps." The right name was "pillars," but the miners at Jordan called them stumps because they were only six to eight feet in diameter. We placed sticks of powder into the stump holes, lit them, and ran like hell. The blast loosened the heavy top, which then rode those stumps down as they crumbled. After the dust and smoke cleared, I had to climb in over the coal, dragging a one-hundred-foot-long steel cable up to the crossbars that remained stuck in the roof. All the while I held my breath and hoped that nothing fell on my head or buried me. As fast as humanly possible, I tied a long portion of the cable around two or three bars and hollered at my buddy to start the post-pulling machine. With the roof rumbling like thunder, I scrambled back over the coal and ran like hell again.

Once the machine had wound the cable tight, those bars let go with a snap. Cracking and buckling, the rest of the coal crashed to the bottom. The post-puller kept the tension on until he hauled the crossbars out to a safe place where we could recover them for future use. We stacked the bars and went back to blast the next group of stumps until we completed the whole heading. Then we'd move on to another worked-out heading and start over, leaving the retreat coal lay until there was a big accumulation. After several headings had been retreated, they moved in the equipment from the active workings and loaded the coal into shuttle cars. No one cared much about the side posts because they were all different sizes, but the company wanted to recover as many fourteen-foot crossbars as possible. Sometimes we recovered fifty in one shift.

Roof falls kill several miners every year. In retreat mining, we created intentional roof falls. The work was so dangerous that I just did my part as fast as I could. Fifteen minutes of preparation and planning, punctuated by a blast and five minutes of pure terror. Over and over and over. From the time I entered the cage, the adrenaline kept my heart pounding and my stomach churning.

That job went home with me. Being in harm's way, day in, day out for seven months took a lot out of me. I became detached from my home life and filled my off hours trying to forget that I had to go back and do it again the next day. That next day could be my last day. Any experienced miner can tell stories about men killed or maimed doing what I did.

Retreat mining can eventually cause subsidence above ground because no block of coal is left in to hold up the surface. When subsidence does occur, the earth's surface sinks slowly over time or can drop abruptly, creating a sinkhole. Subsidence works in peculiar ways and can hit anywhere. It may affect one or two homes in one location and go six or eight hundred feet before it hits another one. A congregation in Fairmont had to demolish their church because mine subsidence ruined the foundation and cracked the outside walls. People living above Barnesville Shaft say, "I can hear my basement crumbling and cracking." Many banks and mortgage companies in West Virginia require homeowners to buy mine-subsidence insurance, but proving that subsidence is slowly destroying your home is almost impossible.

During the time I worked in retreat mining, a revolution occurred in the conventional coal mining process. They stopped using fourteen-foot bars to hold up the roof. A conversation I'd had with a foreman at Barnesville Shaft had forecasted this change. "Bob, in two or three years we won't need those crossbars. We'll just run on in, pull the coal out, and drill a hole in the roof. Then we'll simply insert a long rod with a plate up there to hold the top up." The idea of not using timber seemed unbelievable, but then it happened: roof bolts.

The company introduced the process in stages to ensure safety. Using conventional mining methods, they extracted the coal fifteen feet into a heading. One miner, called a "pin man," used a tape measure and chalk to mark the roof where the drillers had to drill. They drilled six holes, four feet apart. In the beginning timbermen set posts and crossbars first, and drillers drilled the holes up through the crossbar into the roof. Then they brought in a roof jack, jacked the crossbar up, placed and tightened the roof bolt, and knocked the side posts out. When they removed the jack, the roof held with no supporting side posts.

Before long they started using nothing but roof bolts, or pins, and metal plates, or shields, four feet apart. No posts or bars at all! Since the timbermen were no longer installing posts and bars, the company converted them into pin drillers and roof bolters. The classification "timberman" slowly disappeared. The big advantage was no more lugging around and fitting heavy wooden posts and bars. The first time I walked under a pin and plate holding the top instead of a bar, all I could think was, *This is not safe! The roof will come down and bury me alive. I am going to die!* Engineers claimed the roof was as safe as a mine roof can be, but all eyes looked up for weeks after this change occurred.

While I worked with the post puller in the old sections with timber, doing retreat mining, I could relax and enjoy myself for one hour each day. The mine foreman had approached me. "Heard you have a good reputation as a shuttle car driver."

Pleased with this remark, I asked, "Is that right?"

"We need dinner-break relief. You fill in a half-hour for one driver and then the next half-hour for the other. If you do a good job, when a shuttle car job opens up anywhere in the mine, it's yours."

A few months later, I got back to doing what I enjoyed most. Naturally, I didn't luck out and get one of the brand-new shuttle cars from Everettville. I got an old one. It differed completely from the ones I drove at the two other mines, but after a few trial attempts, I finally managed to control my shuttle car. It wobbled, and I had trouble getting around corners. The darned steering wheel had so much play in it that I had to be turning it all the time. Some days I'd walk away from wrestling those cars, cussing or laughing out loud with frustration.

I could tease or joke with most of the men at Jordan. They were all damn good coal miners. Even during hard and hazardous work conditions, someone often said something comical or broke the tension with a laugh. I soon mingled with black and white miners, regardless of their personalities. There was always a Spike, Butch, Slim, Shorty, or any nickname thinkable in our crews. We told jokes, shared food and even drinking water. Most guys carried an extra sandwich in their lunch pail to share with the fellows who worked overtime. We worked together, enjoying ourselves, for at least eight hours underground in the most dangerous and hazardous work conditions.

When our shift ended, white miners and black miners took their showers in separate facilities and went their separate ways. I wondered if the company prolonged segregation by having white and colored showers, or if the white men demanded it. Underground we were equal, dependent on each other, and friendly. Once we hit the showers, a mental separation took place. We were black men and white men, no longer equal.

Many of the miners lived in Jordan, a thriving little coal camp across the Monongahela River from Rivesville. Consol still operated a company-owned store in Jordan. As a convenience for hauling their employees, Consol maintained a ferry and also a barge, which was pulled across the river by a winch-and-cable system. After workers reached the other side of the river, they entered the mine down through a special man portal.

Just for fun one day, I drove my car onto the ferry and rode over to visit the company store. From the ferry I watched belts loading Jordan mine coal into empty barges lined up along the river banks. Destination: Pittsburgh and northeastern cities. With the loading operation on one side, the town on the other side, and all the river traffic in between, it was a one-time experience. I didn't have the patience to take the ferry back across. When they stopped the ferry service in 1955, the miners who lived in Jordan, or nearby Catawba, complained because they had to drive around to a bridge in Fairmont to get to the mine. I heard that an accident with a coal barge prompted them to shut down the ferry operation.

I only worked at Jordan mine from October 1951 until the spring of 1952. Hard times hit the coalfields, almost like a recession. Most companies laid men off or couldn't hire new employees during this slowdown. Sadly, I was among some fifty to seventy-five miners who suffered a layoff at Jordan. The local union contract stated "last hired, first fired." My dad made the cutoff, but I went back on the streets doing whatever I could to support my family.

The ups and downs of my work life affected my home life. We could never get enough ahead to even rent our own home. Two women in the kitchen and raising the kids put a strain on all of us. Unfortunately, my absences, working or hustling for money while laid off, added fuel to the fire. My kids were growing up, needing things and needing my influence, and now I didn't even have a job to take care of them. It was a rough time. I tried to keep my old '39 Buick running so I could be out getting a few dollars here and a few dollars there. Occasionally, the head waiter at the Fairmont Hotel called. "I have a convention with three hundred people. I'd like you to come in and wait table." I never turned him down, but I couldn't be a man without a real job. Joblessness made me feel less of a man.

Halfway through the six months' unemployment compensation deadline, I started haunting mine offices for work. I'd heard that the Grant Town mine hired workers from men who waited outside the office. Eastern Fuel and Gas Company owned the mine, and they had a big payroll. Their new portal was just beyond my old home in Grays Flats. I drove there every day for two weeks with no success.

One day after the crews went into the mine, the general mine foreman, Fred Pitman, put his No Work Today sign in the window. The small group of hopeful men, now disgusted, started wandering away, but I stayed. Mr. Pitman had the reputation among blacks that he would hire us. Through the window I could see him climbing into his coveralls. I went up to the porch, planted my feet, and tapped on the window. He came over and threw that window up with a bang. He was not happy. "The sign means what it says. No Work Today. Now go on home."

My feet wouldn't move. I looked him straight in the eye and came the closest to begging that I ever want to come. "Mister, I need a job. Bad."

His face didn't change. He stared at me until I stopped breathing. The air was thick with me willing him to say yes and him trying to decide what to make of this stubborn black man who refused to take "no" for an answer.

"Have you worked in a mine before?"

"Yes, sir. Four years' experience on the shuttle car, but I can timber, drill, cut, load, or shovel coal."

"Do you have a family?"

"Yes, sir. I got a wife and three kids."

"How long have you been out of work?"

"Almost four months."

He kept staring at me, like he couldn't make up his mind. Then he said, "Son, you need to be working. I have to go in the mine now. You come back tomorrow after 3:00. When I get through seeing all the foremen after the shift, I'll talk with you."

"I'll be here. Thanks."

He shut the window without another word.

Superintendents and foremen dealt with miners needing jobs every day, so I didn't think twice about him being short with me. All I could think about as I sped home was, *He listened. He knows I have experience. Tomorrow I have a chance!* ■

CHAPTER SIXTEEN

Two Years at Grant Town Mine

The next day I arrived an hour early, ready to start work at the Grant Town mine. With a death grip on my dinner bucket, I parked myself outside Mr. Pitman's door. The man would have to trip over me to get from the mine to his office. As I waited anxiously for him to come outside, I pumped up my confidence and rehearsed my answers to his questions.

He noticed me right away. "Good. You're here. I have to talk to my section foremen, and then I'll speak with you." I stood aside as a large group of coal-dust-covered men floated in and out of his office. When the last foreman left, Mr. Pitman called me inside. His manner was friendly. He intended to hire me and asked only a few questions, like what jobs I did best and what I could contribute. "You can start tonight on the midnight shift. Come early for payroll sign up. Go on home now and get some sleep." Like I could sleep! In the middle of a recession, I got a job with one of the biggest coal producers in West Virginia. Federal Coal

Company started the mine in 1901. Though everyone called it the Grant Town mine, the official name was Federal Mine No. 1.

My dad had slaved in the old sections of this mine. On my way to work that first night, I thought about his exhausting work, driving horses and hand-loading coal. I hoped to get the unique opportunity of seeing where he had worked. I never did because the mine had expanded miles from where he'd been. The headings connected, but the old portal my dad had entered, across from the company store, was now big underground rooms where mechanics worked on minor machine repairs.

Though the mine was huge and producing almost twice as much coal as in his day, mechanization had dwindled the 1920s work force from twenty-two hundred to one thousand men. I discovered that I joined a small minority of twenty or so black men in the whole mine. My dad told me he was one of five hundred blacks. Mechanization had slashed the percentage of blacks at Grant Town from 25 percent to just 2 percent. Blacks lost their jobs in far greater numbers than whites as the machines took over the work. I'm not saying they had racist hiring practices in the summer of 1952, but I felt lucky to get on the payroll. They had no black foremen, which didn't surprise me.

The Keystone Shaft, where I entered, went down 265 feet. The cage measured 21 feet long and 7 feet wide and could raise or lower two ten-ton mine cars at a time. It had built-in tracks so the hoist operators didn't have to step inside to load and unload coal cars. Thirty men, or two cars of supplies, traveled from surface to bottom in less than a minute. There were so many men on all three shifts that those working in the sections farthest away caged in first. Then the next farthest section employees went in and so on until all miners reached the bottom.

At the bottom we climbed into rail cars with seats and a cover, or canopy. The dangers of smacking your head on the roof, your elbows on the side walls, or getting hit by a rock shower were a thing of the past. These personnel carriers, as the company called them, sped along behind fast locomotives. Though fancier than a dusty old rail car, miners still called them mantrips, or trips.

Excited about being back underground, I was eager to see how Eastern Gas and Fuel's mining policies, rules, and regulations differed from the three Consolidation Coal Company mines I'd worked. On my initial shift I got a big shock. Everything was completely different! For one thing, Grant Town still had a no-name policy. Besides forbidding foremen to fraternize with their crewmen, the company insisted that all supervisors refer to the miners by check numbers only.

My number was 330. I felt like a prisoner to have someone say, "Hey, 330! You go to Six West and help unload supplies," or later, "330, you go run the shuttle car in Two East tonight." After I agreed, he hurried me along with, "Good, 330! You go ahead." Something like that distracts a man but amuses him all the same. Under my breath, I'd laugh and say, "*Mister* 330 to you." Only my friends or fellow crewmen called me Bob or June, my old nickname from Barnesville Shaft. I'm not James Armstead Jr., but the nickname June stuck.

When I started in July 1952, the Grant Town mine had one Joy Manufacturing continuous miner in place. The wave of the future, this do-it-all machine combined cutting, drilling, shooting, and loading in one process by continually grinding the coal off the face and conveying it directly into shuttle cars. Five men and the continuous miner did the work of at least fifteen men. The high price of the machine, and the labor problems generated by laying off ten to twelve men each time they placed one, caused the mining companies to introduce the continuous miner slowly.

What a beehive of activity! Grant Town mine had thirteen sections with seven or more headings in each section. In the ninety or more work places, the Pittsburgh coal seam, a rich grade of soft coal that lay all across northern West Virginia, was eight feet thick and level. Using the conventional mining process, they left a few inches of coal as a platform-type bench at the bottom of the face. At the top they left about a foot of boney refusal coal, which has a high percentage of slate or rock mixed in with the coal.

According to a paper written for the company by Harry Nichols in 1952, three shifts at Grant Town hauled out one hundred cars of coal waste (rock, shale, and clay) and thirty-three hundred cars of coal a day. Total coal output every working day was ten thousand tons. My first year they hit their highest yield in the history of the mine—two and a quarter million tons. That production made a lot of people happy.

With that kind of steady, pushing progress, however, problems are numerous. From the face to the outside hoist, some coal traveled by shuttle cars and then rails for more than six miles. Each month we had to travel farther and farther to the work areas. Miles of track had to be laid, maintained, and torn up on retreat in the thirteen sections. Rock dusting all the work places was a twenty-four-hour job. Since the mine was gassy and considered hazardous, heavy-duty ventilation fans pulled fresh air through the headings. The Grant Town mine even had a separate air shaft to help ventilate it. Booster fans hung everywhere. Rock dust and coal dust hung suspended in corners. Roof bolting left more room to move mine equipment around, but the company didn't have near enough machines to do the work so most sections still used timbers to hold the roof. As an experiment, they tried using wooden pins and plates. When I saw a few wood pieces holding up the roof, I thought it wouldn't work. They soon found it didn't. The thin stakes broke and the plates couldn't take the pressure from above.

Though production was high and everyone worked at a rapid pace, some methods at Grant Town mine seemed primitive and behind the times. In all the conventional mining headings, cutting machines made only two cuts into the coal face, one across the bottom and a vertical one up through the middle. This lack of cutting put the drillers to a disadvantage. They had more holes to drill, pack, and shoot, which wasted valuable time and was more hazardous because of extra blasting. Plus, that drilling was hard work, even with pneumatic drills. I know because I filled in for the drillers occasionally. Many times during a shift I heard, "Fire! Fire! Fire!" Then kaboom! The earth shook, and coal dust and chunks sprinkled from overhead. Miners were continually shooting new coal somewhere or demolishing one of the seventy-five-foot square pillars in retreat.

After blasting in the headings, the real fun began. Cutting across the bottom, and not at the top, left the roof jagged. Timbermen came in and tried to level the top with a pick, which was next to impossible to accomplish. Since their crossbars were thick and crooked with lots of knots on them, timbermen had to hew them with a sharp ax so they'd fit against the jagged top. Only two big timbermen were assigned to do the backbreaking jobs of picking at the roof and hewing and setting timbers. Every so often the foreman would send extra men to help raise the heavy bars up to the roof on jacks. Precious time ticked away while this went on until the loading machine finally moved in to scoop up the coal. I could never understand why they didn't just cut across the top, like I'd seen them do at previous mines. At the very least, I thought they should put more men on the timber crews, but I kept my mouth shut.

The midnight-shift foreman was an understanding fellow. He had learned from Mr. Pitman that I could operate both battery and electric shuttle cars. Of the thirty-five or more shuttle cars in the mine, only a few were electric. On my second or third night, the shift foreman called me aside. "330, there's no opening for a full-time shuttle car operator at this time, but I will keep you in mind. Your classification for now is general inside laborer. I'll start sending you to a different section with a different foreman each night. That way you'll learn your way around and the foremen will know who you are. Just do whatever they tell you to do."

That's what I did. I loaded supplies, shoveled coal, and ran errands, counting my blessings that I had a job. I learned that a lowly miner with only a number as identification didn't step out of line for any reason. All those men, machines, and active coal faces placed stress on supervisors for high production. They had no tolerance for socializing on the job.

After several nights of sending me from section to section, the shift foreman told me that he put my name on his list as a substitute shuttle car operator. I thought it was good news, but I soon found that substituting in this huge operation had its drawbacks. The first night I got an assignment, he had me go in with the first crew to enter the mine. One of his shuttle car operators in a faraway section had called in sick. The next two nights, the shift foreman had me wait for the last group to enter. I rode to work with three other men, and when I came out late, they teased me. "Look here at this big, important miner, making us wait on him." After a week or so of that ribbing, one of the fellows said, "Seriously, Bob. We never know when you're coming up. Why don't you ask the shift foreman to put you on the same crew every night?"

That night I approached the foreman. I didn't want to make my buddies wait on me and thought I should be assigned to drive the same shuttle car in the same section every night. I asked simply, "How about a steady starting time?" He just smiled at me knowingly, as if he'd heard that question a million times. He didn't even hesitate to let me have it. "All I can do is put you on one of the timbering crews, 330."

That did it! I knew I didn't ever want to carry those huge, old knotty crossbars. I still only weighed about 135 pounds. I didn't want to swing a pick over my head pulling down coal chunks into my eyes and down my back. He had me. "You know what?" I said, grinning. "I believe I'm satisfied the way things are right now. And I will keep my mouth shut."

"Good, 330. I need a driver on Five West. You go in with the last crew tonight."

I never asked for consideration again. When I came out late and told my riding buddies what choices I had, they let up on me and accepted it. Things went along smoothly for several months as I learned the mine and filled in, driving the shuttle cars and drilling shot holes.

Rumors surfaced of spirits haunting the mine. Some said, "Yes, it's the gospel truth. They are here." Others denied their presence. "Can't be. There's no such things as ghosts." I listened to the rumors, but I never heard or saw anything unusual. I didn't go looking for that kind of trouble either. Some of the stories I overheard were eerie. In "Tales from La-La's Porch," a weekly Grant Town news feature in the *Times West Virginian*, former miner and storyteller Larry "La-La" Merico related several unusual happenings. Miners had warned him to stay away from a certain heading in the mine. Disregarding the advice, La-La claims he saw the image of a ghost, "a shadow of a man with a pick through his back, moving along the rib." Rumor said a miner had died years before on that site from a cave-in as his own pickax pierced his body. La-La claimed the sighting frightened him so much that his hair turned gray, right on the spot.

Timbers creaking and air moving in abandoned sections can play tricks on the mind. Several old-timers attested to the following tale. Two miners, one a man and the other a boy, pulled a trolley car through an accidentally open trap door. Trap doors, built into concrete wall "stoppings" acted as air regulators, controlling ventilation. A spark from the car ignited flammable gas and caused an explosion that killed both miners. Some said that for years afterward, on the anniversary of the explosion, that trap door opened and closed on its own.

Two other mystic occurrences took place in the old sections of the mine. One involved a light that moved through the mine with no one in sight. The other was a "ghost trip" heard clickety-clacking down the track that was never seen by anyone. Several miners claimed that they witnessed these incidents. Merico also insists that to this day, when one puts his ear to a pipe that still snakes into the mine, he can hear active mine working noises. Cars on tracks, grinding coal machines, and the steady blast of the death whistle. When a miner died, it was customary to hold the mine-shift whistle open for a long, long time to announce the death.

Fact or fiction? I don't know. When I worked at Grant Town Federal Mine No. 1, it was a noisy, busy place, filled with men moving coal. No quiet time existed to look or listen for ghosts. I did, however, keep an eye out for rats. I heard miners cussing them and laughing about feeding them, but I never had one cross my path. Working around horrendous noise had one advantage. No rats!

None of us saw it coming. One morning at the end of our shift as we stepped off the cage, the day-shift foreman stood in our way. He held up a handful of time cards and shouted over our heads. "There's been a layoff." He waved the cards. "These seventy-five men will be leaving us this Friday. If your card is still in the time card rack, you can withdraw it and punch out for your shift."

Complete silence fell over the crowd of black-faced men. In a tight bunch, we herded ourselves into the lamphouse where the time card rack waited with seventy-five cards missing. Each man coped privately with the fear of losing his job by looking down or straight ahead. No one talked or even whispered. No clanging of dinner buckets hitting the lamphouse floor. No rush to be first in the showers. Everyone stood in shock and disbelief as the foreman called out numbers and handed out useless time cards to the unlucky ones.

I couldn't breathe. Misery spread through the building as the foreman called out number after number. Men reaching high over hard hats for cards were ten-year veterans. What chance did I have? Listening for my number, sure to come, I glanced at my slot in the rack. My card was still there. I blinked. The card still read "330." In slow motion I reached for it, pushed it into the time clock, put it back into the rack, and slipped silently into the colored bathhouse.

From both sides of the partition separating us that morning, I could feel the agony of the men laid off and the contained relief of those who still had a job. But for how long? A layoff this size could be the beginning of the end. Many fellows with three to ten years' seniority over me lost their jobs, but that's the way the contract read. Men with the job classifications that the company needed stayed on the payroll, regardless of years served. What I couldn't understand, but didn't question, was how a one-year general inside laborer like myself kept his job.

One of my riding buddies got laid off. We rode home in silence that morning. I figured someone made a mistake in retaining me, and the ax would fall before the week ended. That evening my shift foreman called me aside and told me that Mr. Pitman wanted to talk to me the next morning.

I went to work as usual, going through the motions and assuming I was right about the mistake. Visions of telling my family, women crying, and me looking for work haunted me during my shift.

The next morning Mr. Pitman stood waiting for me and beckoned me into his office. He shuffled some papers and then looked me straight in the face. "Bob, you have a very good work record. I'm changing your classification from general inside laborer to shuttle car operator so I can keep you on the payroll." I didn't understand how he could do that when I hadn't applied for the change, but I didn't question it. All I could mutter was, "Thank you, Mr. Pitman." I left his office a happy man. His decision to go out of his way to keep me working lifted my spirits beyond words. Not missing work, doing what I was told, and keeping my mouth shut seemed to have paid off.

The layoff brought a strike by the union so we all missed some work. Eventually most of the laid-off miners came back. In the past I had often heard my father and some of the union members argue and debate over whether company layoffs should depend on miners' classifications or plant seniority. Dad didn't agree with the contract but, on a personal level, was glad I didn't lose my job. More than anyone, I understood it was unfair to retain me while others with many years of seniority lost their jobs. Obviously, the strike wasn't just about me, but that is one strike I understood, agreed with, and supported all the way. Lucky for the others, it didn't last very long. Things got back to normal within a few days.

The night foreman started sending me out each night to various sections to run the shuttle car. Most of the battery-operated ones were new enough to hold a good charge, so I didn't have a preference for the coveted electric ones. I discovered they moved operators around from section to section to even up production so no one section shined or fell behind. A close friend of mine was an excellent shuttle car operator. Some nights they scheduled us to haul coal on the same section. That section foreman respected us, believing that he had the two best shuttle car operators hauling coal for him that shift. We saw by his manner that he assumed he could count on the highest production, and we worked to deliver. The midnight-shift foreman eventually named us "the two buggy devils," and we carried that name all over the mine. We had a good time and didn't mind all the attention.

Although I was quite happy with my work life, I drove an exhausting pace and had to sleep most of the time I was home. The tension there mounted to the breaking point. My wife decided she needed to be on her own. Not knowing how that would work out, she left the children with me. My mother and my sisters, Clara and Barbara Jean, adored the children and assured us they'd be in good and loving hands. Though I'd have liked for the kids and I to have had our own home, the practical solution was for all of us to remain in the same house where the children had constant care. As it turned out, Mom and my sisters did a great job of raising my three children.

At the Grant Town mine I survived still another layoff. This one was massive and permanent; three hundred men lost their jobs, all in one day. Some men had been there twenty-five years. The company had bought and placed tons of mining machinery and streamlined many work areas. They stood up to the union objections. In my case, nothing but a long, expensive conveyor system could replace shuttle cars hauling coal inside. My classification held, and I stayed. One example of company cutbacks did affect me. They added one minor step to my job and laid off the man who had done that step, just pressing a button to forward the rail cars. The electrician simply moved the button down so that I could reach it. Thirteen sections, thirteen men laid off.

They mechanized other jobs. In one example of company shrewdness, they installed pneumatic drills on the back side of the cutting machines and furloughed fifty drillers. The first night at Grant Town after the major layoff, they loaded just as much coal as the previous night. The business decisions worked, but the miners and their families suffered.

Forty percent of the miners working when I started two years before were gone. Many sold their homes and moved away to find work. No one blamed anyone specifically. The mining company had to keep up with their competition or go under. New mining machines caused layoffs and growing unemployment, but their size and efficiency brought excitement to those miners remaining on the job.

Every miner, including me, felt insecure about his job. Every time I started a new job, I believed that it would last forever, but here I was in my fourth mine. I was only twenty-five. The economic instability of the industry made me feel lucky to get back to work within a year after each layoff. When a man enjoys his work as much as I did, he's hooked. At that time, no advice or reasoning allowed me to even consider another way to make a living. I worked hard and gave each job assignment my all, even when I simply shoveled loose coal. I learned to enjoy each work day because a layoff could be just around the corner.

Work continued without any major disruptions for another year. Then Mr. Pitman called me into his office. I didn't suspect a thing. He said, "Bob, I got bad news for you."

My heart moved to my throat, and I choked out, "Yeah, what's that?"

"We have a service man returning from the army. The company, by federal government rules, has to give that man his old job back. You're the last shuttle car operator on the hiring list so I have to terminate you."

I felt as if he'd punched me in the gut. Boom! My time at Grant Town was over. I was never mentally prepared for a layoff when it happened. I hid the sadness that fell over me, shook his hand, and said, "I understand. I've enjoyed working here."

One month short of two years, I lost my job. What could I do? Nothing. The union representatives came to me and said there was no other solution. I had to take it. Company policy, the federal government, and even the mine contract stacked against me. As lousy as I felt about losing my job, I knew the guy deserved his job back. I had no choice but to accept it. In June 1954, I ended nearly two years of employment at Federal Mine No. 1 at Grant Town.

Back on the street again. Allowing myself only a few days to recover, I started making the rounds. I discovered the Fairmont Hotel needed a day-time bell captain. Since I'd helped them any time I could for the past several years, they hired me. With unemployment and tips at the hotel, I survived, but for five months I was miserable.

I had traded my 1939 Buick in on a 1950 Buick just before I got laid off. My car payments were $58.26 a month. They were a hardship after my layoff, but I was determined not to lose my car. One day when I got home from the Fairmont Hotel, my mom said, "There's a guy been here looking for you from the bank." My car payment was one day overdue. Like a vulture, the bank had apparently sent someone to see about it.

"Mom, did the mailman pass by yet?" My $60.00 unemployment check was due to arrive that day.

She pulled back the curtain. "No, but I see him coming up the road."

As I looked out the door to check on the mailman's progress, here came the bank man, climbing up our porch steps. Without looking at me, he asked, "What time will the mailman be here?"

"Soon," I replied, not exactly sure what he planned to do.

He plopped into a chair and said, "I'll wait." We sat on the porch in silence, waiting for the mailman. I felt humiliated not to be trusted by my own bank and fought to hide my anger. When the mailman arrived at our door, the bank agent took out his pen, had me open my check, and sign it over to him for my car payment. He had the $1.74 change ready for me. My check for two weeks' unemployment was gone, but I still had my car and $1.74.

In the late fall of 1954, I was on my way to the post office, walking across town to First Street, when a guy yelled at me. "Hey, Bob, did they ever call you back to Jordan?" I recognized him as a motorman who had survived the layoff at Jordan in the spring of 1952.

"No! What do you mean?" I dodged the Friday afternoon traffic to cross over and find out what was going on.

"They called a couple guys back. And they got some new guys out there. You have seniority over them because they weren't on the layoff panel." I knew he referred to the list of classified, furloughed workers.

For two days I was agitated. Early Monday morning I rushed down to Jordan to see the superintendent about my classification on the panel list. The company had me listed as a post-puller helper, which was incorrect. Staying polite, but adamant, I explained, "I worked here at Jordan for eight months. Soon after I started, I was a post-puller helper. The last thirty days on the job, however, I operated shuttle cars exclusively. This list should show me as a shuttle car operator. Now you have new operators from other mines when I should have been recalled."

He listened and said, "Let's go over to the personnel office and pull the files of all furloughed miners. That should be accurate." Within minutes he found that I should have been listed as a shuttle car operator. Since I was correct, I made another step forward that could have easily backfired. It wasn't a hustle for "free" money. At the time, I felt I'd been wronged and deserved compensation. I stood up to the man and said, "I should have pay starting back when the first outsider was hired."

He didn't get angry. We kicked it around for awhile, me trying not to be too anxious and him keeping his control of the situation. Some superintendents feared unions but still wanted to hire whomever they pleased and play by their own rules. Any minute he could have said, "I don't like your attitude" and dismissed me from the office, and from the list.

Cautiously we met in the middle. Finally, he said, "I can't give you any retroactive pay, Bob, but can you start this afternoon?" I lost one battle, but won the war. Without hesitation, I said, "Yes, Sir. I can do that." After thanking him and getting the payroll sign-up particulars, I left, rejoicing in going back to a mine where I knew people. My dad had been at Jordan since 1951. I hoped we could get on the same shift.

Within a few weeks something happened less than twenty miles away that jolted me into taking a hard look at what I was doing. On Saturday, November 13, 1954, Farmington No. 9 blew up, trapping fifteen miners. A second explosion killed a rescuer. The uncontrolled fire that raged on forced the Jamison Coal and Coke Company to seal the mine with the fifteen men still inside. Had the blast come during a normal work day, hundreds would have died. Six months later they opened the mine and recovered the bodies for a decent burial.

We all knew deep down it could happen anywhere, at any time, but when it did happen, and so close, everyone in the industry was affected. Survivors, though they had escaped death, were out of work. For months, you could spot a miner's wife on the street from the looks of worry and dread in her eyes. I drove near the Farmington mine, stood on a hill, and watched the billowing smoke. I read all about it, saw the pictures of the suffering families, and felt a strange restlessness until they brought out the bodies. Even with this tragedy, I still had to admit that I liked what I was doing. I didn't want to do anything else, and the potential dangers of working underground were not going to stop me. I often wondered how many of those fifteen miners felt the same way. ■

CHAPTER SEVENTEEN

Jordan Again and . . .

Men who hadn't "blended with the coal," as I did on the first day at Barnesville Shaft, often chose to give up coal mining after a mine disaster. Pressure from terrified loved ones saying, "That could be you" or "I can't live in fear all the time" pushed them to choose a factory job or something else that was above ground and safer. The only two things that gave me any thought to getting out of mining were the sudden layoffs and the uncertainty between jobs. Once back inside a mine, I forgot those negatives.

To make a little extra money and to keep a safety-net job available, I stayed on as a bell captain at the Fairmont Hotel. They needed me and allowed me to schedule my hours around the different mine shifts. A couple of weeks after the Farmington disaster, I had Sunday evening work at the hotel. When business was slow, I could sit on the couch in the lobby and rest before going on midnight shift at Jordan. That Sunday had been a hectic day, and I was exhausted. The weather was rainy, the hotel was quiet, and I dropped off to sleep.

An older gentleman, wearing a trench coat and a flop hat, came into the lobby. The lady at the desk banged the service bell. I went to the desk. She said, "Bob, check this gentleman in." Nonchalantly, I checked him in, not paying any attention to the register. I picked up his bag, got us the elevator, and escorted him to room 526. We chatted about nothing, and he tipped me. After I came back down, I went back over to the couch to continue my nap.

The lady at the desk banged on the bell again. She called to me, "Bob, don't you know who that was?"

Startled, I said, "No. I checked him in. Is everything all right?"

She started to laugh.

"What's wrong?" I asked.

"That was John L. Lewis."

I didn't even know it. The moment had passed me by. If I had been wide awake and aware, I'm not sure what I would have said to him. Thinking about that woke me up. He apparently came to Fairmont to take care of union business connected to Farmington No. 9. From the time I was a little boy, my father spoke of this man with reverence and admiration. For seven years I had been paying dues to the UMW, and here was the president of that powerful union. My union. I felt like I had missed an opportunity. For what, I'm not sure. Maybe just to shake his hand and say, "It's a pleasure to meet you, sir." What a story to tell when I got to work! I'd met and exchanged small talk with the famous John L. Lewis and didn't even know it. I took a load of teasing about that.

During my absence from Jordan mine, nothing much had changed. Most of the old-timers had accepted my return as natural. Though I had been away from Jordan nearly three years, I adjusted to the awkward Jeffrey shuttle cars again. For my first couple of years there, the mine's production increased a little each year. I worked five and sometimes six days a week and enjoyed being a buggy devil. As always, I began to believe this job would last.

We continued to live with my parents. They supported me by taking care of my kids and keeping us all fed. My older sister Clara lived at home also. She cleaned houses for people and still found time to fix my lunch bucket every day. I contributed money for groceries and paid Mom for the charge accounts that she used for my kids' clothes. Everyone in my family was supportive through the difficult time when I divorced my wife.

The changes in my personal life were nothing compared to what was happening in national politics. Finally, the federal government got involved in the separation of the races. The movement had started with a 1951 lawsuit for a little black girl in Kansas named Linda Brown. Her parents wanted her to attend a neighborhood white school instead of riding miles on a bus to a black school. After defeats in the lower courts, the Browns appealed to the Supreme Court. The result was the famous *Brown v Topeka Board of Education* decision that said, "Separate educational facilities are inherently unequal and unconstitutional." We followed the case closely and celebrated the decision but didn't know how soon it would affect Dunbar School.

Many schools in the South dragged their feet for two decades. In our area of West Virginia, the change came within one year. The issue challenged the school district and the city, but we were glad to have the doors to equality start to open somewhere. Eleven years passed before we could go in and sit down in a public restaurant.

After the Supreme Court ordered all schools to integrate in May 1954, sport enthusiasts in Marion County wanted to have one rousing competition between the white high school and the black school before integration occurred. For years the two schools debated which one had the superior athletes. West Fairmont High, the white school, always had a larger enrollment than Dunbar, the black school, but both had outstanding, often championship, football teams. Rumors had it that the years that Dunbar had powerful teams, West Fairmont did not want to play them. The years that West Fairmont had powerful teams, Dunbar declined. Every year one school declared, "You have too good a team!" In reality, before desegregation, Dunbar played in a statewide black athletic association for schools their size and West Fairmont played in a white athletic association with much larger schools. Before 1954 it might have been illegal for them to play one another. In any case, it never happened.

West Fairmont extended an invitation to Dunbar to play the first football game between colored and white schools in West Virginia. With cooperation among the coaches and principals, the "Big Game" went on the regular season schedule in mid-October 1954. The buildup and anticipation excited the schools, the parents, and especially the players. Everyone talked about it and argued who would win. I placed my hopes and a small wager on Dunbar.

Over five thousand fans attended the game in the East-West Stadium. Both teams fought hard with excellent sportsmanship. West Fairmont won seven to six. That historic football game was the only athletic event ever staged between the two schools. With extra security, no racial incidents of any kind occurred. Today, many of the players remain friends and still talk about that football game. I thoroughly enjoyed it!

When the schools in Marion County desegregated, the student population shifted around. Dunbar School closed for awhile and then eventually became a middle school. The school board changed the name to Fairmont Junior High. My old principal, William Armstrong, and the black community petitioned to get back the old name, Dunbar School. All who opposed the name change to Fairmont Junior High, including the NAACP, claimed that the name Dunbar had more meaning and character than Fairmont Junior High. The school had been named after the black poet, Paul Lawrence Dunbar. In 1971 the school board reversed its decision, and the name changed back to Dunbar. Winning a struggle such as this was new and unusual for blacks, and we relished the success. The only school I attended in Fairmont, Dunbar School, is seventy-one years old and still houses fifth and sixth grade students. Just like anywhere else, though, new schools or consolidation could change that in a minute. That's the way of old school buildings.

Another local building, the Watson Hotel, fell to ruin and decay. The owners put their time and money into their more productive investment, the Fairmont Hotel. In 1956, seeing the once-elegant Watson Hotel torn down brought back old memories, but its time had passed. When I worked there as a maintenance man, it was already deteriorating. No one wanted to restore it, so they just leveled it.

My dad retired from mining at Jordan mine that summer. Since he'd entered the mines in Alabama as a young boy, he thought fifty years was long enough. Dad never got out of the habit of planting a huge garden. After he retired, he threw himself into it with the energy of three men and produced enough vegetables to can for weeks. He did this year after year. Besides the garden, he took on home repairs. All the things he never had time for when he was a miner got his full attention. Even when I had other plans, he drafted me to help him.

Late one fall I looked forward to going to a local championship football game. The morning of the game, my dad cornered me. "We have sidewalk work to do."

"Well, Dad, okay, but about 12:30 there's a big game downtown. I think I'll go."

"No, Son. You're not going to a game today. We're going to finish this sidewalk." I tried to compromise, but he wouldn't listen. That was it. I worked on the sidewalk.

He never made me really angry at him because he generally treated me with respect. I, in return, respected him for all he did for me. That incident did upset me, however. I was thirty years old, and he wouldn't let me go to a football game. He ruled the house and those in it.

Dad taught me to respect authority. His domination contributed to my being a good employee in the mines. Like at home, I never questioned my orders from supervisors. Even if I thought their way of doing things was stupid or inefficient, I kept my mouth shut.

Jordan had years of good coal left to mine. To increase production, they planned to install ten-ton haulage cars. All miners dismissed the idea and wondered among themselves, *How in the world are they going to put ten-ton cars in this mine?*

Previously, the largest car in use held only four tons, but the company's solution to prepare for the change was incredibly simple. Cutting machines took eighteen inches off the turns by shearing the corners. Unfortunately, the company didn't replace the shuttle cars right away. Since they only carried between six and eight tons, we had more trips and more pressure to fill the new haulage cars. I had to put more hustle into the job. Before long we found out that placing bigger haulage cars into the mine was only the first step in a major plan to increase production.

They installed it over a weekend. Jordan's first continuous miner, a five-foot ripper, sat ready to mine coal when we arrived one Monday morning. The old loading machine was in place behind it, but a new shuttle car sat parked about one hundred feet back from the coal face. Frank, an old friend of mine, had received training by the manufacturing company to run the continuous miner. One man from each shift worked with the trainer for several hours a day on a demonstrator. Frank was a third-generation coal miner, born and reared at Jordan coal camp. We were timbermen together at one time. When he heard the company planned to bring this new piece of equipment into the mine, he hung around the superintendent for months asking, "When is the new machine coming?" Frank wanted first shot at running the new continuous miner. If a fellow already had the training from a previous mine, or had experience from there, they would use him. When the continuous miner came into Jordan, Frank got the job for our shift.

The shiny new miner and shuttle car were in the heading I generally started working. Thrilled as I was at the possibility of seeing these new machines go into action, I didn't assume anything. Several of us walked around the miner, admiring the technology. Approaching the shift foreman, I said with a devilish grin, "Buddy, that's a lot of iron in a coal mine. Does it work?"

"Let's hope so," he replied. "We got enough money in that machine and training three men to run it. Bob, did you happen to see that new shuttle car sitting back there?" He had my attention. If it wasn't going to be me driving it, he'd have already sent me somewhere else.

"Yes, sir. I did. Would you like me to start it up and see how it sounds?"

He laughed and smacked me on the back. "Bob, how would you like to be the man who hauls the first load of coal out of here from that miner?"

I don't know if I said anything back to him. At that moment the foreman signaled Frank to start up the continuous miner, and the heading filled with an incredible roar. The wheels on the ripper dug in as it started moving up to the face. I stood and watched as the bits attached to the five-foot-wide belt ground into the coal face. It gouged out the coal from the top to the bottom and then back up to the top. Coal spilled back through the miner onto the bottom. Frank moved the machine back and over and started the process again, roof to bottom and back. By the time he moved it to the last five-foot section, the loading machine's claws had started flexing, gathering the coal. I bolted for the shuttle car and turned the key, adding to the trembling noise. As the first chunks emptied off the loader into my new shuttle car, the miner disappeared into a cloud of black dust.

They said the churning bits, which looked like fat, sharp icicles strapped to an oblong-shaped cutter drum, ripped out eight tons in a minute. The drum hung on a central bar so the back end could swing up as the front end cut down the face. All I know is that, in no time, my car was full and I pulled out. What an exciting day! And a busy one. I maneuvered the shuttle car into that loader and dashed to the ten-ton haulage cars and sped back again countless times.

The continuous miner was like a new toy. That first day, Frank nearly shook from excitement. During a break he walked around the miner, admiring it, and asked, "Bob, you think you're going to learn that machine?" I answered, "No, Frank. I'm going right back here and stay on my new shuttle car. It's a nice one. I'd just as soon they'd drop those old Jeffreys in a pit somewhere." He laughed in agreement, aware of our struggle with the erratic Jeffrey shuttle car.

After about six or seven months, the continuous miner operators found that the job was more hazardous and more demanding than they had expected. One Sunday night the section foreman said to the crew, "We have to go back in there and get that stump of coal." He was referring to the one remaining pillar supporting the roof in a large mined-out room. Frank ran the ripper down across the pillar. Directly above his head, the roof started shaking. He leaped off that continuous miner and ran back away from the potential danger. Luckily, nothing happened. After he collected himself, he said, "Bob, I want you to learn that machine." No way was I going to get involved in that situation. I had not earned the classification. Besides, I figured he would only let me do the job when conditions were hazardous. I shook my head and replied, "No, Frank. You begged for it. Now you stay with it." With his eye on the roof, he grumbled and climbed back on the machine.

Within a few months another continuous miner was installed, and then another a few months later. New loaders and new shuttle cars followed. The company investment for each heading was probably close to a million dollars. Men lost their jobs, of course. We knew they would. For the first time in years, however, I felt secure in my own job. I'd been working at Jordan mine four solid years without a layoff.

Away from work, I had my mind on women and my brand-new 1957 luxury Buick. I had driven old cars for twelve years, and I just decided to treat myself to the best. That blue-and-white beauty caught my eye in the car lot, and despite the price tag of $4,105, I had to have it. The monthly payment of $127 was outrageous and gobbled about a third of my month's pay, but I didn't care. No matter where I drove in West Virginia, Ohio, or Pennsylvania, everybody raved about that car. I kept it shining clean inside and out. Heads turned as I drove by, and I heard "Whoa! Look at that car!" My favorite was "Take me for a ride, honey?" Wherever I parked in a big city, I had women sitting on my car when I came back. The Buick was a magnet, and I didn't mind that at all.

At twenty-eight years old, I was still a young man, now divorced, and I became involved with quite a few women in Fairmont, Clarksburg, and Morgantown. When I was out gallivanting around, dancing at the clubs, sometimes I wouldn't get home until 2:00 A.M. on a Saturday night. Even if she had to preach in the morning, Mom waited up for me, reading her Bible. She never went to sleep until I came home.

She'd call out, "Bobby, is that you?"

"Yes. It's me." She never nagged me, so I didn't dread her being up.

"Well, come here then." She'd small talk a little bit, careful not to ask what I was doing out so late. Then she read me a scripture from the Bible and went to bed. I suppose she worried about my running around because one night, she got agitated and declared as righteous, "Son, you got three devils in you. A woman devil, a fast-drinking devil, and a fast-dancing devil."

I wasn't sure what she wanted to hear so I just mumbled, "Yes, Mom. I think you might be right about that." There was nothing else I could say without getting into a religious discussion, which I definitely avoided. She "permitted" my father to drink so there was nothing she could say about her adult sons drinking as long as we didn't shame her or the children.

Soon after that discussion I became involved with a young girl named Zelda Gay Holloway. Two friends I ran with also had sporty cars, and we enjoyed driving around West Fairmont High as school let out. The girls admired our cars and flirted with us. They coaxed me to take them to the Dairy Queen for soft ice cream, and I did that quite often. One day Gay was with the girls and said, "You girls aren't going. I'm the only one going today, and I'm going to sit in the front seat."

We got acquainted with one another that day. She said, "You know, I never had soft ice cream before you took us there. You bought me my first Dairy Queen." Gay also told me she was one of the first black kids sent to Miller School during desegregation. That was the white school in my neighborhood that I had to walk past to get to Dunbar. Since I left school in the mid-1940s, I missed the turmoil of desegregation. After Miller, they sent her to West Fairmont High. One of the principals greeted them with "You know, I'm not ready for you black kids, and you black kids aren't ready for me." My sympathy went out to Gay and her friends having to make that adjustment. She said it wasn't easy.

I knew from the start that I was almost thirteen years older than Gay. Because of the age difference, I tried to keep our relationship a secret from my mother. Though Mom didn't nag me, she did stand in judgment of my escapades, pronouncing them good or bad. Since I was on midnight shift, my mom took Gay's calls when I slept through the day. One late afternoon Mom said, "I know you have a lot of girlfriends, Bob, but there's some young girl calling here for you." I acted as if I didn't know whom she meant. My sister Barbara Jean was around Gay's age and knew her, but she didn't let our secret out for awhile. Another day when Gay called, my mother asked, "Who are you? What's your name?"

Even though Gay knew trouble might follow, she spoke up and told her the truth. "Mrs. Armstead, I'm Gay Holloway."

"Holloway? You girls are young! Bob's divorced, but he's thirty-one years old. I think he's too old to be dating you."

Gay stood right up to my mom and said, "My mother knows about Bob and says it's all right with her."

Gay told me all about it, but Mom never said any more to me for about four months. Then it got to be too much for her to stay quiet. Barbara Jean finally told her all about Gay. That's when my mom discovered that Gay was only eighteen. Her judgment was that Gay was much too young for me. She sat me down one evening. "That little girl who calls here for you? I found out who it is. She's one of those Holloway girls. You're an old man compared to her. I'm going to call her mother and tell her to make her quit calling here."

"You do what you have to do, Mom." I knew she would make the call and didn't resent her for it. She was forward and always wanted to do the right thing. She thought Gay's mom didn't know how old I was. Gay's mother surprised her. Gay was home and overheard the conversation on one end. Afterward her mother told her all about it.

My mom said, "I understand your daughter's very young. Do you know that Bob is thirty-one and has three children?"

"She's over sixteen. She can decide for herself who she wants to go out with." Mrs. Holloway's feelings on the subject gave my mother no other choice but to stifle her objections. I'm a peaceful man and was glad the resolution came that way instead of a family blowup with hurtful words flying.

Gay came and met my mom, and it started from there. Our relationship was out in the open. Within a short time, my mom said, "She'll make you a nice wife."

We dated about a year. One evening when Gay, her girlfriend, and I were in Morgantown, I hit a culvert. My Buick only had a few thousand miles on it so I was angry with myself. Since it was already late, I had to get those two girls home. A cab seemed my only option, but I didn't consider the expense. We dropped the girls off first. When I got home, I realized I only had eight dollars. I handed over all my money and started to go inside. The driver yelled, "Hey, Buddy. You owe me sixteen dollars!" Mom heard the disturbance and came outside.

She asked me, "What's wrong? What's going on here?"

The driver spoke loudly enough for the neighbors to hear. "He still owes me eight bucks!"

Becoming exasperated, Mom glared at me. "Well, pay it!"

Like any man, not having enough money embarrassed me. Since I was five years old, I carried enough money in my pockets to take care of myself. Old humiliations came back. I was also mad about my car and not thinking straight. "I don't have it, Mom. I gave him eight dollars. That's all he's going to get." I knew it wasn't right, but I walked away from the whole situation. Mom and my sister Clara scraped up the other eight dollars and paid the man. We never spoke of it after that. They hadn't seen me do anything they considered dishonest before and didn't understand what had happened to me. No way could I explain how I felt.

A couple of weeks later, the garage called that my Buick was ready. Insurance paid for the damage, but I had a one-hundred-dollar deductible. One hundred dollars was a lot of money. Since I gave my parents a large portion of my paycheck and had the big car payment, I didn't have the deductible money.

Mom said, "Your car is ready. What are you going to do about it?"

"Mom, I just don't have that kind of money right now. I don't know what I'm going to do."

She said, "Go talk to your dad."

His response was simple and logical. "Well, Son, I guess you're going to have to wait until you get paid."

Mom talked to him for quite awhile and then slipped me the one hundred dollars. "You paid a lot of money for that car. Your friends have cars. I want you to have it. Don't worry about paying me back. I won't take it."

My brothers and sisters said as often as they got the chance, "Mom spoiled you. You were a momma's boy. You could get her last dollar." It comforted me and embarrassed me when my Mom spoiled me. But she did. Even when I was a child, she did extra for me. For instance, I hated vegetables. I just couldn't gag them down. Everyone said that's why I stayed so scrawny. Mom fixed a pot of green beans or other vegetables for everyone else. Then later she'd come back into the kitchen and fry me bacon and eggs. I knew she did it so I wouldn't go hungry, but I came to expect it. How often I heard "Uh huh. Momma's pet. Bobby is Momma's pet."

I felt grateful to have my parents' kindness and support any time, but especially in the summer of 1959. My friend from another shift called me and woke me up in the middle of the afternoon. He had the sound of doom in his voice. "June, you better get down to the mine. There's a big layoff, and I think you're in it." As I scrambled to get dressed and out the door, the world moved in slow motion around me. The mood in my house went somber, and all I could think was, *Not again! Please, not now!*

My name was on the list. I had five days of work and one paycheck left. Seventy miners lost their jobs. Sixty-nine men and I were back on the streets. Consolidation Coal Company claimed poor market conditions. "Can't sell the coal, can't keep a full work force."

That last day was tough. I shook off the depression and jumped back into hustling every way I could to make a dollar to help my mother and father. Although they weren't financially able to do too much, I always appreciated their help with the kids. I went back to odd jobs as I had done in past years. I gambled at cards and hustled pool for money on the side. A major question bothered me the moment I saw my name on that list. One of my dad's neighbors and former co-workers brought it out into the open. "How is Bob going to make all them car payments since he got laid off?" He asked the wrong person. Mom got furious and said, "Don't you worry yourself about it. He won't lose it!"

To help me, the bank reduced the monthly payment from $127.00 to $92.92, still a big payment for that time. When I lost my job, I had sixteen payments left to go on the note. Even though I felt desperate at times, I didn't rob anybody or knock anybody in the head to get the money. I became a good pool hustler during those months. Two or three days before my car payment was due, I was often $30.00 or $40.00 dollars short. Somehow I always came up with the money. Gambling, shooting dice, or any way I could think of. My brother Joe had a habit of sending me a little money when I was laid off. An envelope from Joe often showed up just in time to pay my car note. Sometimes I wondered if another family member conspired with my brother to help me, but I never asked.

In December I got a job, a very low paying job, but I held onto my car. That was an accomplishment. One obligation I paid, without fail, was my union dues to the UMW. As long as I paid my dues as a contract miner, the time, even time laid off, counted toward years served and pension accumulation.

A friend of mine received a job offer at one of the largest funeral homes in Fairmont, but he was afraid to work around dead people. He asked me, "Could you work around bodies?"

I didn't even have to think it over. "That wouldn't bother me."

"Then go and talk to the owner, Mr. R. C. Jones. Maybe he will consider hiring you. The pay is not coal miners' pay, but I know you need work."

I got dressed up in a white shirt and tie and went to see Mr. Jones the next morning. He hired me immediately. My job was to be a custodian, keeping the place clean, and to answer the telephone when everyone was out with a funeral. The pay was only fifty dollars a week for six days, nine to five. If someone scheduled a Sunday funeral, a common occurrence, I had to work seven days a week for the same amount. My instructions were to wear a white shirt and tie to work every day so I always looked nice if a customer came in. I knew the work would be clean and easy, but my, the low pay depressed me.

Gay and I married two weeks later, on December 24, 1959. We rented our own place nearby. My children stayed with my parents. They had been living in the same home with them for all those years, and they wanted to stay. Besides, we had our first child, Anthony, on the way soon afterward. Taking care of four children all of a sudden would have been very difficult for Gay. She was only nineteen. Financially, the next few years were the lowest ebb in my life. Coal miners earned $26 a day, or $130 per week. Here I was, trying to support a new family on menial wages. Every mine layoff pulled me back so far that I never got caught up.

Since my hours were mostly daylight hours, I didn't mind being alone with the bodies. I adjusted to it and didn't let the creepy atmosphere get to me. Scary moments? Sure, but I prided myself in being fearless. Except for maybe one incident. We had nine bodies in the building, which was unusual. Four bodies lay upstairs for viewing. Four were downstairs in preparation, and there was one in the cooler, awaiting relatives from out of state. We had had a funeral service so I had to clean up afterward. I passed the embalming room door and went outside to empty the garbage pail. The embalming door slammed behind me! That sent chills up my spine. Like a dead person got right up off the table to shut that door. I later figured out that the wind blew it shut, but I stayed shaky and apprehensive for several days.

The embalmers had a morbid sense of humor and played pranks. We had a room with eight or ten caskets on display. They sent one man up to dust off a specific casket for a possible sale. One of the embalmers hid behind it. When the prank victim started to dust it off, the man in hiding pushed it out. They said that guy practically tore the place apart getting out of there.

Occasionally we made out-of-state trips to pick up bodies, and I drove the Cadillac hearse. The closest crematory was in Pittsburgh. Whenever a family wanted a body cremated, I had to drive it to Pittsburgh and return with the ashes. They trusted me to carry money to the bank, sometimes three times a day. During a big funeral I helped with parking and sometimes drove a family car to the cemetery.

Soon after the federal government imposed the one-dollar-per-hour minimum-wage law, I approached Mr. Jones. I figured the increase in pay I deserved by law would only be ten dollars a week. That amount was nothing to him but would be a major help to my family and me. He apparently expected this conversation and had his answer prepared. "Robert, you are not covered by that law because this is a small business." I didn't argue, but the outcome frustrated me. Six months later I went in to see Mr. Jones again. "I've been here three years without missing one day of work. I think I deserve a raise." He was ready with his reply. "Robert, I can't afford it." I knew he could afford it. He just didn't want to give it to me.

From that point on, my determination to secure a better job increased every day. Several times a week I left home around 6:30 A.M. and drove to the mines. I even tried to get back into Jordan. Recession had hit the coal industry hard, with no end in sight. Hundreds of coal miners were scuffling around the offices, trying to find work, so I always got no for an answer. One mine at Fairview, Loveridge mine, had a large work force, but they weren't hiring or replacing men who left. After these disappointing attempts, I had to rush back to be at the funeral home by 9:00 A.M. What I wanted was to go back into the mines.

Gay and I really had it rough. Our second son, Michael, came along only thirteen months after Anthony. We were so proud of those boys. My work schedule allowed me to be with them. Without support from my parents, however, we would have all starved to death. Gay was dutiful in sticking with me during those hard times. Even after getting my car paid off, we struggled to live. Only God knew when it would end!

During our first years of marriage, we had one personal adjustment that took time to resolve. I visited Mom and my kids often. We'd come home from someplace, and I'd drop Gay and the boys off at our house and go to my parents' home. After about five minutes, the phone would ring. My mom was sensitive. "That's your little wife," she'd say. "She's calling for you." When I'd come home, only a hundred feet away, Gay would blast me. "You had to go see that woman." She told me she thought my mom and I were too close. "You even still got your momma 'fixing' for you." She was referring to the occasional weekend lunch I took with my parents and my kids. I sat her down and tried to explain. "My mom takes care of my kids. I love her. We're close because she has my three kids. I didn't have anyone to turn to but her and my sisters. It's that simple."

One day Gay went down to Mom's house and cried. "Mrs. Armstead, Bob doesn't love me. He has all his love for you. Bob's got too much love for you." My mom explained how she saw it. "No, it's different. I've helped him raise the children. He has two kinds of love. He loves me and his children. And he loves you." Gay had to outgrow those feelings, but as she matured, she saw the difference. That turmoil didn't affect me like it did Gay. I felt lucky to have such a good family, full of love. And I appreciated Gay wanting to be my wife, despite the fact that I didn't have a good job that kept up with the bills.

During the summer of 1963 a friend of mine, who was only one of four blacks employed at the Loveridge mine, asked me for a special favor. Though he worked full time for Consol, he kept his job as head waiter at the Fairmont Hotel when they had big dinners. An ambitious man, he also had a catering business on the side. He employed twelve other men to help him serve big parties. He called me on the phone and said, "Bob, I have a banquet this weekend. I'm a little short on waiters. Could you help me out?"

"Just tell me where and when."

"Be at the Country Club Field House in Fairmont at 6:00 P.M. this Saturday."

That evening changed my life. ■

CHAPTER EIGHTEEN

Loveridge, 1963–1968

The banquet held at the Country Club Field House was for Loveridge mine supervisors. As I waited tables, a foreman I knew from Jordan mine caught my attention. "Bob, what are you doing for a living?"

Choosing not to tell him, I replied, "Filling time until I can get back in the mines. I've got my application at every Consol mine around here."

To my surprise, he led me across the room and introduced me to the Loveridge superintendent. "You need a buggy man at Loveridge? Here's one of the best shuttle car operators in the county."

The superintendent looked me over and asked, "Is that true?"

I didn't hesitate one second. "Yes, sir. That's the truth."

"You be in my office at 9:00 Monday morning. I think we can use you."

"I'll be there." The rest of the evening was a blur. All I could think of was getting home to tell Gay.

Two days later I had a new job at Loveridge mine. Classified shuttle car operator at twenty-six dollars per day. Being hired there was one of my biggest thrills in life. Loveridge was Consolidation Coal Company's "prima donna" of all their northern West Virginia operations. Named after George Love, some called it Consol's Billion Dollar Baby. The mine was only ten years old and had the best equipment money could buy. Though I could write off my funeral home job, I decided to keep my part-time bell captain's job at the Fairmont Hotel. I'd been with them for many years, and the manager said he wanted me to stay and would go back to setting the schedule around my mine shifts. My plan was to keep the job a year or so, in case Loveridge didn't work out.

When it opened, a rumor circulated that Loveridge would be lily-white. Experienced miners that had worked at other Consol mines, including No. 63 mine at Monongah, got top priority. One black employee, a longtime miner at Monongah, got laid off there with years of seniority. He went on his own behalf to Consol's main office in Monongah and talked to the president of all northern region operations. I heard that the topic of Loveridge's lily-white policy came right out into the open. The black miner confronted the president with the policy, and the president hired him immediately. The first black man to enter Loveridge was courageous, and I admired him.

Shortly thereafter, 3 more blacks came on the payroll, and that number stuck for three or four years until I was hired on June 10, 1963. I was number 5. The work force numbered nearly 225. I already knew the 4 black men working there, and they greeted me with open arms. With only 5 blacks on the payroll, of course, we had no black foremen at Loveridge. Quite a few of the other miners were friends and acquaintances from other mines. They, too, seemed glad to see me. I was thirty-six and eager to get to work.

On my first day at Loveridge mine, after riding down in the cage, I couldn't believe how spacious the main line was. Twenty-ton cars, twice the size of Jordan's new cars, ran freely there. Men and vehicles moved every which way in the well-lit corridor. Instead of getting into a mantrip, as I had expected, I rode in a rail jeep to our weekly safety meeting with my new section foreman and the other six men in his crew. He introduced me to all the fellows and assigned me to my shuttle car. The electric shuttle car was easy to adjust to, but the haul ways were wet and muddy. Getting back to driving in muddy bottom after the long layoff took me some time. My assigned section included six active headings, all in the same condition.

The continuous miner was a twin borer, a huge machine that cuts in two circular patterns that mesh to make one deep cut. A shaft with three giant arms loaded with bits rotated one way, and the other identical shaft rotated the opposite way. As it ground into the face, a chain penetrated the coal and pulled it out behind onto the loading machine. Our section was hard to cut at all the faces. The miner operator had to stop the machine and replace the bits four or five times during a shift, which slowed down production. Some days that twin borer went through as many as 130 bits. Around the clock for three shifts the machine ground coal and wore down cutting bits. We were lucky if we could fill twenty of the twenty-ton rail cars. That's not much coal. We struggled in that section for a couple of months and were glad to leave it behind.

A special, gigantic twin borer made it happen quicker. Manufactured by Marietta Company and nicknamed Big Mary, this machine was huge because it cut rock. Big Mary must have weighed about sixty tons. Her circling pieces that came together were so big that we called them washtubs. Mary's washtubs had to cut a lot of rock to get to the coal. In a normal section without rock, the twin borer could cut forty tons of coal in half an hour. With increased production from this type of machine, the mining companies could afford to buy one every couple of months until all the sections had a twin-borer continuous miner.

This unique miner made an arch of the roof. My dad retired without ever seeing a twin borer in action and could not understand the arch. He grilled me about it several times.

"I want to ask you something again, son. How far do you guys penetrate into a heading?"

"We go in 110 feet or so."

"All the time the shuttle car and the loading machine are in there, you don't have anyone bolting the top behind you?"

"No, Dad. It's not necessary."

"When do you pin?"

"After we get all the equipment out, then we bring in the roof-bolting machine. Crosscut intersections are the only places that need roof work, Dad. We put four or five bolts above the intersection."

Each time he looked at me as if I was lying. "What holds the top up everywhere else?"

"The arch."

"Suppose the arch breaks?"

"The arch doesn't break, Dad."

"Uh, uh," he said. "That doesn't make sense to me. I couldn't work that way." Then he'd walk away, shaking his head and muttering to himself about "blamed foolishness."

After I'd been at Loveridge eighteen months, I graduated from shuttle car to loading-machine operator. The loading job paid two dollars more a day, which was good, but three other important things gave me incentive to get off the shuttle car. First, I got bored with it. I kept thinking that I'd been doing this for fourteen years. I had to move on to something else. Second, driving back and forth, and especially up the ramp to the dump, currents of cold air hit me in the face. I'd always worn long johns under my coveralls, but at Loveridge my bones got cold and stayed cold. Behind the continuous miner the cold air didn't blast me in the face. The whole work area was considerably warmer because the miner threw off heat.

Finally, I realized that if I got on the loader, I could begin to get experience on the continuous miner. Loading-machine operators had to learn how to run the miner in case the operator was absent. I knew that more experience on more equipment could mean the difference between working and being laid off in the future. Also, at that point, I believe I moved from the safe area of just trying to keep a job into the more interesting area of wanting to learn all I could in the coal mine. I became determined to remain in Loveridge mine for the remainder of my working years.

I always loved the work, no matter what the specific job. The atmosphere of working underground suited me. After only a few days on the loading machine, I found that working right at the coal face where the action was, what we called inby, suited me even more. The work, the environment, the danger, and the minor negatives challenged me. I liked that. For instance, getting clean after a shift at the coal face was a challenge. I needed a twenty-minute shower to remove the ground-in coal dust from my pores. I learned to actually scrub my eyes with soap. After my shower, I put Vaseline around my eyes and ran a tissue across to remove the coal dust. That process cleansed the skin, but on the way home, the tear ducts washed more of the dust down under my eyes. Every day that I worked in the mines, the first thing I did when I got home and put my bucket down was wash my face again. If a miner didn't work at it, the dust stayed on his face and around his eyes, giving him the look of a startled owl. White eyes peering through black circles. I could always spot a newcomer by his black circles.

Another challenge was the "cat-eye," or midnight, shift. I didn't particularly like the night shift, but it agreed with me because we didn't have as much supervision. Mine inspectors didn't come out at night. Not that we took chances, it was just less troublesome. The midnight shift was hazardous to some because they couldn't sleep through the day. I often heard, "Bob, I didn't get but two hours sleep today." I got too much sleep on midnight shift. I'd get in after 8:00 A.M., read the paper, and either go to the Fairmont Hotel for a couple of hours or go to bed around 9:00. Gay had to come up at 6:00 P.M. to wake me for dinner. Though I got plenty of rest, the schedule made me cranky. I would just sit down to enjoy a movie in the evening, and I had to go to work. Some weeks it seemed as if all I did was work, sleep, change clothes numerous times, and drive back to work.

Like anyone else in the mountains, I had to allow extra time to get to work in winter with ice and snow on the roads. Since the loading-machine work was so demanding at Loveridge, many times I had to pull off the road on my way home and doze off for about twenty minutes. This need was worse after a midnight shift. For convenience and a safeguard, most miners had a riding buddy to push at him and say, "Hey, wake up!"

Danger hung in the air everywhere in a mine. An exhausted miner, half paying attention, increased the odds for an accident. Sometimes things happened because men were ignorant of conditions or blind to the danger. I witnessed an accident that occurred as a result of competition, tied with one instant of carelessness. It could have been fatal.

When I first started operating the loading machine, a friend of mine ran the continuous miner. He didn't want me to learn his machine too well because when he left to eat, I could outcut him in that half-hour. He never stayed away more than fifteen or twenty minutes because he didn't want me to show him up. This competition was in his mind, not mine. One day he went to lunch, and I started to run the continuous miner. A black guy took over my loading machine. Loading machines had one peculiarity. Even when the operator cut the power, inertia made their digging arms continue to rotate for five to ten seconds.

I had my attention toward the coal face but knew that a pile of coal was accumulating behind me. I stopped the bits running for the loader to catch up. Suddenly, I heard a piercing scream.

The continuous miner operator, back from lunch early, had climbed over the top of the loading machine instead of waiting for the arms to slow down and stop. Luckily, the claw arms stopped in time, and though his leg was caught, he appeared to be in one piece. My first instinct was to grab at him and pull him to the floor. He yelled, "Don't pull at me. I think my leg's cut off!" By then blood flowed through his coveralls onto the loading machine. We shut everything down and helped him get out of the claws. Blood gushed into his boot. While the loading-machine operator took off his other sock to use as a tourniquet, I took my knife and cut his boot off his foot. Since he was a big guy, we had to get three other miners to help us carry him to the mantrip and then on out to the emergency car.

That machine almost sliced his leg off below the knee. He was very badly injured but did not require amputation. I got a call at home after he'd been in the hospital a few days. He wanted me to go to court and be a witness, saying the accident was the loading-machine operator's fault for not shutting the machine off when he saw him. I wouldn't go because the operator had stopped power to the machine. The incident was my friend's fault for not waiting until those arms had completely stopped. Everyone on the section knew what had happened. I didn't help him get a claim against the company.

After about six months' recuperation, he came back to work. The first thing he said to me was, "You and your buddy owe me a pair of boots." He didn't seem to be joking, and he didn't crack a smile. He was serious.

"For what?"

"You cut mine all to hell."

Since I couldn't believe what I heard, I just walked away. Later, I told my loading buddy about it and added, "That's a hell of a man, isn't it?"

He said, "Yeah. We should have just let the SOB bleed to death."

The accident was a close call, and we felt we had acted swiftly and probably saved his life. I guess the man was joking, but what a way to say thanks! That was his gratitude—a smart remark. We didn't buy him any boots.

Another incident at Loveridge could have cost me my life. The regular continuous miner operator was off, and the section foreman assigned me to run the twin-borer miner. Halfway through the shift, I had to change the bits. I was between the machine and the coal face, up front with the working parts. After several trips, I yelled back to the loading-machine operator, "Come up here and turn on the switch to forward these bits so I don't have to keep running back and forth." I assumed he knew what to do.

As he reached for the switch, he said, "I'm not sure which switch to push."

I only heard "not sure," but every nerve in my body exploded. I hollered, "Hold it! Don't touch that switch!"

He threw his hands up to show me he hadn't done anything. I stepped away and took a few minutes of deep breaths to calm my pounding heart. If he'd pushed the wrong switch, the miner would have lurched toward the coal face and ground me up. I heard about a man who was changing bits on a full-face ripper in another mine. Whether horseplay or not, somebody turned on the machine. That man was gone! Dead and gone!

My regular position as a loading-machine operator suited me. Word got around that I was the best loader operator. The mechanic on my section told another loader that he ought to come to my section and learn from me. A man nicknamed Big Boy relieved me on the loader when I went for dinner. When I came back, I could see his shoe print in the floor where he had struggled to run the machine. His shirt was soaked from sweat. He had to take it off and lay it on the power supply to dry. The mechanic teased Big Boy. "How come you sweat so much? Bob Armstead can load all day, and you don't see a drop of sweat on him." I enjoyed my reputation. Following old advice, I let the machine do the work.

Foremen on different work shifts often asked me to operate the continuous miner for them, but I always refused the offer. Many, many times I substituted on the miners when operators were absent. I didn't ask for a classified job as a full-time continuous miner operator because I simply didn't want to do it.

From the beginning years of mechanization, the accepted thinking in coal mining was that black men could not learn or could not adapt themselves to the new techniques of producing coal. Company policies surrounding mechanization forced black miners to leave the industry as the machines took over. For machine jobs, mine superintendents sought coal miners who were loyal, dependable employees. Although many black miners were steady and reliable, the offers went to white men. Even into the 1960s, 90 percent of all continuous miner operators were still white men, even if they were reluctant. Many miners wanted the classification of mechanic, the most desirable job in the mine. Mechanics in a big operation had to wait for an equipment breakdown. Until that happened, they filled time by running errands, or kept themselves scarce.

Running a continuous miner earned a man three dollars more a day, and with the job came a lot of pride. A man got more respect in the mining community if he had this top job on the section. People figured that if a man got to that high echelon, a section foreman wouldn't fool with him because he could slow down production. Though it was the top job, by the time I learned to operate a continuous miner, the prestige, glamour, and novelty of the position had begun to fade. It carried a lot of responsibility, and the roof danger and eating dust made it hazardous work.

For a time, when we had seven active sections, I substituted for a miner operator two out of five days a week. I never refused to fill in for a man who couldn't come to work. At Loveridge mine some considered me one of the best, and they kept asking, "Why don't you take that miner?" I always replied, "No, no. I'll stay with my loading machine."

One day, as I operated the loading machine, the mine foreman said, "Hey Bob, I hear you're a pretty good operator. How about signing up to run a miner?" I put him off. "No! I'll help out with it and learn that way." Another time, my buddy had a flood at his home, and we knew he'd be off to get things straightened out. When I came in, the foreman said, "Bob, you know you've got to be the operator until John comes back." I replied, "I know, and I'll do it. The only thing about it is this: I want to sign a paper that releases me from being the full-time operator in the future." He couldn't understand why I opposed having the job on a permanent basis so strongly that I wanted it in writing, but I got what I wanted. We signed a paper that said I was under no obligation. Once I knew I was free to do what I wanted with the job, I got myself into one speed—fast! I put pressure on myself to mine as much coal as humanly possible that day.

A twin-borer operator has to stop and change twelve bits during the shift. When I yelled I was ready to go, the loader said, "My God, Bob! You're already done with them bits?" That day I broke a company record. I loaded forty-six cars of coal. The word got around and several miners told the foremen, "You should get Bob to be the operator." I repeated myself when he asked me again. "No. I'll fill in until John returns, but I won't do it."

Besides eating dust, the main reason I didn't ever want the full-time continuous miner operator's job was simple. Eight or ten years ago they wouldn't have even offered me this job because I was black. If I'd have been ambitious and gone after the job, they wouldn't have given it to me because I was black. So I wouldn't do it now. Pride? Yes. But that's how I felt.

For weeks after that, I rode high on the feeling of accomplishment and renewed respect that setting a new record brought to my work life. Then I got the wind knocked out of me. My dad called me at 1:00 in the morning. "Bob, you'd better come out and see about your mom. I think she needs to go to the hospital." The date was January 15, 1966.

Never weighing more than 120 pounds, Mom was small and frail and had been a diabetic for eighteen years. My sisters diligently gave her insulin and food on time. She hadn't been feeling well for weeks and spent most of her time lying on the couch. One of her joys during those weeks was Gay and I bringing our two boys to see her. We had recently gotten them a puppy, and we brought the puppy in with us, filling the house with activity and laughter. Every day for the last week before Mom collapsed, my sister said she asked, "Where's my little boys and the puppy?"

As soon as I got to the house, I helped Dad get her into the back seat of my car and drove her to the hospital. By the time we got to Fairmont General, she was gone. She died quickly of a heart attack and didn't suffer any longer.

I took a week off work. Since my mom and I were close and she had spoken to me about whom to call and what she wanted done when she passed, I took charge of the arrangements. She'd written down exactly what hymns and Bible scriptures she wanted for her funeral. "Bob took over Mom's service" was a criticism I heard, but that's the way she wanted it. Dad never showed his emotions, but I could tell that losing her was hard on him. My first family were teenagers and still living with my parents. Barbara Jean continued watching out for them. By then, however, they had gained much of their independence. The death of a parent is a sorrowful time. I missed my mom and, along with all my family, grieved her passing for a long time.

For the next two years I continued my work as a loading-machine operator, content with watching how production flowed and learning little things about the mining industry to help me do a better job. Then one day in the late spring of 1968, something at work took my attention and filled my thoughts day and night. I was sitting on the bench inside the lamp-house, waiting for my section's time to enter the mine. Approximately ten minutes before I had to get on the elevator, the general mine foreman on that shift came up to me and put his hand on my shoulder. "Bob, have you ever thought about going to classes to be certified as a mine foreman?"

I told him the truth. "No."

"Well, you take a couple days to think it over and let me know your decision." He stepped back into his office and closed the door.

What he had asked me didn't affect me at first. Then a strange feeling came over me. As I rode the cage down six hundred feet to the bottom, I felt as if I was in a trance from the words. Then I said to myself, "Why don't you think it over?" As the shift progressed that afternoon, the question the shift foreman had asked me kept revolving in my mind. I couldn't help asking myself, *Why me?* Like a long-playing movie, I reviewed my time in Consolidation Coal Company mines. As the shift moved to the halfway point, the question changed. *Why not me?*

After working on and off for thirteen years for the same company, word gets around to management whether a man is a good or bad employee. I realized I had a perfect work record. I had been at Loveridge mine for five years, accident-free, with lost time only for the death of my mother and a few days for sickness. Eight days absent, at the most, in five years. During one sequence I worked twenty-seven days straight. I never turned down overtime shifts. I could operate most machines on any of the sections.

The foreman's words stayed with me during the entire shift. I loaded coal and thought, *What should I do? What should I tell him after I make my decision?* The main thing that bothered me was my keen awareness that this mine now had 440 men on the payroll and still only 8 or 10 blacks. On the positive side, a black minister, Deacon Fred Dooley, had paved the way in management at Loveridge. He'd been working as a foreman for three years and had gained acceptance. Through the years I worked with black men and white men, both younger and older, and tried to maintain a friendly, level-headed personality. But if I was ever put in charge of a crew, they would undoubtedly be all white men. How would they handle that? How would I?

Somehow I got through the shift. When I arrived home around 1:15 A.M., Gay was waiting up for me, as usual, so we could discuss the events of the day. She knew I had something on my mind. Finally, I told her what had happened. "The foreman asked me about taking classes for the Mine Foreman's Test." She showed her surprise with silence for a time. We discussed the positives and the negatives. Then she said, "I think they made a nice gesture. If the company thinks that much of you, you ought to consider doing it. You're the breadwinner in the family, Bob. One way or the other, this has to be your decision. You do what you want to do."

After a few days of thinking things over, I decided to challenge myself, take the opportunity, and go for the schooling. I had some insecurities, but I definitely wanted to try for it. I took the certification classes at the armory in Marion County for two weeks that summer. U. G. Carter, a black man who'd been a federal inspector and mine foreman, taught gases and fires, the most difficult section. My friend from Loveridge and I were the only two blacks in the class with ten other white guys.

The courses of study included mine safety, production of coal, and proper ventilation of mine air. Ventilation is extremely critical to mine operations. From the intake air produced by powerful fans outside the air shafts, to channeling it to the face of each section, to pulling it out by return airways. Poor ventilation can cause fatal illness and a buildup of explosive methane gas, present in every mine. How to protect employees and fellow workers and how to produce coal in a safe manner were the two main priorities of the classes. We also learned laws, rules, and regulations, first aid, ways of ventilating a section in case a fire broke out, proper roof control, and methods of rock dusting. All the terms and much of the material were familiar to me, but I had so much specific knowledge to learn in two weeks' time.

Soon after the class ended, we joined another black miner and drove to West Virginia State College near Charleston to take the examination. Someone had read that West Virginia's mining program had certified only 320 black men in its whole history. We had hopes of increasing that number. West Virginia University in Morgantown had been desegregated by federal law since 1955. Still, after thirteen years, black men had to go to the former West Virginia Colored Institute for mine certification tests. The white foremen candidates in our class went to WVU. Driving 125 miles instead of 20 miles because of skin color was ridiculous, but we set our sights on the challenge ahead of us, not the inconvenience.

Fires and explosions were the troublesome parts of the test. Scoring was so critical that missing just a few items caused a failing grade. On the map test, neglecting to put in one detail threw the whole question out. The test results took ninety days to filter back to me. What an agonizing wait!

My buddy and I both failed the test. I had messed up on my map test and missed a couple of other questions. The day after being notified that I had failed, the general mine foreman who had encouraged me to take the test pulled me aside and asked, "You got your results?"

"Yeah. I didn't make it."

"I know. I got a notice on it." He stared into my eyes. "Bob, don't be discouraged. You're a young man. You still got time. Go back again."

I told him I'd think it over. I knew I shouldn't let this opportunity slip by. The foreman was right: I was only forty-one years old. By then, I knew I wanted to be more than just a machine operator for the next fifteen to twenty years. My buddy didn't have confidence. He said, "I think I'm done with it." We discussed it and kicked it around for a couple of weeks. Finally he decided to try one more time. We knew a test date was coming up on a Saturday. We arranged to take off for Charleston right after our midnight shift ended that Saturday morning. We took the test over and sweated out another ninety-day wait.

My buddy called me on the phone when the results came back. The foreman told him before we got our notices in the mail. "We made it, Bob! We're mine foremen!" Gay and I were both so happy. By then I had determined to take the test again and again until I passed. Thankfully, that worry was over. Though I had been very happy at Loveridge, I could hardly wait to get to work each day and see how this certification status would affect my work. The future held the promise of change.

A horrible tragedy made me more determined than ever to learn everything, every day that I could. The date was November 20, 1968, one week and one day before Thanksgiving. I was on midnight shift. About 5:30 in the morning a couple of fellows on my section thought they heard a thump or felt a tremor. I didn't feel it myself, but I don't doubt that they did. Before I left the mine at 7:30 A.M., the news penetrated the lamphouse. One statement spread like wildfire. "Number 9 went up!"

Consol's Farmington No. 9 mine had exploded. ∎

CHAPTER NINETEEN

Loveridge, 1968–1975

Everyone was in shock. We knew No. 9 had a midnight shift but had no idea how serious the explosion was. At the closest point, about eight hundred feet separated one Loveridge heading from a heading at Farmington. The tremor felt on our section was the first blast. Many more followed. Frantic rescue efforts started right away. As I drove home, the radio described billowing white and black smoke and flames pouring from two of the eleven portals. The mine spread out over forty-eight square miles underground. Because so many escape routes existed, hope continued. Twenty-one men miraculously got out or were rescued. The company report that evening: more than seventy miners trapped inside.

Morning papers displayed stone-faced dignitaries and union people arriving in Farmington. I had bell captain duty at the Fairmont Hotel when all the media started coming in and filling the hotel. The governor came. Curiosity seekers choked the main road from Fairmont into Farmington. I heard about the media circus out there and chose not to go. The news reported the scene as heart-wrenching. Being a coal miner, I couldn't watch women and children weeping for their trapped husbands and fathers on television. Reporters bothering the poor families, just for a story, disgusted me.

Fires spread, and small blasts continued to hinder rescue operations. Then another horrendous explosion, like a volcanic eruption, wrecked portal buildings and dashed the last hopes that the men could survive. Fifteen major explosions and four minor ones forced the company to a difficult decision. On November 30, Consol repeated the action taken by Jamison Coal and Coke Company at the same site in 1954. Ten days after the initial blast, to stop the fires and ongoing explosions and to protect nearby communities, Consol sealed the mine. The official death toll was seventy-eight.

I knew one man who died in the Farmington No. 9 disaster. We grew up together in Grays Flats until his parents moved to Fairmont when he was about ten. He was Bill's age, one of his good buddies, and a heck of an athlete. We played softball together. Since he was an only child, his parents spoiled him. Even during the Depression, I thought he had everything a kid could want. He had been working day shift. He and his section foreman didn't get along so the company transferred him to midnight shift before their disagreements came to real trouble. The night the mine went up was his first time to work midnight shift. They never recovered his body.

The mine stayed hot for months and months. In September 1969, the Department of Mines ruled it safe to begin recovery operations. Clearing shafts and building new ventilation took weeks of work. They eventually found fifty-five bodies, but twenty-three were never recovered.

As with any mine disaster like Farmington, not only do families lose their loved ones and their means of support, but the surviving miners' jobs disappear. The company placed some men in other mines but not the hundreds of men who needed work. Men who came to Loveridge from Farmington told me that it was a clean, well-ventilated, smooth-working operation. The newspapers said it had a reputation for being hot and gassy, but I had never heard that about Farmington. With the fires and explosions destroying everything, no one could ever pinpoint the exact cause.

The same thing could have happened any time at Loveridge. In 1963 a spark from a continuous miner set off methane and caused a fire at Dola that killed twenty-two men. Six months before Farmington, four men drowned at Hominy Falls when a continuous miner cut into an abandoned mine full of water. Twenty-one crawled to safety, but the underground sea hampered rescue. Five days later rescuers found one group alive, and ten days later they found another group, nearly starved. Unpredictable incidents brought death in the mines. The numbers at Farmington stunned the public. That tragedy happened close to us, and we all knew we could be next. Personally, I had learned over the years to ignore the fear. I couldn't be effective if I allowed the fear to cripple me.

The Farmington mine disaster in 1968 was a turning point in two ways. Before Farmington, an average of one hundred coal miners died in mine accidents every year in the United States. Because of the disaster, the government created the Federal Mining Health and Safety Administration to watchdog the industry. The death rate declined by 80 percent after 1969. Secondly, the UMW fell apart, splintering into two opposing sides. One, led by UMW president Tony Boyle, said coal companies had the right to change conditions at their own pace. The other side, led by Jock Yablonski, supported miners' rights to an immediately safer working environment. He campaigned for Boyle's job, saying the Farmington disaster was a symptom of all coal companies' neglect of their employees. After he lost the election, Yablonski, his wife, and daughter were murdered. Everyone believed Boyle was behind the killings and lost faith in the union. Four years later a jury convicted Tony Boyle of ordering the murders.

The Farmington disaster made me more alert to the hazards surrounding me. I paid closer attention to the safety meetings and the monitoring work done by foremen. For my own safety and for those around me, I carefully plotted escape routes from wherever I worked. If something happened, I wanted to know exactly what to do and where to go. Even with this in mind, I did not pursue becoming a section foreman right away. I wanted to gain more experience and to pay attention to what foremen did from section to section.

When a man gets West Virginia mine foreman certification, he is eligible to be a fireboss. Firebosses walk the mine checking for gases and reporting any problems. As soon as I got certified, the mine foreman asked me to fireboss weekends. In large mines like Loveridge, two or three firebosses cover the whole area. Since the mine was idle, the atmosphere was darker than usual, and quiet. Hearing the roof working in an empty mine disturbed me at first, but I adjusted and came to ignore it. We divided all sections equally and kept in touch by telephone. That way, if one of us got his jeep off the track or had trouble locating a section, another fireboss could help him. With head lamps and big flashlights, we monitored for gas accumulation and also watched for water problems. We got paid time and a half on Saturdays and double time on Sundays. Usually, I worked one weekend day, sometimes two.

Besides firebossing on the weekends, I continued to run the loading machine during production days. Within a few weeks I got notice that I could go on salary if I wanted. I couldn't decide whether to do that or not. Firebossing one or two days paid well. Salaried foremen had more responsibilities, and I thought the pay was about the same. I got into a groove and felt satisfied with firebossing as my only added responsibility for about a year.

One day the superintendent, Kay Franklin, cornered me. "Come into my office so I can talk to you." He invited me to sit down. "I want to know if you are interested in going on company salary. Are you?"

I said, "Let's talk about it." We discussed the situation for half an hour, and when we had finished, I told him, "I don't feel qualified or ready enough yet."

"Bob, if you change your mind in the future, let me know."

I was asked the same thing three or four times in the following months, but I felt I had much to learn before taking on a foreman's job. Studying the books was a two-week cram session. I wanted to study foremen's techniques of being a boss and listen to the crews discuss the foremen to see whose ways got the best results. I wanted to learn Loveridge inside and out, including ventilation, mining preferences of the top management, equipment placements, and exactly what each man should be doing to earn his pay. Each time anyone asked me, I said, "I'm thinking about it." I wanted to know everything so I didn't have to look foolish and ask any questions. I didn't want anyone to think I was ignorant or couldn't do the job.

One arrogant friend of mine ran a continuous miner. He said, "Ah, Bob. I wouldn't go on salary. They're hard on the bosses here, and you may get fired. Bossing is too much responsibility." His negative attitude got to me. I said, "Let me tell you something! Every man who steps on that cage has a responsibility. What the hell! I might as well go for it. If a man can't take criticism, he doesn't need to have a job. As long as I know that I've made a mistake, I'll take the criticism and learn from it."

About that time my oldest son from my first marriage came out of the service and needed a job. He wanted me to get him on at the Fairmont Hotel as a bellhop. I refused. I told him it was menial work and he needed to find something that paid well. After a few weeks of looking, he called. "Could you see if you can get me on at the mine?" I told him, "All I can do is ask. I'll talk to Mr. Franklin." When I approached Mr. Franklin, he said he'd think about it. Two weeks passed before another Consol mine, Blacksville, called my son for an interview. He got the job.

I knew Mr. Franklin was slick and told Gay, "You watch. He's going to call me in about that salaried foreman's job as a reminder that he helped my son. He won't say that. He'll just expect me to do what he wants this time." That's exactly what happened. Mr. Franklin called me in again. "Bob, what do you say now about going on salary and becoming a section foreman?"

"Let's talk about that. I think I need more experience—"

He cut me off. "Let me think about that, Bob. Let me be the judge. I think you're ready."

We talked for an hour about what to expect and handling this type of problem and that type. I valued his experience and learned a lot. He respected me and believed I could handle the job as a foreman. I finally said, "I'll sign the papers."

"Good! We'll put you on ninety-day probation. If you have any problems with any of the bosses or the men, you come straight to me."

In 1970 I became the third black foreman at Loveridge. Two years is a long time to keep yourself in training. The friend I tested with became a foreman about a year before I did so he, too, chose to take it slow. As black men, we had more than a job to lose if we weren't competent. My probation was only four weeks instead of the normal three months. That boosted my confidence.

Besides increasing my take-home pay considerably, going on salary meant that when the union had a strike, as management, I continued to work through the strike. Gay commented that a regular monthly check helped with home finances. Even a three-day strike threw the budget off. I had just purchased a home and felt that, for the first time in my life, I finally had security for my family and for myself.

Gay enjoyed a couple of my contract perks as a supervisor. I received a check for a clothing allowance once a year to buy work clothes. Also, for ten dollars a month, a rental company brought two uniforms and then replaced them with clean sets every week. I got denim shirts, slacks, and coveralls. The underground temperature outby, the areas near the ventilation shafts or the portals, could be as low as twenty degrees in winter. I had to wear thermal underwear, but I could shed my rented work clothing and change into dust-free regular clothes. After laundering ground-in coal dust for ten years, that was a big bonus for Gay.

I understood the change to being a supervisor involved more responsibilities. Safety programs had improved mine conditions, but coal mining still ranked up there with steel mill and construction work as the most dangerous.

Bob and Gay, 1975. Courtesy of Bob Armstead.

Soon I would be the one responsible for keeping my section employees safe. To broaden my experiences, I chose to fill in on several different jobs when employees were absent. For instance, I drove the locomotive, pulling as many as thirty twenty-ton cars. One pulled the train in front, and one pushed from the back. When we came back in empty from dumping into the silo, they said all that was visible was the first six yellow cars. Then nothing but a yellow streak. We traveled sixty miles per hour inside the mine!

At Loveridge mine, night trains brought in about 150 empty hopper cars. Within an hour and a half, the tipple loaded all of them. That's a hell of a lot of coal! Two engines in front to pull and two behind to push hauled it out of there. When they left Loveridge, they were "spinning and smoking," trying to get that heavy load started. The satisfaction of seeing a full train pull out was tremendous for me.

Some days I ran errands throughout the mine in a rail jeep, a small personnel carrier attached to an electric trolley wire. It had a telephone. In that job I learned every inch of the mine and got familiar with all the miners. By running the mantrip, I hauled miners I would be supervising in the near future. As assistant shift foreman, I got assigned to supervise men working with hydraulic jacks and roof bolters. Another day I had to oversee drilling or loading work. Each day was different, and I looked forward to going to work.

If a piece of equipment or a continuous miner got covered up, especially on a Saturday, the shift foreman would call me. "Bob, the mine foreman and the superintendent are up there trying to get that miner out. Go up there and get it done. I'll give you three or four men." If the mine foreman had to transport any piece of equipment three or four miles from one end of the mine to the other, I got the job. To move a piece of ten- to forty-ton equipment, I had to take strict precautions. My rail jeep had to have fire extinguishers and a mine ax, in case of fire. I had to supervise the area we traveled through. Most times equipment transport ran on tracks. The work was unpredictable. One spark could lead to a disaster. We might get the equipment moved only one hundred feet and boom! The weight broke a rail or the equipment fell off into the mud. Then we had to stop to jack it up and put ties under it to be able to move it back on the tracks. This time-consuming procedure was exasperating.

One afternoon an arrogant shift foreman (he and I had had words) barked an order at me. "Move that miner across to section three. Be careful. And I want you to call me every hour." Each time I called, he asked, "Where are you located now?" I told him, and he hung up on me. By 7:00 P.M. we had the miner in the crosscut just where he wanted it. I called him.

He asked, "Bob, where are you now?"

"You told me number two block on section three?"

"Yeah, what's the trouble?"

"Miner's in the crosscut."

"You're lying! Tell me again, Bob!"

I ignored him and asked, "What you want me to do with these three men?"

He didn't answer me. After a long silence, which I thoroughly enjoyed, I said, "I'll find them something to do," and then I hung up on him. I gave the men an hour and a half for dinner.

Mistakes some shift foremen and section foremen made influenced me. I hated being yelled at and ordered around like a servant, so I vowed

I'd never do that to my men. Sometimes a foreman couldn't see his way of doing things was slow and inefficient. I watched, learned, and got my own ideas of how to do things better and faster. I looked forward to trying them out when I became a section foreman.

That day finally arrived. I'd been expecting it for two weeks from the way the shift foreman had been watching me. He came into the lamphouse and yelled, "Hey, Bob. Get your lamp and get ready to go."

I was almost certain what he wanted, but I walked over to him and said, "What do you mean?"

"I'm short a section foreman. I want you to get ready to go in and take over his crew. Take your time. The mechanic and the miner operator are certified also. They'll help you, if you need it. Don't worry about making a mistake. If you make a mistake, you won't make it twice." I knew he meant there was too much on the line—miners' lives—to make the same mistake again.

Naturally, I was nervous but excited. I knew all the men on the crew, seven white men, and had worked many shifts with all of them at one time or another, but I didn't know how they were going to react. This group of miners was one of the highest coal-producing crews at the mine. Although I had the jitters, my first shift went well. They all responded, and we mined more coal than expected during my first shift as a supervisor.

A few days later the shift foreman pulled me aside with some good advice. "Bob, you got seven men up here. Every day they are the same guys. They all got different personalities, but what you've got to do is make a crew out of them." I learned a lot from him. He was right about the men. One day they'd be cheerful, and the next day they'd be surly. Sometimes a man had family problems and couldn't concentrate. Even though they had different personalities and work habits, I enjoyed blending them to make one combined crew. I ended up being a father, a doctor, a lawyer, and everything to them. Understanding their ways and attitudes could be a challenge, but I got into a habit of trying to be a good listener. Many times a man doesn't want advice; he simply needs someone to listen. The result of my kindness to them was that they worked hard for me, producing endless tons of coal. My crews took pride in their jobs.

We got the second full-face ripper, nicknamed "the corncob," on my section. The working end of this continuous miner looked like a huge round drum, loaded with bits, and it ground the whole coal face in one downward roll. At a quarter of a million dollars, the full-face ripper was a big company investment. Equipment on any given coal-producing section by 1973 was worth nearly $3 million. Loveridge had six sections. We were lucky to have the first new miner in several years. After that, there was no stopping us for production.

On the daily report, we usually stayed either first or second on any of the three shifts that we worked. At the first of the month, I checked the production sheets. "Bob Armstead's crew . . ." for however many times we topped the list. Usually every month or every other month, we'd either be first or second leading the sheet in production. My crew earned the record for thirty-one days of production at Loveridge mine.

Things didn't run smoothly all the time, however. The shift foreman sent me a guy nobody wanted to bother with because he was a complainer and wouldn't listen. Adam worked with me several times and did all right, so they assigned him to me. He drove a shuttle car. Every shift something was wrong. He'd call me that he had a bad switch, the car was out of oil, it wouldn't steer right, or something else was wrong. One day the shift foreman said, "Bob, you're going to be down about an hour. I called a mechanic to fix the portal feeder." "Down" meant no power, no production. At the coal dump, about one thousand feet from the section, the portal feeder that kicks the loaded cars forward had quit working. I signaled that I understood and then assigned the men to check machines, cables, or shovel—whatever chores needed to be done. John, an excellent bolt-machine operator, had already started roof bolting at an intersection that had power. Since I didn't want Adam working alone, I sent him to help John. Before he left, I got in his face and said, "Do not operate that bolt machine!" He promised, "I won't."

Since we were down, I went on a check of the headings in my section for methane. I came around the corner, and there was Adam, operating the bolt machine. I stood watching them for about ten minutes. John looked at me, and we stared at one another. Finally, it got under my skin that this guy had defied me, so I stepped in and said, "Hold it, Adam! John is the operator. You were supposed to help him." John said, "Bob, he's doing all right. Let him run it." I trusted John, so I let Adam get some time on the bolt machine.

My next instructions were very clear. "After you get that done, you guys go to section one and bolt there. Adam, help John get the machine over there, and then you give him the supplies. Do not bolt. I'm going to drive over and check on the progress at the dump. Adam! You hear? Do not operate this bolt machine!" He assured me. "I won't, Bob. I won't." I felt certain that he would obey my strict order. It did not occur to me that he would defy me again.

I was at the portal feeder when I saw two fellows running down with their lights flashing. I yelled at them, "Hey, where you fellows going? You're supposed to be—"

"Bob! You got an accident up on the section!" We jumped in my jeep and took off. We didn't take time for explanations, but from their heated directions, I knew the accident site was the roof-bolting work, and I knew who had caused the accident. *Adam, what have you done?* went over and over in my head.

When we got there, Adam lay all twisted and moaning in pain. A line curtain, used to channel the air in and take it out, hung near the bolting area. Somehow Adam got his light cord entangled with the stem of the bolt machine and the curtain. When he went to penetrate the drill into the top, the light cord wrapped around his arm and almost tore it out of the socket. All John could say was, "Bob, you can't tell him nothing. It happened so fast."

I called emergency, and they took him to the hospital. Safety inspectors came and measured everything, including the curtain. I told them exactly what had happened and that he had defied my orders. John told them that he had instructed Adam how to move that curtain back before installing the drill. He didn't listen. They didn't fault John or me. At the hospital his wife told me, "Adam liked working for you. None of those other SOBs liked him." All I could think of to say to her was, "He did the best he could." Adam had several operations on his shoulder, at least one of them in Pittsburgh. He didn't work in the mine again because he lost the total use of his arm. Adam died within a year. I don't know why. I felt bad for his family.

When I was assistant day-shift foreman for ninety men, I had to be on the bottom by 7:30 in the morning. Since we operated three shifts and the ongoing coal extraction in each section was unpredictable, a regular job assignments list was impossible. My first job of the day was to point the miners in the right direction. I finally got on the section about 8:30. Before the first shift of the week, we assembled the men and discussed safety for fifteen to twenty minutes. After a safety meeting one Monday morning, I told this kid, "Jim, I want you to shovel this loose spill coal here from the loader off the last shift. You'll find the shovel up the heading there. Straight up. Turn two blocks to the right, and one block to the left." He said, "OK, Bob" and took off.

Time passed. Too much time. I knew the kid had experience around the mine and asked each man I met, "Have you seen Jim?" No one knew where he was. One guy reassured me. "I heard you tell him where to go to get a shovel. Your directions were clear, Bob."

"Man, it's been almost an hour. I've got to find him."

When I finally found him, he didn't have the shovel and got very defensive. He blurted out, "Bob, when I was in the army—"

"This is not the army, son. This is business. I told you exactly where to go. That was an hour ago."

We got the shovel, and I walked him back to the spill coal. I don't know if he was killing time or not. Like in many situations with crew members, I had to give Jim my trust. He was a good worker. I couldn't criticize his work. I believe Jim simply didn't know his right from his left and got lost. I couldn't understand how these young people didn't know their directions. What a waste of time! That's the type of thing a foreman had to work his way through without laughing or getting angry.

The mines had electrical resistor boxes where we could plug a little stove in and have about five amps. The top had bars, and we placed a huge piece of metal across those bars to cut down on the heat. Around dinner time guys lined up their sandwiches on the "rotisserie." Gay wrapped mine in aluminum foil so they wouldn't burn. Some single guys just carried a can of beans. One day a guy we called Beanie put his can on the "mine microwave" and went down a section. Somebody called out, "Where's Beanie? Tell him to get back to the dinner hole. He forgot his beans and they blew up." Beans flew everywhere! All over the walls and the floor. They stuck to our sandwich wrappings and burned onto the stove, giving off a horrible stench. We gave thanks for good ventilation, but what a mess! What can a foreman say when something bizarre like that happens?

At times I had a good section foreman and bad conditions on the section. We did the best we could to mine coal. Other times conditions were excellent, but I'd have a bad section foreman. Mean and arrogant, he wouldn't listen to anything. His attitude affected the men and the coal production. Those circumstances gave me the incentive to learn more about handling the men and running the sections with top efficiency.

As the mine advanced, the company sank another shaft to get the personnel closer. I took the first midnight crew into the new portal at Flat Run. Previously, we had entered at Sugar Run portal. After Flat Run, they opened Miracle Run between Fairview and Pennsylvania. Miracle Run came in twelve miles from where I had started in 1963. That's how far the mine had advanced: twelve miles. The Pittsburgh coal seam still being mined at Loveridge supposedly runs all the way across northern West Virginia to the Ohio River.

I continued alternating as a section foreman and assistant shift foreman for several years. I felt good about the job I was doing. Not arrogant, but confident that I could handle anything that came my way. To protect my men, I tried to practice safety by the book. If something potentially dangerous happened, I didn't hesitate to shut down production. If two guys didn't get along, I split them up without blame, knowing well that personalities don't always mesh in a pressure situation. We were always under pressure to get the coal out and to keep our area free of hazards.

In a man's personal life and his work life, choices of what to do, or what not to do, come every day. He generally has time to weigh the good and bad consequences of the choices he makes and the actions he takes. At Loveridge, with many men depending on me, or standing and waiting for my judgment, I learned to make choices quickly and suffer the consequences. With years of experience behind me, my decisions were usually sound and correct. Not always. One time, reason and good judgment left me. In the early part of the century, I could have been hung for what I did.

During a midnight shift in late March 1975, about twenty minutes before quitting time in the morning, my loader operator and I had a disagreement about rock dusting. Before our shift left the work area, company policy stated that all surfaces had to be rock dusted. Special sprayers were used to spread the white, powdered limestone. Rock dust mixed with the coal dust particles so they wouldn't explode. This guy had been arguing with me about my instructions for several weeks. I don't remember if he just didn't want to do it or if he didn't think it needed done. Maybe he had coal running and didn't want to stop. I insisted he do the work because everyone else was busy with other jobs. The loader operator came up to me several times, shaking his finger in my face, telling me he wasn't going to rock dust.

I warned him, "Don't do that! Don't be shaking your finger at me. Back away from me." I repeated those words several times. He didn't back off. He stayed in my face. The incident went from this guy not listening to his supervisor to threatening me on a personal level. All of a sudden, I lost control. I punched him in the face and knocked him down. I hit an employee, a white employee.

The shift ended abruptly. We shut down and climbed into the jeep to go outside. An eerie feeling hung in the air as no one spoke a word all the way out. By the time we got to the lamphouse, the news had spread to top management that I had hit my loading-machine operator. As I approached the mine foreman's office, he met me at the door and directed me inside. He was very upset. "I'm disappointed in you, Bob, but mostly I'm surprised that you took this inappropriate action on your own. You have always been faithful to this company's rules, policies, and regulations, but in this case, you used bad judgment." I knew the company had to do something about what I did, but his choice of words told me that my job was in jeopardy. I didn't defend myself, but I wanted to. He didn't ask what happened so I stayed quiet.

He continued to rail me out. "Management and I have always supplied you with extra manpower to produce coal on your section. Now you do this."

I retaliated. "I know you did. I appreciated that, but I always produced tonnage to balance the wages for the extra manpower, didn't I?"

The office became silent. Absolute, deafening silence. He was obviously mulling over whether he should let me go right at that very moment. As the general mine foreman, he had the power to do it. He motioned me to go and turned away. He didn't say, "You're fired!" But I knew I was in deep trouble. I went in, took my shower, and then headed out to my car. Several of my foremen friends waited for me, telling me that troublemaker had it coming. I told everyone, "I don't want to talk about it."

What a long twenty-two mile drive home! I was one of only four black section foremen in northern West Virginia. I liked my job and wanted to keep it. Then this happened. I wanted to turn the clock back. Gay was up when I arrived home at 9:00 A.M. As soon as I entered the kitchen door, I set my dinner pail down and said, "You won't have to wash or pack a lunch in this for awhile."

The look on her face! "What happened?"

I told her what I had done. At first she could hardly speak from shock, but she recovered and found some choice words for me.

"Settle down now," I said. "I'm only forty-eight. I'm still a young man with mining skills and years of experience. I'll get work in another mine. Don't worry about it. I'll take care of it."

I sat down to read the morning newspaper and drink a cup of coffee. I began to calm down. As we discussed our future, the kitchen door flung open with a bang. My longtime friend, a foreman at Loveridge on another shift, and his wife stood in the doorway. "I heard, Bob. Now these things do happen. What are you going to do about it?"

"I haven't decided. Maybe there's nothing I can do."

"Yes, there is now. You should go out to Monongah and talk to the president of Consol's northern mines. He's got five or six mines. You know something like this has probably happened before. Tell him exactly what happened and that you didn't mean for it to happen. Maybe everything will be OK."

"I don't want to talk to anyone about it right now." I was getting nauseated from all the stress. "I don't feel good."

For an hour, he coaxed at me to go see the president. Since he could see I wasn't going to say, "Yes, I'll do that," they left. I knew he wanted to help, but I also knew I'd have to think long and hard about just showing up in the president's office. After a few more minutes of discussing plans with Gay, I said, "I'm going to bed. Please take the phone out of our bedroom." Of course, I couldn't sleep. An hour or so later I heard the phone ring and the door open. Gay said, "The Loveridge superintendent wants to talk to you about the incident."

Like me, Mr. Franklin had had time to calm down. He said, "Don't come to work tonight, Bob. Some of the hourly employees may want to strike because of your actions. You be at the president's office in Monongah at 8:00 tomorrow morning. He wants to talk to you. I'll be there also, but I'll probably be a few minutes late." Mr. Franklin and I had always gotten along well. I believe that because my crew was one of the leading coal producers in the mine, he chose to treat me with respect and kindness, even though I was in trouble.

What a sleepless night! I got up around 6:00 A.M. so I wouldn't be late for the biggest appointment of my life. The outcome of this meeting was beyond my control. Hanging in the balance was my job, our home, and the future for my family and myself. When I arrived at the president's office, the man astounded me with his warm reception. He even made a joke. "How about that Muhammad Ali fight last night? Heavyweight title bout and he wins by a knockout!" Then he looked at me sideways to see my reaction.

With nervous laughter, I said, "Yeah, I had one also."

He got down to business quickly. "Yes, you did, Bob. What happened out there?"

I explained the incident the way I saw it. "The company pays me a nice salary to run a production crew to produce coal. This employee wanted to take control. We had a difference of opinion, and he stopped production to argue with me for about seven minutes. Everyone stopped working to watch us. That cost the company production of about 120 tons of coal. He was shaking his finger in my face. I told him to stop doing that several times." He knew I hit the guy, so I avoided saying those words. A kind of sparring on my part. The president, whom I had met several times when he toured the mine, said, "I can't condone what you did, Bob." Then he spoke of keeping control without violence. He did not speak of termination.

Within a few minutes the door opened and Mr. Franklin walked in. He spoke directly to the president, saying he did not want to lose me. I was shocked! The president asked me, "Would you consider transferring to another mine?"

"Yes, I would. I need the job."

"Bob, you already have a job. With this company. I need a foreman at the Four States mine. Go back to Loveridge and get all your belongings and meet with the superintendent at Four States this afternoon at 2:00." The meeting was over with that statement. I thanked him and left, still in shock. He didn't fire me! I could hardly believe it. I really didn't want to leave Loveridge but knew I had no choice, not after what happened. I was lucky and grateful to remain a section foreman. Lucky to have a job, period.

After picking up my stuff, I went home to share the news with Gay. We couldn't have been happier. Four States was a big operation, just outside Worthington. My drive to work would be considerably shorter. I didn't know what to expect, but the superintendent at Four States greeted me wholeheartedly. He could not have been more welcoming. I became his first black section foreman.

Loveridge to Four States—what a drastic change! ■

CHAPTER TWENTY

Four States

Conditions at Consol's No. 20 Four States mine were deplorable in April 1975. I had heard rumors that it was bad, so nothing surprised me on my first day. As I toured the mine, slopping through water, every face was a stranger. New job, old mine, no friends. I needed this job to work out and wanted to be a good section foreman. At least I still had a job.

What a challenge! The haulage line, called main north, was six miles of bad tracks. Running twenty-ton cars across unstable bottom and through water resulted in a lot of wrecks and lost man-hours. The mine had a slurry pond inside and a huge slurry system outside to hold some of the water. We tripped over pumps and hoses lying everywhere. The pumping system worked overtime. Suppressing the water conditions was nearly impossible and kept a man busy on all three shifts. He'd pump the water from where it was high to where it was low. The joke was that they wore the water out, trying to control it and keep it moving away from the work areas.

So why bother messing around in this old deteriorating mine? The coal. The seam was identical to the high quality at Loveridge, and there was a hell of a lot of coal left to mine. Consolidation Coal Company bought a twenty-year lease on Four States mine in 1969 and, despite the conditions, had plans to expand. The mine was only about one-third the size of Loveridge with four sections in operation. Three sections had a twin-borer continuous miner advancing and one section had a Jeffrey ripper doing retreat mining. Out of the approximately 225 men on the payroll, only 5 others were black. Most of my crews were white. They adjusted to me as a new section foreman, and we began to understand each other. I found the fellows to be good and willing workers. Things went along well.

After I'd been at Four States about a month, a man came over from Loveridge. He put his hand on my shoulder and said, "Bob, it's pretty rough here, isn't it?"

"Trying to mine coal? Yes, it is."

"You got a record left at Loveridge."

"A record?" I didn't follow what he meant. "How's that?"

"A company record, Bob. For thirty-one days you mined at least thirty twenty-ton cars of coal. That's six hundred tons a shift for thirty-one days straight."

"That's right, but I didn't know it was a whole company record." I set that record with seven men. Sometimes I only had five, but they were a good crew.

"Well, it is. Keep up the good work, Bob."

I had a bounce in my step for weeks, thinking about that record. A couple of months later I received an invitation to the Loveridge supervisors' banquet. Since I had been a foreman there, the invitation didn't come as a complete surprise. I felt honored to be included but wondered if I was going to take a ribbing for the knockdown incident. What I didn't know was that they planned to recognize me for the production record. The announcement came as a total shock. I received a framed certificate, my first achievement award since my boxing years. The recognition from Consolidation Coal Company felt great! The applause was nice, too.

I'd been a section foreman at Four States about a year and a half when we got a new production manager. That job entails running around on different sections, showing crews how to get at the coal more efficiently. A production manager can also openly advise foremen how to manage the men. We got a notice one particular day that he'd be on our section. After that announcement, all the guys were nervous. Someone watching over us wasn't a welcome thing. We put the power on and then took about ten minutes to eat. That day I had to move equipment, and this production manager walked along with me while I made assignments. Most of the guys knew their jobs, and it was my habit to give instructions as a question. "Joe, how about you doing this? Jim, how about doing that?"

After we'd mined about an hour, the production manager said, "Hey Bob, come on over here. I want to see you." His voice had an edge to it. Though I didn't want to leave the work site and wondered what the heck he wanted, I walked with him to where we could talk above the noise. We sat down.

"I want to ask you a question, Bob."

"What?"

"Do you have any trouble with these guys here?"

I pointed to my face, referring to my skin color, and asked, "What do you mean? Because of this?"

"No, not really. I noticed that you ask them to do this and that." All of a sudden, he got hot. "Damn it, Bob, don't you ask them. You tell them!"

I said, "Well, I hear you." I didn't answer him or agree with him. This man was a former mine foreman at Consol's No. 95 Robinson Run and deserved respect, but he'd only observed us part of one day. I worked with these guys every day. They knew me. I never addressed a man harshly or ordered him to do anything. I never cursed an employee. I treated them like I wanted to be treated, even when stupid stuff tried my patience.

For instance, one time I had to move a long continuous miner cable. At four inches thick, plus the covering, those cables were heavy and hard to handle. The men got one behind the other and tried to pull it. They were stepping on each other and struggling. I said, "Hold it fellows! You're pulling against yourselves. Get about ten feet apart. That way everybody's got ten feet of cable, and you're pulling even." I learned this stuff from experience and passed it on. I could have cussed their stupidity and shouted the right way to do the job, as I'd heard others do, but then they'd either feel humiliated or angry. There's enough stress underground without having somebody criticizing and yelling orders all day. Although I was a supervisor, responsible for coal production, the men came first.

I never got anybody fired. If I found people sleeping, I chastised them, but I never turned them in. One man had the job of shoveling coal onto a belt. He'd left his place, walked down to the dump, and was pushing buttons for rail cars to move forward. I found him there and said simply, "Don't be caught down at the dump anymore." Somebody else snitched on him, and it got back to the superintendent. He called me in and asked, "Bob, why didn't you fire him?"

"He didn't put anyone at risk—"

"Disobeying a supervisor's instructions is serious. There will be a hearing. We'll sort it out there."

I said, "I understand" and left the office. At the hearing, I stood by my position. The miner didn't get fired.

Besides defying instructions, a man could get fired for alcohol or drug use on the job. One midnight shift a miner gave me a hard time because he was drunk. I made him shovel loose coal so he couldn't hurt himself or anyone else. The next morning the superintendent called me in and said, "You had a man drunk on your section last night. You should have fired him."

"No! He didn't belong on my section in the first place. I only had three men, so the shift foremen sent him to me as a replacement. He shouldn't have. Someone should have stopped that man before he came in and sent him home."

He stared at me as he thought it over. "You're right." Nothing more came of it. The man got a second chance because someone else made a mistake.

In 1976 I became the assistant day-shift foreman. No longer responsible for production on a specific section, I helped the day-shift foreman with scheduling, moving equipment, and management of the shift. I enjoyed the regular schedule and hoped it would continue. I did have to serve a week of night work from time to time.

Just as I settled into the job promotion, my father died. During his last five years or so, he'd gotten close to his religion and found comfort in it. From years of working in coal dust with no protection, Dad suffered from black lung. Though luckier than some, because he lived to be seventy-five, he never got a penny of compensation for his condition. Dad lived out his life on his pension, struggling for breath. He used an oxygen tank for the last six weeks, but he just got weaker and weaker. Coal dust coats and scars the lungs, and the victim dies of asphyxiation, like with emphysema. My younger brother Joe couldn't work because of his health, so he and Dad had lived together for many years. That was a rough time for all of us. Both our parents gone. I was fifty years old.

I knew my father was proud of the work I did, and that helped me to keep going, but the grieving stayed with me. I'll admit my new position required a lot of perseverance and patience. The psychological skill needed to handle ninety to one hundred men and direct them to their jobs every day exhausted me. All of these employees had different personalities, likes and dislikes of job assignments, and differing opinions of company policies. Often they came to work sick or with a sick child or other problems at home. Most were good men, but we had a couple of hell raisers who were hostile. If they couldn't settle something by the end of a shift, the next morning I saw them marching into the superintendent's office with their demands. The problem was always conditions—intense conditions.

The shift foreman I assisted was difficult. I nicknamed him "Hard-Way" because he did things in an antique fashion, that is, the hard way. He lacked imagination. Somewhere, I got the ability to see through a problem and find a solution.

Moving multi-ton equipment was one of the most difficult tasks at Four States because of the water and bad track. On several occasions I helped speed up the process. I liked the reputation it gave me. One midnight shift when I came in, the previous shift foreman called to me as I entered the section. "Bob, we've been wrestling with this miner all evening and still don't have it where it's supposed to be." Everyone was grumpy.

I could tell by the way my boss, Hard-Way, talked that he was planning to continue with the method that wasn't working. I didn't argue with him. I simply ignored him. After I heard the call that the previous shift foreman had left the mine, I took control of the situation. We moved the equipment within an hour. Hard-Way stood by and watched, but he didn't say anything. He and I butted heads over procedures several times, but he was my boss.

Saturday work was optional. When I went around with the sign-up sheet for who wanted to work Saturday, the men asked, "Bob, who's working?" If the schedule said Hard-Way, they said, "No, Bob. I'll pass. He dogs you to death. If you're going to be here, I'll work." I never had trouble getting men to come in on Saturdays when I was the shift foreman. I appreciated their confidence.

Nature doesn't always cooperate in a coal mine. Sometimes things happen beyond anyone's control. The closest I came to losing a man on the job happened at Four States in 1980. My emotions moved from terror, to frustration, to joy, to pure anger. I had a man covered up, and then trapped, for what seemed like a year and a half. In reality the time was only eight to ten minutes.

We were working near a wall that had been mined over the weekend. Left standing, it had settled enough that we could cut a hole through it for ventilation, which was the law. We mined nearby for a couple of hours and set a crib block next to the wall to hold the roof. The crib block's square-shaped layers of timbers provided ample support for the roof. Tim Sanders wasn't the loader operator, but he came up to relieve the continuous miner operator for dinner. Just as Tim started penetrating with the miner, we heard a big clap of thunder. Boom! The roof fell, burying Tim along with the continuous mining machine. The crib block still stood after the fall, but the cap rock slid sideways and got between the roof and Tim's head. The crib block saved Tim's life, but the sliding cap rock put terrible pressure on his head.

We could hear three hundred thousand tons of rock rumbling overhead and Tim's muffled hollering. "Bob! Bob!" Tons of rock lay on the machine and more were ready to come down. We had to get him out! I dug until I got his head exposed. I yelled, "Come out of there, Tim!" He shouted back, "I can't! I'm hung up. I need a wrench. My safety cord is caught. Get me a wrench to unloosen this nut and get my light out." His cap light cord had gotten wrapped around one of the machine levers.

Feeling the panic coming, I yelled, "Forget the light! You don't have time! Come on!" But he kept yelling for the wrench. The mechanic was too scared to get close to the rumbling overhead so he threw him the wrench. I don't know if Tim loosened the nut or yanked the cord loose with the wrench, but twenty seconds later, he was trying to squiggle himself out. Then he quit moving.

"Tim! Come on! She's coming down!" Big and little chunks were raining down and the noise was getting louder and louder.

"Bob, I can't!"

"What's wrong now?"

"My belt's hung up! Get me a knife!"

Time was running out! Shaking with terror, I went in to him, grabbed his belt, cut it with my knife, and dragged him out. We scrambled and took cover about twenty-five feet away from the roof fall. Ten seconds later all that rock came crashing down with a roar. Dust flew everywhere. When he turned and saw the roof fall, Tim stared at the heap of coal and slate. "Bob, you mean to tell me I was under all that rock?"

Between my calming deep breaths, I said, "Yes, you were."

"I'd have been a goner."

"Yes." There was nothing more to say.

The cap rock crushed his hat in, but that hard hat saved him from certain death. I couldn't believe that Tim had no broken bones or open wounds. Unfortunately, the pressure had crushed his teeth. Several teeth had parts missing.

After all this trauma, I saw the superintendent coming. Though I still had the shakes, I knew Tim was going to be OK. This superintendent saw things differently. He liked to swear. He came up to me and said, "Bob, you got all these so-and-so cables lying around here . . ." He didn't ask if anyone got hurt. He hadn't even seen the site where Tim was covered up, and he chose to criticize me. Swearing. "You know the inspectors will be coming up here, and on and on and on." That got me. I didn't listen for long. I walked past him, heading for the cage. I could have hit him with a sledge.

The shock of what could have happened hit me after I got outside. As I filled out my fireboss book about the accident, my hands still shook. I took my time with it because I was so nervous. Reliving the incident, on paper, didn't help. The day-shift foreman stood nearby, ready to go in. Nobody liked that foreman. As I prepared to leave, the foreman stopped me, folded his arms, and said, "Bob, how soon will they get that miner out?" He was referring to the continuous mining machine. That went bad with me. His attitude sickened me. I mumbled, "I don't know" and brushed past him.

I drove home, sat down in my living room, and cried like a baby. After I recovered, I got mad. I called the assistant mine foreman to come over to my house, and I vented my frustration. "I came within an eyelash of getting a man killed, and all they're concerned about is when that miner will be able to cut more coal." He agreed that some officials had no regard for the men. That whole thing took a lot out of me.

When I came in to work the next evening, the continuous miner was free from the roof fall and actively mining coal. Someone said it took about ten hours to uncover it. Tim Sanders lost three days' work. He needed reconstruction dental work. The company paid for that and for the three shifts that he lost.

On Tim's first day back to work, I could see he was eyeing the continuous miner and thinking about his accident. I asked, "Are you going to run that miner?"

"I don't think I should, Bob. I'm afraid of it."

I saw the fear in his face. What I said next made both of us uncomfortable, but his future in mining depended on it. "Tim, you have to. If you don't do it today, you'll be afraid of it forever. Go on up there now, and get to work."

He did what I told him. I kept an eye on him through the lunch hour. Tim later told me that I was right in making him do what he didn't want to do. I knew from others' experience that the first day back after an accident was critical. He could have refused and walked away, but he didn't.

Anytime an accident occurs, the company wants to know everything. Where were you at that time? Did you take safety precautions? Did you give instructions? Supervisors go under the gun when they get a man hurt. If an accident causes the immediate death of a miner, the supervisor has to go in front of the National Safety Council.

During 1982 I received a promotion to safety but often filled in as a shift foreman. In safety inspection I walked the mine, checking work practices and machinery. I had to be on constant lookout for potential hazards and safety violations. One job in safety required that I walk the returns. A return is a mined-out heading used as an airway to suck bad air outside after it has swept across, or ventilated, the active workings. You could call it a bad-air wind tunnel. Some returns stretched three thousand feet one way at Four States. Most had standing water and mud. If I came up to a roof fall, I had to crawl over it and then arrange to clear it out so the air could flow freely again. The work wasn't hazardous, but it was hard. Mud and water! The walking I did was level but often through low areas, which is hard on the legs and back. Besides treacherous walking, I wore eighteen pounds of equipment: safety lights, self-rescuer, and methane detectors.

During this time my son, Tony, started working at Blacksville mine. He only worked there for three years, but for that time, he was a fourth-generation coal miner. I don't think he ever missed but three shifts, one to have a tooth pulled. I took pride in his work record. One night we talked about mining at the dinner table. Since he was new to the job, we discussed getting along with bosses. Word around the coal mines said that when a young miner started working, veteran miners told him, "You do as I say if the boss isn't around. You do what you can to please the boss, but don't bust your ass."

Tony told us of his day's work in an air return. He helped set up four-feet cribs, stacking them to hold the roof. The day-shift crews irritated him. "They don't do much. We do it all. Like I told my buddy, 'We're going to do our work, but we aren't going to bust our asses.'"

I saw red! "Hold it, Tony. Where did you get that phrase?"

"Oh, I don't know. The guys just told me, 'Don't bust your ass.'"

We discussed it awhile. Then I gave him my view. "You haven't been in the mine a year. Don't use that term. You do what you can. You do your part." He said, "I understand, Dad." He told us about shirkers on his crew who sat down on the job until they saw a light coming down the belt. Then they'd hop up and get busy until the foreman left. I'd seen it myself, and I understood his frustration, but I didn't want him to have the attitude of a shirker, ever.

Just as the first cutting machine in the Grant Town mine started a revolution in my dad's work, the longwall brought a drastic change to my mining experience. What an incredible system! I helped install the longwall at Four States mine. It took about a month. In preparation, a permanent layoff of one hundred men took place, and one or two sections closed down. Just like in the 1930s, this revolution cost men their jobs.

The best way to describe a longwall mining operation is to picture two long tunnels running parallel to each other about eight hundred feet apart. Between the two tunnels is nothing but coal. Then cut a tunnel across from one side to the other at one end so it looks like a large U. The longwall mining operation gets set up in the coal seam, across the bottom of the U, and works up through the coal to the top of the U.

We anchored a continuous, three-thousand-foot-long conveyor belt to the roof so that it hung suspended. The conveyor belt hauled the coal from the longwall to the dump inside the mine, where it got hoisted to the surface. In a slope mine, the belt runs directly out the portal and dumps the coal into the processing plant. The shearing machine, or shearer, that ground the coal off the face, had a corkscrew design with cutting bits along the edges. Water sprayers, attached to the bits, helped to keep the massive amount of dust under control. The coal tumbled down onto an attached pan line belt that moved it on out to the conveyor system. In the longwall tunnel we installed big hydraulic jacks on movable frames. Attached to the jacks and at right angles up against the roof, a movable metal canopy, called chocks, hung out over the shearer and the pan line.

When in operation, the shearer grinds across the eight-hundred-foot distance (the bottom of the U) and then back again, gouging out the coal. The chocks and jacks move along with the shearer to support the roof. Where the coal is mined out and the chocks have moved on, the roof falls in behind. Unmined coal and the longwall operation are on the front side of the eight-hundred-foot tunnel. On the back side, behind the line of jacks, is the "gob area," consisting of rock and waste that falls after the longwall mines out the coal. The original crosscut disappears as it fills up after the first few passes through with the shearer and the roof support system.

Setup was critical, but once installed, the longwall system cut and moved coal out with incredible speed. No loading machines. No shuttle cars. Just cutting and moving coal out on the belt. Miners operated the buttons and monitored the operation, making sure the shearer, jacks, and belts worked properly and that methane gas stayed below acceptable levels. Machines did virtually all the work, but dangers existed. Water everywhere made surfaces slippery. One bare wire could electrocute a man standing in water. Moving jacks could easily trap a man's foot. Rock fell from the exposed roof between the chocks and the coal face.

The biggest danger was that first break in the roof. What an incredible experience! Behind the longwall operation, where all the coal had been mined out, a massive underground room grew larger and larger. Years of training couldn't prepare us for the tension that this ever-expanding emptiness poured onto jangling nerves. Above the roaring longwall machinery noise, we could hear thousands of tons of rock grumbling and cracking as it tried to fill the empty void below. When the roof finally collapsed under the pressure, an avalanche of boulders, rocks, and dust crashed to the bottom, filling up all that empty space. The air, suddenly displaced by tons of rock, blasted past us like a hurricane wind.

Words can't describe what it's like to be that close to that much power. Like a tidal wave of dangerous energy. After the first break, we stood wide-eyed, speechless, and struggled to keep our hands steady enough to keep working. I've heard that in some mines, when that first major fall came, men simply walked out of the mine and away from mining forever, saying, "That's it for me! Can't do this anymore!"

Sometimes I supervised the longwall operation and the self-advancing roof support system. The responsibility challenged me, and I never lost respect for the incredible technology that came together to produce the longwall. For the year following its installation, coal production nearly tripled, from 350,000 tons to 1,000,000 tons. If my father, or miners like him, came back from the grave and walked into a longwall coal mine, they'd be struck dumb with amazement.

We later replaced the chocks with huge units called shields that were a similar, but more efficient, method of supporting the roof. These monstrous shields also had a horizontal jack that pushed against the shearer and kept it pressed against the face. Miners moved the individual shields by remote control.

Not far from the active longwall, we opened up a new section and started mining with a brand-new twin-borer miner and loading machine. I helped move a half dozen older mining machines into an abandoned heading for storage. We cut into Dent's Run, an operation that hadn't even started mining as yet. The previous year the company had installed a conveyor belt system inside a new half-mile-long sloping tunnel to the outside. This belt, nearly five feet wide, was to haul coal from our longwall, two old sections, the new section, and from the new operation to come at Dent's Run. Included in the rumored $13 million price tag was a brand-new automatic rotary dump at the base of the slope. I could walk down there and see bright lights shining everywhere and coal running up the slope on that belt like a never-ending black snake. It was an incredibly modern haulage system, built to serve a gigantic operation.

The company had to eliminate jobs, always a sad occurrence, but it excited me to see all these operations come together. Great expectations for Four States and Dent's Run working together brought confidence to everyone. Certain their jobs and futures were secure, miners bought homes and cars. With only two years or so to go until my retirement, I knew I would retire from Four States mine.

Suddenly, it all went away. ■

CHAPTER TWENTY-ONE

Four States, 1984

I n the fall of 1984, I did safety work and filled in as a supervisor wherever needed. The events of one particular day left a lasting impression on me. I was the assistant day-shift foreman. Ten minutes before I got on the cage, the shift foreman asked, "What are you going to do with those flats of cribs?" He was referring to several flat rail cars loaded down with short timbers.

"Like we've been doing every morning for over a year—take them to the longwall. Why?"

He looked grim. "Take them up there, but don't unload them."

Puzzled, I shrugged my shoulders and mumbled, "OK." After I issued instructions on the flatbed of wooden cribs going to the longwall, I rode to main north and started checking rails and cars. Karen, a new employee who had only been working three or four months, stopped me and asked, "How many people they going to lay off today?"

Spreading rumors irritated me, so I cut her off abruptly. "Girl, don't you start that!"

"I heard there's going to be a layoff, Bob."

"I didn't hear anything of the sort. Just forget it."

Fifteen minutes later, about 8:30 A.M., I walked across the tracks and noticed the maintenance foreman sitting against a wall, eating his sandwich. He stopped me. "Bob, how many men and how many foremen are they going to lay off today?"

Here it was again. "What are you talking about?"

"I heard there's going to be a heck of a layoff and a lot of foremen are going. You don't know how many?"

"No. That's the first I heard of it." Not exactly true, but I discounted what Karen said because she was new. I figured someone was teasing her to scare her. I couldn't ignore the statement twice in such a short time. When I found the shift foreman, his sad face confirmed the news. It was 9:00 A.M. "Bob," he said, avoiding direct eye contact, "we have a situation. Have your men install those cribs at the longwall and brace those shields. We're running until 11:00 this morning, and that's it for the longwall."

There it was! Something terrible was about to happen, but I couldn't bring myself to ask what else he knew. For now, I didn't want to know. I walked to the longwall, my stomach churning. I helped the men unload the crib blocks to support the new eight-ton shields we'd just installed. As the jacks moved on, crib blocks had to be wedged in under the shields to support the roof. I didn't tell the men what I'd heard because I didn't know the whole story and didn't want to worry them.

At 11:00 A.M. the longwall shut down on schedule. Shutting down tons and tons of production was serious business, but the other sections kept mining coal. Any time I met anyone, we exchanged bewildered looks. One hour before the shift ended at 4:00 P.M., the mine foreman gathered everyone together. "This is not a layoff. It's a shut down. The superintendent got a call from Consol headquarters in Pittsburgh. He didn't know anything about it until he got the call. They said, 'Shut her down.' Only foremen in tomorrow." No one said a word. I couldn't believe my ears. Dumbfounded at this unbelievable news, we shut down and went home.

The longwall had been in operation a little over one year. One day the new section was mining, and the new belt was hauling out as much coal as it could hold. The next day, nothing. At the top of production, they shut down everything with no explanation. Development at Dent's Run came to a halt. All that money invested. Hundreds of contract miners, who now faced unemployment, didn't return to work the next day. The other foremen and I walked into an eerie underground tomb. Mining ceased forever at Four States mine.

On a personal level, I couldn't adjust. I'd been comfortably working mostly day shifts for seven years. At fifty-seven, the thought of change, looking for work, or worse—forced retirement—really upset me. I suffered from nausea and sleeplessness for a week. Rumors floated around. Consol's lease expired in a couple of years. Maybe that was it. Water problems had worsened in some areas. Maybe that was it. For the first few weeks, we disassembled and moved out equipment, trying to make sense of the whole thing.

We removed eight or ten of the newest power supplies, or rectifiers. We took the longwall shearer out and the one hundred eight-ton shields we'd just installed. We disassembled the new twin-borer miner that had just started on the new section and brought it out along with a couple of other twin borers. When I firebossed, checking for methane, I saw a section with a continuous miner and two full shuttle cars ready to dump onto the conveyor belt that sat idle. The scene looked as if the men had simply stopped for the shift. I found other sections where they stopped mining and left the machines and coal sit. Good coal lay in cars everywhere. The six older, but still functional, continuous miners that I'd helped to store sat dust-covered in the abandoned heading.

Within four weeks the equipment removal slowed down to minimal stuff, like cable and trolley wire. Then the word came. We began preparations to install twelve seals. I helped to supervise putting in those concrete walls. We placed them about one hundred feet apart and reinforced them with steel. Seals serve only one purpose. They contain water. The company planned to flood the mine. Within two weeks everything left inside would be under water. Twin-borer continuous miners, loading machines, shuttle cars, track-loading machines, thirty-ton locomotives, forty-ton locomotives, over one hundred twenty-ton cars. Millions of dollars worth of equipment, enough to start up two mines, did not come out.

I knew a guy who was building a house and wanted one hundred feet of the longwall cable. It was nice copper cable with a thick black jacket. When he asked if he could have it, a company official said, "Don't you touch an inch of it. It goes underwater, and it all goes back to taxes." Taxes! When I heard that, I shuddered. Equipment and equipment, and coal, and coal, and blocks of coal, and more coal. Miles and miles of coal could have been mined out of Four States. What a waste! I was there when they brought the man cage up about halfway and dumped tons of gravel into the cage and the shaft. I watched as they turned the outside slurry loose and flooded it. Millions of gallons of water. If there was a rat down there, it drowned.

I couldn't understand it. Nobody could. Why put that much money in a mine and turn around and shut it down? All that coal and all those experienced men. For taxes? Maybe, maybe not. No one offered us an explanation, but that was normal. Perhaps some federal and state inspectors would have more in-depth knowledge about the particulars. Of course, they couldn't say *why* it happened. Only the men at the top knew why.

A couple of days after the flooding, in November 1984, the superintendent called me in. "Bob, we're keeping a skeleton crew here to maintain and guard the outside buildings and equipment. Some foremen have been retained. We're retaining you as a safety inspector. Next Monday, you go up to Robinson Run for an inspection. You'll be working there."

What a relief! Soon to be fifty-eight, I was too old to be looking for work with another company. Robinson Run was a new mine and another new experience ahead of me. I felt very fortunate and blessed to have a job. When my future supervisor's name came up, I didn't show my concern. My newly assigned safety foreman had been at Four States as the general mine foreman, so I knew him. We had some hard days because we couldn't get along. Mentally, I put Four States behind me and hoped for the best.

When I arrived at Robinson Run, I found that my supervisor had made a 180-degree turnaround in attitude. The conditions were far better at Robinson Run than at Four States. That probably helped him be more relaxed. Not so many worries. Also, there's a big difference between being a mine foreman with production as your main concern and being in charge of the safety department.

He greeted me with a handshake but got right down to business. "Bob, you'll work twenty-two days a month for me. Six days one week, five days the next. You'll be working out of Jones Run portal. I'll introduce you to your new supervisor over there." He turned away like he didn't want to look at me. As he turned back, I noticed he was smiling like he had something to put over on me or a bit of information he enjoyed keeping from me. "There's something else, Bob."

"Yeah?" I didn't have a clue why he was acting so odd. "What's this all about? What are you up to?"

"She's a twenty-three-year old woman."

"You're joking with me, right?"

"No, Bob. No joke. Your new supervisor is a woman. A very young woman. Now, don't be alarmed. She uses a lot of profanity."

He left me speechless for a moment. When I recovered, I just shook my head and muttered, "This ought to be interesting." ∎

CHAPTER TWENTY-TWO

Women in Coal

In the days before I reported to Robinson Run in December 1984, I worried about the big adjustment facing me. Thirty plus years underground working for men, and I get assigned to a woman boss. I knew what it took to be a foreman, but I didn't have the vaguest idea what to expect from a woman in that position. The whole thing seemed like a cruel turn of events. Usually, I'm easygoing and don't let things bother me, but a woman for a boss—that bothered me. I couldn't help thinking about how women had come into the mines. They definitely weren't welcome, for many reasons.

Superstitions against women in the mines were strong in West Virginia. Northern West Virginia miners believed that if a woman entered the workings, the mine would suffer a spell of bad luck. When I worked at Grant Town in the 1950s, I heard the superintendent say, "A woman better not ever try to darken my coal mine." In southern West Virginia, miners believed that if a woman entered the mines, one of two things would happen: a miner would die or the whole mine would blow up. Supposedly, a woman, disguised as a man, worked in the southern coalfields for many years. No one seems to know anything about her, so it could be a tall tale.

In Marion County mines, if a woman came in with a party of visitors, the miners immediately dumped their drinking water, an unmistakable sign of a walkout. Then the entire work force left for the day. Mine operators got the point. They respected this superstition and would not think of allowing a woman to enter their mines. Although live women never came inside, many miners believed that dead ones frequently passed through as ghosts in search of their mates. I never put much stock in superstitions about women in the mines, alive or dead.

I'd read about England, Scotland, and Japan using women and young girls to transport coal to the surface in the early years of primitive mining. In shaft mines, they carried coal up winding stairways in wicker baskets strapped to their backs. With the baskets held in place by a leather strap around their foreheads, the women hauled coal for twelve to fourteen hours every day. In drift mines they hitched a woman to the front of a mine car with a belt around her waist and a chain between her legs. Another girl pushed the car from behind. If her husband or father was a miner, a woman shared in this work as her lot in life.

Since operators considered women bad luck during the same era of primitive mining in West Virginia, male Negro slaves hauled coal with baskets and wheelbarrows. Later they pushed small wooden-wheeled cars with their heads while crawling on their hands and knees. If the slave was lucky, a big dog, harnessed to the front of the car, pulled most of the weight. Ponies, mules, horses, and paid drivers replaced slave labor after the Civil War. This system of hauling coal continued underground until locomotives came into use in the 1930s.

During the World War II manpower shortage, women sorted coal in processing plants. No operator considered letting women dig coal underground. When the soldiers came back for their jobs after the war, coal companies sent the women home. In 1972, a federal law made it possible for women to apply for any available job. Miners were dead set against women invading their territory, but it was inevitable. Forced by the federal law, the 1974 UMW contract included women miners. Before I left Loveridge in 1975, I heard that some area mines had hired women, but Consol avoided the issue. Before long, women turned away by Consol sued the company, forcing it to implement a hiring policy.

Logically, I knew it wasn't fair to keep them out. Women's unskilled jobs paid less than two dollars an hour. As general inside laborers, they could make eight or nine dollars an hour. Like other miners, however, I dreaded the changes needed to accommodate women and the turmoil I knew their presence would bring. My generation was raised to respect and protect women. Younger men were more hostile with their language and their actions. Some mines became a war zone: male versus female. Everybody in the area, inside and outside the industry, had an opinion on the subject. Many felt that each woman who took a man's job denied him the opportunity to support his family. Naturally, miners' wives opposed women coming in and possibly tempting their men.

At a store in Fairmont, a clerk asked me what I thought about women coming into the mines. I told her the truth as I saw it. "They have every right in the world to get a good job and to earn nice money. A coal mine is about the only place in the area where they can do that. But it's going to affect the men, the way they act and the way they talk. Some men, when they enter the mines, every third word is a cuss word. They'll have to change because the women won't put up with it. Men can be standing around talking, and one of them will leave the group and go around the corner to take a leak. They won't be able to do that any time the urge hits them because the women will be right there. Those things could be problems." I didn't tell her my fears of sexual harassment and bad feelings from the men about the women being underground. I dreaded the first encounter, but I knew it was coming.

When I heard the company was going to hire a few women at Four States, I told a couple of the fellows, "We already have 220 women in this mine."

"Bob, what do you mean?"

"Some of you guys cry worse than women. Big strong guys. You assign a meager job, and they cry about their assignment." That shut them up for awhile.

Though I didn't think that a mine was any place for a woman, I tried to take a wait-and-see attitude. Where I might have respect for them, I worried that a lot of men wouldn't care. I knew they would deliberately say things because a woman was there. They would urinate in front of them, saying, "Hey, you're down here. You want to be like us and get paid like us?

Then you're one of us. You'd better get used to it." The men didn't hold back their crudeness and curses. To embarrass the women, men brought in obscene magazines, and they harassed them.

One girl worked under my supervision at Four States. Karen was only five feet tall and slender. Like other new employees, she started as a red hat, which meant she was on probation for three months. Miners with red hats got more detailed instructions and received more allowances for making mistakes. Karen earned a black hat because she did well. She shoveled coal and put herself into it. The men didn't appreciate her being there in the beginning. She intended to stay and held up her end of the work.

Karen came to me and said the men were harassing her and bothering her. She wanted me to do something about it, but I couldn't do anything unless they were touching her. Even if they had touched her, my instructions were to refer it to the general mine foreman. Walking that fine line between all those men and one woman was difficult. I felt terrible not coming to her immediate defense. I knew that if I made a big deal about it and criticized the men, their attitudes would have changed for the worst toward Karen, and toward me. I told her the men had been warned to leave her alone and suggested that she go straight to the superintendent and try to get him to make the changes. She ironed it out somehow because she stayed.

Another woman came to Four States while I was there, but we didn't work together. She didn't last. If a woman could get through that first week of lifting and being on her feet, she might make it. The danger was exciting for awhile, but then that, and the hard work, caused many women to quit. I suspect that's why she left, but I don't know for sure. Maybe she let the guys' tricks get under her skin.

Privacy was a big issue with women. I know of one large company in the area that didn't make any accommodations whatsoever for their women employees. They designated one specific mined-out heading that the women had to use for the bathroom. Every day women took their chances of getting walked in on because no curtains existed for privacy. I didn't agree with that. At Loveridge, the company provided an outside trailer for the women to shower and to use the bathroom. Two black girls, sisters who came up from the South, worked at Loveridge. They found that someone had bored holes in the trailer as peepholes and complained about it several times. No one did anything. They finally sued the company and got a big settlement for sexual harassment. I heard of another peephole occurrence where a company had sectioned off a corner area in the main bathhouse for the women. The partition was secure, but before long, they discovered peepholes cut from the outside of the building. Women didn't take that type of blatant harassment for long, but they couldn't control other ways used to discourage them and make them quit.

Some companies intentionally hired small and overweight women and then assigned them to heavy work, like lifting fifty-pound rock-dust bags. They suffered, trying to keep up, and couldn't work for long. Then the company said, "Well, we tried it. This woman thing didn't work." Another tactic was to schedule women with children on the second shift so they wouldn't see their kids except on weekends. Also, they'd schedule married women on permanent midnight shift to make their husbands mad. No man wanted his wife "out all night." Even for single women, adjusting to midnight shift exhausted them, and they decided it wasn't worth the hassle. Many didn't realize these strategies were intentional to get them to quit.

Some bosses made no allowances, or they would order a woman to do a dangerous job that could cause her to get hurt. They might assign a small woman to the construction crew, loading and unloading cement blocks for eight hours. When that happened to a woman who tried to do a good job, the men often pitched in to help her. Most women worked at general inside labor jobs. They shoveled loose coal, rock dusted, or assisted with belt work. Very few worked around the face. Most companies considered training women to operate machines to be a waste of time. I never felt that way. Some ambitious women kept applying for machine jobs until they finally got a shuttle car or learned to run a scoop. I only know of one who became a continuous miner operator.

Quiet or backward women didn't cut it. If a woman wanted something, like a job change or to run a machine, she had to be a little mouthy. Those without courage to speak up for themselves got run over and stayed in a meager job, like shoveling coal. They also suffered the most from sexual comments and tricks, like "greasing." To grease a woman, several men dipped a hand in mechanic's grease and brushed her in delicate places at every opportunity. Men also tested a woman to see if she was easy, or to see if she planned to work hard. Some men only harassed a woman while she was a red hat. After she earned a black hat, they let up on her and treated her more equally.

Rumors circulated from mines that lacked leadership. Miners got away with criminal behavior and did not even get reprimanded for groping, gang grabbing, assault, or open threats of rape. I couldn't understand how anyone in authority could let bullies get away with that kind of harassment. Knowing this was going on in other mines, I felt bad for the women who just wanted to keep a good job. I realized that every one of these women was someone's wife, sister, or mother. I tried to treat each one the way I would want others to treat my own wife, sisters, or mother, if they ever decided to work in a coal mine.

If Gay and I disagreed about how to do some little job around the house, she'd tease me. "You know, Bob. I think I'll go and get myself a job in the coal mines. I just hope I don't ever have to work for you." I'd get her right back. "Girl, I wouldn't have you working for me." She knew my smart remark referred to our disagreement, but she also knew how I felt about women working underground.

Some women came in determined to get respect from the men immediately, but they had to be tough. I heard about one woman who, on her first day, made an announcement in the dinner hole. "You guys can say anything you want to around me, but you will not touch me. If you do, the first chance I get on the outside, I'll shoot you. Count on it." They left her alone. Since she was older and carried aspirin and first-aid items for everyone, she got the nickname "Mom." Another woman my buddy worked with yelled loud enough for the whole section to hear, "You touch me again, and I'll kick you in the face! Then I'll call your wife and explain to her why you don't have any teeth!" Naturally, the guy backed away and never touched her again. Neither did anyone else.

When a woman reported harassment to a supervisor, sometimes her situation got worse. A reprimand could make a man meaner and give him incentive to put his accuser in harm's way. A smart woman demanded a transfer if she filed a harassment report, but then the suggestion that she just quit and get out of mining might be thrown back at her. They really had it rough before the companies started needing "quotas" and had to hire so many women. Then the foremen cracked down on the men. A third reprimand for harassment brought dismissal.

Sometimes relationships developed. One man at Loveridge got involved with a woman and lost his wife over it. I heard rumors about men and women having sex in the mines, but as far as I know, it didn't happen anywhere that I worked. A foreman who messed with the women lost the respect of his crews, and that caused him more trouble. The men who respected women and didn't approve of the harassment going on were often afraid to voice their opposition.

The impression that every woman got harassed by every man simply wasn't true. In a work force of three hundred men, a few men with no morals caused trouble for the women. Sometimes a gang mentality took over, however, and others joined in to be one of the guys. In a group situation, one man's bad attitude could infect the whole group. Pointing out her weaknesses, or even flaws in her appearance, poisoned the other men. Then the teasing started. Before long, a situation like that could turn hostile.

Depending on their personality, their work ethic, and the men they worked with, some women got along fine. Men who respected women and didn't mind working with them could become very protective. Some might disagree, but I noticed a change in the mines after women started working. Men, brought up to be tough, take risks for granted. Women are natural protectors of their children and their families and, as a rule, aren't risk takers. I believe the presence of the women, and the idea that women needed protection, caused the men to take less risks. In warning a woman not to do this or that, men started to heed their own warnings. To say that safety conditions improved because of women entering the coal industry may give them too much credit, but I believe their presence had a positive influence on safety.

I was happy to be finishing out my mining career at Robinson Run. I knew I'd have my hands full in the safety department, but I was glad to not have to deal with the stress of production work. All I had to deal with was being fifty-seven years old and having a young woman for a boss. ∎

CHAPTER TWENTY-THREE

Robinson Run

onsol's Robinson Run No. 95 mine opened in 1968 near Shinnston, West Virginia. I was at Loveridge, working on my certification. Harrison Power Station, directly across the mountain from Robinson Run, needed a steady supply of coal. Shortly after the mine started production, an elevated overland conveyor belt to Harrison Station connected the coal supply and the demand.

Four years later, in 1972, Consolidation Coal Company installed the longwall operation at Robinson Run. Publicity for the mine, and for the company, filled the newspapers, radio, and television news. Though I was content at Loveridge, I thought that Robinson Run sounded like a great place to work. Three years later Robinson Run installed their second longwall. For several years the mine also had active sections extracting coal, but by the time I arrived in December 1984, the entire coal production came from the two longwall operations. Ironically, the year I began my job in this highly productive, modern mine, Grant Town Federal Mine No. 1 started laying off hundreds of men. Like other West Virginia communities suffering a mine closing, Grant Town started to take on the appearance of a ghost town. Putting all those miners out of work didn't seem right.

Although nearly six hundred miners worked three shifts at Robinson Run, only about a dozen blacks and the same number of women were on the payroll. I was the only black foreman. Linda, my new boss, was the only woman foreman. I was never completely comfortable working for a woman, but we got along OK from the beginning.

Linda was slender and a little taller than me. She didn't have too many feminine ways about her, but working in a man's world, that was fine. I could tell she was a go-getter. I nodded agreement throughout her introductory speech. "Bob, I'm in charge of the Environmental Dust Control Program at this mine. You'll assist me in this work. I do what I'm told, and I expect you to do the same. I can get along with just about anybody as long as they do their work. This is a big mine so there's plenty to do. The safety supervisor is over both of us." She waited for my reaction, but I stayed quiet. "You have safety experience, right?"

"Yes. I was in safety at Four States the last couple of years, but not every day. When they needed a foreman, I filled in."

"You know both sides of the work then. Come on. I'll show you around." She had spirit and a pleasant personality. I liked her.

As we toured the longwalls, I could tell she was very knowledgeable. Linda told me the safety department had seven people for three shifts and that the main office was at Robinson Run portal. The mine was spread out with two satellite portals, one at Jones Run and the other at Oakdale. I'd be working at one of these locations on the day shift each week. She told me the rules and regulations she had for her staff, like the daily checking of inspectors' books. Any unresolved problems got passed to my relief on the next shift.

After the tour, she sent me to the supply house to pick up my equipment. From there, I had to check the water-sprayer system on the longwall nearest to Oakdale. Then I found the area where two full-face-ripper continuous miners were penetrating the next longwall headings. The miners developed the entries on three sides of the longwall. By the time installers put the longwall in, the continuous miners were done. They moved on to start developing for the next longwall location. Each continuous miner had a loading machine and two shuttle cars. The last assignment on my first day was to have the two operators back up their miners so I could clean the screens of coal dust. These modern machines had roof bolters attached to the back end so they could bolt and mine, bolt and mine. Very efficient combination.

As I got more familiar with the layout, I realized that my hunch about Robinson Run was correct. It was a great place to work. I especially liked the variety of safety jobs and the freedom to move around all day. Sometimes I wondered how I had ever run a loader, standing and pulling levers, day in and day out. Safety work was much more interesting. I can only think of one irritating negative. The equipment strapped to my belt weighed me down. Every miner at the coal face had a methane detector on his belt. I had to carry an anemometer to measure air flow, a safety lamp and methane detector to monitor gases, a walking stick about forty-two inches long and a special hammer to sound the roof. I also had to wear a self-rescuer, complete with a one-hour supply of oxygen. Most of the time I tried to keep a supply of respirator masks so a miner could get a clean one from me anytime. All that equipment weighed about eighteen pounds. I clattered when I walked through the ankle-deep rock dust. With safety goggles and a mask on, I'm sure I looked like a lumbering monster from a science fiction movie.

Besides scheduled assignments, I took air and methane readings continuously. Since blackdamp accumulated in unventilated areas, I used the safety lamp to check for this suffocating gas. I repeatedly pounded and poked at the roof, looking for hollow, or "drummy," roof. If I found drummy roof, I had to report the area immediately. Others explored the potentially dangerous roof condition and often ordered additional support to prevent a roof fall.

Linda and I got along well. She was radical in her use of colorful language, but a woman had to be radical to survive as a supervisor underground in a male industry. I never felt as if she used her language against me.

I spent most of my time working out of the Oakdale office. To manage the large work force, each portal had its own superintendent, general mine foreman, and crews of men. When I had to work every other Saturday, the safety supervisor held a meeting in our office. He had a strong conviction that every safety employee had to adopt. That was: "Production and safety go hand in hand. No production, no payday. But whatever you do, you have to do it safely. It is a very delicate balance." He told us that if a production foreman complained to him about one of us shutting him down, then he knew we were doing our jobs. As a former production foreman, I knew production considered the safety department a necessary evil they had to endure.

Robinson Run had mined over two and a half million tons of coal consistently for several years, and the company expected that output to continue. Our watchdog unit had to take care of our own business, but we also had to consider the business of production. That was the delicate balance.

Where I went in at Oakdale, the cage went down 342 feet. Electric trolley wires hung over the rails to power locomotives, mantrips, and jeeps. Unlike other mines I'd worked, Robinson Run had good roof conditions and also good bottom, a soft fireclay. The longwall shields rested on pontoons so they wouldn't sink into the clay. Because of the slope of the mine, water ran to low areas, where pumps took it up to the surface. Conveyor belts hauled coal from the longwalls to the dumping points. Rail cars took it out the Robinson Run portal to the processing plant. From there, the overland belt to the Harrison Power Station picked up about 60 percent of the coal. The rest poured into a steady line of coal trucks.

Since my official job title was "dust sampler," I slowly got involved in getting the men to carry in dust pumps, an apparatus that monitored inhalable dust in their work area. A machine operator had to wear the pump for one day. We sent the removable disks that trapped the coal dust to a federal lab for analysis.

Getting an accurate dust sample, and one that passed the test for compliance, was a problem. Some miners thought we took the samples to deny them black lung benefits so they wanted a sample that was rich in coal dust. No one could make them understand. To camouflage the test, a miner might intentionally "pack a pump," or place the pump inside a dust collector or cover it with coal dust. When I gave an operator a dust pump, I had to watch him carefully throughout the shift so he didn't mess with the sample. To get some men to cooperate, I had to joke with them. "Tom, I know you don't want to do this today, but I got a car payment due. If you don't do this for me, I'll get fired, and then you'll have to pay my car payment." That kind of persuasion usually got the business done faster than being a hard-ass.

Besides working as a "dust man," I constantly watched for safety violations and hazardous conditions. With only two safety inspectors on a shift, we couldn't be everywhere. We knew that when we walked out of an area, a miner would probably remove his respirator, or breathing mask. Masks are nasty, sweaty things that clog up fast. Knowing they took off their respirators when I left, bothered me. I knew firsthand, from my dad's experience, what that meant. To be more comfortable, those men elected to join the legion of other forcibly retired miners who couldn't leave their homes without an oxygen tank hitched to their belts and little plastic tubes stuck up their noses. I didn't see myself as saving them from that fate, but I hoped that my constant reminders might make a difference. If I walked through an area and spotted someone without a respirator, I got his or her attention and pointed to my own mask.

Earphones or earplugs protected us from hearing damage at the long-wall. The noise was so deafening that no one cheated on that regulation. Conversations were impossible unless we walked a long distance away from the shearer. Rumbling machinery and the constant grinding of coal at the face rattled teeth and bones. If I spent a day at the longwall, I could feel the vibration in my feet and legs most of the way home.

Safety glasses were mandatory at all times, but I knew they were a pain. The eye-protection part fogged up and needed to be cleaned often. Sweat ran down around the eyes. The company strictly enforced this regulation, and I had to issue disciplinary slips to miners who were caught not wearing safety glasses. Three slips brought dismissal. Few miners risked getting that third slip.

We tried to keep everyone in compliance with rules and regulations as much as possible, but it was an hourly struggle. Everyone had to wear steel-toed boots with pants or coveralls tucked inside the boots. Just moving around caused the pants' legs to blouse, creating the hazard of getting them caught in equipment. We had to keep telling the men to tape their pants' legs down. I finally started carrying tape with me.

When a fan went down, our department got the men out. We coordinated with the mine foreman who had ordered the evacuation by taking a roll call outside. If the mechanics couldn't get the fans going, the men went home with half a day's pay. In winter, power outages forced us to evacuate the mine several times.

A large union mine has two to four federal inspectors inside at all times. Their presence kept us on pins and needles. Federal safety inspectors could put pumps on men at random. We never knew where or when that might occur. Sometimes they tested one man's intake for a whole week. Inspectors started at one end of the mine, worked their way through, and then started over again. West Virginia state inspectors also had the authority to shut down production for a violation.

For the two years I was at Robinson Run, I worked for Linda. On several occasions during our joint inspection tours, some older fellows hollered for me to come and speak with them. Linda walked on ahead. Someone in the group said, "Bob, you probably know a lot more about a coal mine than she does." After the first time this happened, I prepared a little speech to stop their tongue-wagging about me, a veteran miner, working for a young girl. I'd say, "Yes, that's true. I probably do, but she's got a master's degree in safety. I respect that. She definitely knows her safety, and she's my boss. So that's it. That's all there is to it. She's my boss." They mumbled things like, "Well, yeah. I guess you're right. Bob, I hear you. Nothing you can do about it." I guess I disappointed them by not complaining or bad-mouthing her, but that wasn't my way. When Linda asked what they had wanted, I always told her, "Nothing." I often wondered if she thought I resented working for her, but I never did. I did what she told me to do. As far as I know, she never complained about my work or about me.

By the middle-to-late 1980s, men had accepted that women were now a permanent fixture in mining. While I was at Robinson Run, a man and woman met on the same job, fell in love, and got married. I knew the guy from Four States. Not only did they work together, but they ate together every day. He brought his bucket, she brought her bucket, and they spread out their lunch between them. Some of the guys teased them about that, but as newlyweds, they obviously preferred each other's company. They didn't mind spending the whole day together, which I thought was unusual. I got a big kick out of their togetherness.

As part of my job, I taught safety classes at Llewellyn, one of the old portals for Farmington No. 9. Federal law said each miner had to have eight hours of safety instruction every year. A large segment of the work force had to go in on a Saturday and move from class to class for different subjects. Although they got paid time and half for the day, some tried to engage in horseplay. I kept control because I believed the classes were important. One thing I taught the miners was how to avoid injuries, like how to lift and how to squat properly. When employees came to the office with a muscle strain, the company had to ask them, "Weren't you taught how to prevent this injury? Who was your teacher?"

Mechanics had a lot of strained muscles and backs. They fooled themselves that they could lift a two-foot-square motor weighing 250 pounds all by themselves. Instead of calling for help, they'd wrestle it with a crowbar and strain their backs. I reminded them the UMW contract said that a coal miner was not allowed to lift over 50 pounds, and that being "macho" was just plain stupid. After women struggled with 50-pound rock-dust bags for several years, the size of the bag went down to 25 pounds, a more manageable weight. Some strong men and women could carry two at a time and stay within the contract guidelines, but I advised them against it.

I also concentrated on protective wear, like safety goggles, earplugs, and respirators. When I first started in mining, no one paid much attention to protective wear. Discussions about respirators and the inevitable black lung were dramatic—sometimes heated and sometimes calm with resignation.

The classes broke the routine of safety work in the mine, and I enjoyed that break. Of all my jobs in the mines, I believe I liked the work as a safety inspector at Robinson Run the most. Modern equipment that doesn't break down and stall production makes a big difference in how contented foremen and miners are with their work. Most of the contract miners at Robinson Run were friendly and tried to cooperate with the safety department, and with the jobs I had to do. They were a younger generation and, for the most part, treated me well.

I must have tutored and trained hundreds of men in the coal industry on how to run machines or how to do something without getting hurt. At Four States and Robinson Run, I told at least a dozen young men, "Son, why don't you go to get certified? You may work ten or twenty years in the mines. Look at all that time. When it's over, you'll just be an old retired coal miner. The company has good benefits. Why don't you try for it?" Some came back to shake my hand and say, "Bob, your advice paid off. I'm a certified foreman. Thank you."

In the early months of 1986, I started thinking seriously about retiring. I knew that within one year I would meet the forty-year mark and be eligible for full retirement. Though my actual years underground were closer to thirty-five with all my layoffs, I qualified. Retiring at age fifty-nine, still in good health, appealed to me. Most of my older mining friends didn't get to retire because they had contracted black lung and had to quit. I rode the fence of "should I or shouldn't I" for several months. Then the climate started to change at work. For the first time in my years in the mines, I stopped looking forward to going to work. The reason was fear.

One evening I shared my feelings with Gay. "They're bringing in college kids as supervisors. They've earned degrees that say they're well versed in mining procedures. Being older and experienced, I know more about the dangers. They know their stuff on paper, but for them to go and make decisions which affect me and hundreds of others—they scare me. If I stay with it, I think they're going to blow me up." Sharing the fear that I'd kept inside for months was difficult, but I needed her to know the truth. "What do you think about my retiring?"

She didn't hesitate to give me her opinion. "It sounds like it's time, but it's your decision, Bob. You do what you have to do. I don't know what's it's like down there. Is there something specific that happened to make you feel this way?"

"There's a young black guy, a real smart aleck. I made a suggestion to him today. He said, 'Look, old man, I'm a college graduate. You can't tell me anything that I don't know.' He's one of those young punks you can't even suggest doing something the right way. They all have such confidence and know-it-all attitudes. I'm not comfortable with the risks they're taking. I've never had a lost-time injury in all these years, but I feel like I'm pushing my luck. I think I'd better get out while I can." Talking it out helped me to make my decision.

"It's settled then," Gay said. "You do it now, if you think you have to."

"I'll work to my forty. That'll be in January. I'll get things started for then."

Just knowing I had the plan to leave got me through the weeks ahead. When my dad started working at Watson mine in 1925, the yearly death toll for miners killed in West Virginia was almost 700. During my first year in the mines (1947), 250 men died mining coal. Safety regulations had reduced that number to less than 20 deaths a year. Still, all it took was one explosion. I didn't want to be a statistic.

No one at work knew of my fear. In the mining industry, I had held my tongue on numerous occasions. When I heard remarks and hurtful slurs at my back, I kept quiet. Occasionally, I took action, but mostly I walked away, silent. Keeping a job was more important than putting someone in his place or winning a battle of wills. My upbringing taught me to avoid arguing and subjects that might lead to an argument. It wasn't easy because when I was young, I was feisty and combative. As an adult, I learned that speaking my mind too often caused negative reactions and hard feelings. That's why I tried to adopt the habit of keeping quiet if I had a contrary opinion. Arguing with the young know-it-alls about dangerous risks would have brought negative attention to me. I avoided confrontations and swallowed my growing fears.

Another development had caused me to lose enthusiasm for mining. For several years I'd noticed that the younger generations of contract miners complained continually about conditions, their assigned jobs, and the bosses. In my opinion, Robinson Run was a modern, safe mine with great working conditions, but a portion of the work force were negative about everything. Also, many only did what they had to do to keep their jobs. My dad and I worked in water up to our knees and breathed bad air most of the time. No legislation existed to protect us. A miner accepted the risks and did the job. We didn't think of complaining because we had to support our families.

If one of these complainers came in and had to work in a particular area that wasn't the best, or with a foreman he didn't like, he'd say, "Oh, I'm sick. I've got to go home." I saw this pattern starting at Four States. I had to take guys out of the mine because they didn't like what I told them to do and claimed they were sick. They'd go to a doctor, get a slip, and get paid for the time. Some had fake slips. They'd just sign them like a doctor, with bad handwriting, and get paid. I had to go along with it because someone could slap a discrimination suit on me and say, "How did Bob know whether I was sick or not?" Some would even fall down and pretend they got hurt. As a supervisor, I saw this happen even when a guy got mad about something and simply wanted to go home. It disgusted me, and no one seemed to know how to stop it.

Escaping this negative atmosphere, and getting out before a catastrophe occurred, kept me on the track to retirement. I wasn't thinking about Gay's age, or how much longer she'd be working. Maybe if I'd considered that aspect more carefully, I wouldn't have retired when I did. Part of me was nervous, leaving my friends and knowing I'd have no place to go every day. Some company officials showed their surprise when I put in for retirement, asking, "Why now, Bob?" Though I had always believed in telling things straight, I held on to my right to stay quiet about my reasons. I simply said, "It's time. Forty years is long enough."

For every five years of service, Consol gave their loyal employees a little black box with a gem in it. I consolidated them: two diamonds for fifteen years each, and two rubies for five years. I got to select a ring with the word "Consol" stamped on it from a catalog and had the stones set in it. Gay had given me a beautiful ring years before, which I preferred to wear, but the Consol ring was a nice memento to keep. The ring and a get-together that my friend Tom arranged ended my mining career.

Driving away from Robinson Run that last day in January 1987, I felt sad it was over, but lucky to have survived it. Many didn't. I'd lost a lot of friends and acquaintances to accidents, death, and black lung. All those faces paraded past me that day.

With few exceptions, I enjoyed every day of my work life. Not many people can say that. At age fifty-nine, I felt young and healthy and free. I looked forward to spending the rest of my life in fresh air and daylight. ∎

CHAPTER TWENTY-FOUR

Retirement, 1987

Like anyone who retires, I enjoyed the first month. I slept in and did whatever I wanted to do. After one month, I got bored. I missed Gay during the day, and with energy to burn, I started getting restless.

That first year I got an early start on my garden. Behind our home I'd worked on having a nice vegetable garden every year, but I planned a bigger and better one. When the plants started coming up, I watered and weeded every evening. If anyone came to our house after the sun passed from the yard, Gay had to say, "He's out there in the garden." I didn't come in until I finished the work, no matter who came to visit. The only help that Gay provided was picking. She kept coming out and picking my vegetables before they were ready. Finally I had to warn her, "Woman, stay out of my garden!" We had a lot of fun teasing each other about my prime vegetables and her wanting to get her hands on them.

I heard about a job that interested me. A private concern had bought the old Fairmont Hotel. They closed it, completely gutted the inside, and renovated it into apartments. They called it East View Unity Apartments and had rented out eighty-five units. The housing manager, Danny Summers, hired me as a temporary night watchman for six months.

Most of the tenants were elderly women, and they kept telling me how secure they felt with me there. Close to East View was a nightclub that had rowdy customers on Friday and Saturday nights. Cars honking and screeching their tires scared the tenants. Some folks from the nightclub came over and banged on the door to come in and use the bathroom. On those evenings I stayed in the lobby area to discourage any vandalism. Other times I patrolled the halls to be sure everything was quiet. I know they appreciated me because I often received a piece of pie or cake as a treat. At Christmas the women showered me with homemade gifts, like wall hangings, pictures, and tins of cookies. They spoiled me.

I knew from the time I took the position that it was only for six months. Although I had to walk home at 4:00 A.M., and had a strange sleep schedule, I enjoyed that job. It was different from anything I'd ever done, and I hated to leave. I didn't think I'd ever get a part-time job that I enjoyed as much as being a night watchman, but I was wrong.

One day Tony delivered a Federal Express package to the *Times West Virginian* newspaper office. They asked him if he knew anyone who might like a part-time job. He said, "My dad's retired. He might consider it." They told Tony to send me down to see them. In January 1991, I joined the circulation department of the *Times West Virginian* as a customer service representative. I still work with them. When the news carriers miss a customer for some reason, or the newspaper ends up wet or damaged, I deliver a replacement copy. For seven years I have delivered replacement newspapers five mornings a week, Wednesday through Sunday, all over Marion County.

What I like best about the job is meeting new people. No matter how much trouble it is, I take the newspaper right up to the house. I think it is a courtesy to do that. Several people have said, "You can't depend on these young guys anymore." That makes me feel good.

Once I went up to knock on the door. I hadn't seen a BEWARE OF THE DOG sign. That dog came out of nowhere, barking and leaping after me. I took off for the car as fast as I could run. Soon I heard a little girl howling with laughter at the sight of me breaking my neck to get to my car. Her mother yelled, "He won't bite!" People who put up a BEWARE OF THE DOG sign are either trying to scare people away or they believe that someday their dog just might bite someone. I had no intention of giving that dog the chance to make me his first surprise victim. I stayed in my car. They had to come to me for the paper. We laughed about it, and the woman said over and over, "He doesn't bite. He's never bitten anyone." Now I definitely check for signs before I open my car door.

The people at the *Times* seem to appreciate me. I feel as if they really need me. If they call me on one of my off days, I go in if I can. It doesn't pay much, but there's no stress or pressure. I like doing something because I want to, not because I have to. One nice thing: I don't have to wear special clothes or carry heavy equipment around my waist to deliver newspapers. Gay teases me. "Bob, your britches are falling down. Tighten up your belt!" I tell her, "Yes, I know they're falling down. I had all that stuff hanging off me for too many years. Now I want to feel loose."

After I'd been with the paper a couple years, I thought of an additional way to make some money. An old barber shop had a shoeshine bench they weren't using. I asked for it and got it. I brought it home and fixed it up so it looked respectable. That was in 1994. I set up the bench at Middletown Mall in White Hall, just south of Fairmont. For about six months I took my shoeshine kit out to the mall every day after I got home from delivering papers. In the beginning I had lots of business, but it slowed down as stores closed and moved elsewhere. I decided it wasn't worth my time to be there for a few loyal customers. Several of them called me after I left the mall to see if I had set up somewhere else. I decided against that, so I retired again, from my own shoeshine business. A few customers, who had depended on me, brought their shoes to my house. I encouraged them because it gave me something to do.

One thing I like about retirement is being able to watch boxing on television through the day and into the night. I watched some old black-and-white films of Joe Louis fighting. He knocked them all out. Of his twenty-five fights to defend his title, I believe nearly twenty were knockouts. When Joe knocked a guy down, Jack "Chappy" Blackburn stood up there, ready to put the robe on him. Chappy knew the guy wasn't going to get up. If he got up, it was suicide. My boys don't remember Joe Louis. I always told them, "Joe Louis was the best. He was better than Ali." That's what I think. Of course, when the younger generation came up, they only knew about Muhammad Ali, but Joe Louis was the greatest!

I tried to pass on my love for boxing and other sports to my boys. When they got to be six years old, I gave them boxing gloves. All the kids in the neighborhood enjoyed coming to our basement to box. From my tutoring, the boys developed into good boxers. I tried to stay with them. They played baseball and Pop Warner football. I assisted their coach in football and saw all the games they played up through high school.

Being a sports enthusiast through the years, I have acquired a few insights and opinions about how things have changed. For instance, one development in boxing disturbs me. Matchmakers are just in it for the money, and they don't care who gets hurt. When a fighter gets knocked out two or three times in one year, I believe it's time to revoke his license. They'll match up a kid with eighteen knockouts, two decisions, and two losses against a guy with twelve fights, ten of them losses. That's like putting a Rottweiler dog out there on a puppy.

Boxing was dirtier when I was an amateur. There was a time when a referee might find a horseshoe in a fighter's glove, or a piece of metal clenched in his fist. That's dirty. Also, now the enclosed glove makes it impossible for guys to thumb each other. When the thumb was free, I had people poke me in the eye with their thumb while in the clinches. Doing away with those temptations was good for boxing. Like with other sports, though, big business has taken over. I see Mike Tyson clearing millions of dollars in one fight. That was unheard of in the past. Sports used to be the players competing to thrill the fans. Now it is about big business and money.

There are many black athletes in all sports. They are well compensated for their efforts and their talents, hundreds or thousands of times more than the black athletes in years past. When I was young, the majority believed that a black man was too dumb to become a quarterback in high school or professional football, a star on a basketball team, or even a pitcher in major league baseball. I can't comprehend how fans at a sporting event can cheer for predominantly black teams, and hostility toward blacks still exists in this country. At a big game, with sixty thousand whites and four thousand blacks scattered in the crowd, some black athlete makes a touchdown and everybody cheers like mad. Then when the game is over, many whites go right back to the old ways of exclusion and fear.

The Civil Rights Act of 1964 was supposed to equalize the races. In the thirty-four years since then, some blacks have made achievements, but I don't think that much has changed. It's better now, but it will never be equal. We don't hear about lynching or vandalizing homes anymore, but there will always be prejudice. Because my skin color is different from the majority of people, I feel that stigma of color. Many whites think I'm not as good as they are. I feel as if I don't have a prejudiced bone in my body. Prejudice is taught. If kids hear their parents say things about blacks, they'll think it's OK for them to say the same things. Soon they believe that is the right way to think. That seems to be where the hostility begins—at home.

By the time I was sixty-seven, I started slowing down. Gay had to tell me to quit gardening. The work had become a chore, stooping and crawling around on my knees, so I agreed to give it up. That was hard.

After I had retired from mining, I enjoyed the opportunity to spend more time on preparations for the Dunbar High School reunions. The first one, held back in 1972, had brought together over six hundred former teachers, graduates, and students. A friend of mine, Rudolph Laster, and I discussed the idea for a couple years prior to that. A bunch of us got together and got the ball rolling, electing officers and making formal plans. I got very involved with that first one. It was a huge success.

We still draw a big crowd to our reunions. Over the Fourth of July weekend every three years, we have a variety of events to remember our school and to get reacquainted with former classmates. We have several dances, a banquet, and a picnic—something for everyone. We even have a little memorial service at the school to remember those who have passed away. I enjoy looking over the old pictures and articles displayed at Dunbar during the reunion weekend.

Through the years I have served on various committees, like the picnic and entertainment committees. At the 1984 reunion, they elected me vice president for one term. From the beginning I have enjoyed working hard to help make a memorable celebration for those who take the time to come back and visit. At the 1996 reunion, the president, John West, presented several of us with an engraved plaque as a sign of his appreciation. I felt honored to receive one of these beautiful plaques.

Like the black church picnics of the past, those blacks who have left the area arrange to come home and visit their families every three years. That way they can also enjoy the Dunbar High School reunions with old friends and former classmates.

After the last reunion, I decided it was time to check with my doctor about my shortness of breath. I knew I had black lung, even though he concluded that I didn't. I drove to Charleston for the official testing. It involved a stress test and endless breathing into a machine. The official report said I had 5 percent reduced lung capacity, the beginnings of black

Bob after receiving his Dunbar Reunion President's Award plaque, July 6, 1996.
Courtesy of William Armstead.

lung. I knew from others' experiences that it probably wasn't enough to claim benefits, but sometimes, when the state budget had lots of money, a miner could be successful. I decided to start the process and get my name into the system.

Company lawyers made it difficult for me to receive a settlement. They scheduled a group meeting with several others seeking a claim. Within a few minutes after I heard my name, I heard "Denied," and it was over. Private lawyers won't take a black lung claim because it is a no-win case. For every lawyer a miner can afford, the companies hire more and better ones. Black-lung benefits are extremely hard to get. The federal standards are so high, a miner has to be practically ready for an oxygen tank to receive any compensation. The West Virginia state standards, though less strict, won't open a benefits case if budget money is limited.

The clean air legislation in 1972 went a long way toward getting coal companies to monitor their dust problems. Since that time, not all companies have been as conscientious as Consol. Our safety department at Robinson Run had strict rules and policies. The federal inspectors at that mine did their job of protecting the men. From what I understand, some companies still don't take the standards seriously. They cheat on the samples and get away with murder. That's where the problems lie. Everyone's bickering. The companies complain that standards are too high and too expensive to maintain. The federal government says, "The companies are not doing their job. How can all these perfect samples be right?" The coal miner loses as the battles continue.

For many years I didn't wear a respirator because no one made me. This past summer, in 1998, West Virginia testing showed that I have 15 percent diminished lung capacity. I expected it to be higher because I needed to rest more and more. Black lung was inevitable for me. It's a hazard of the job, just like potential explosions or roof falls. Of the thirty active miners who died in the United States in 1997, seven of them died in West Virginia mines. The statistics claim that in the same year, ninety miners in the United States died of black lung, but that figure is entirely too low.

Thousands of miners died from black lung before dust control was enforced. They received no compensation whatsoever. An article I read stated that between eight hundred and one thousand miners and former miners suffer from black lung today. That kind of misleading statement makes me furious. I have personally come into contact with half that many black-lung victims. I'm more inclined to agree with another article stating that thirty-six hundred currently working miners have black lung and thousands of retirees have it. The same article said that over fifty-four thousand coal miners' deaths can be traced to black lung and its complications. Somebody came up with the idea of a class-action suit, like those people who took on the tobacco industry. That may be where the answer lies for all the miners who have their disability benefits denied.

Though I had retired, I continued to read everything I saw in the news about mining. I've kept up on the legislation and what the state and federal governments are doing to help underground miners. Part of my interest is because of my campaign for compensation, but I also have an interest in those younger fellows I worked with who are still on the job.

Last summer Gay and I drove her godmother to Morgantown to the doctor. In the waiting room I sat next to a young man. He was about twenty-two years old. We got to talking about mining. From our conversation, I picked up that he was from Mannington, West Virginia. I asked, and he said he was.

"You live in Mannington? I used to work at Four States mine."

"My dad worked at Four States."

"What's his name? Maybe I worked with him."

He said, "Tim Sanders."

I almost fell through the floor. Without thinking, I said, "Your dad worked for me, but I almost got him killed." The look on his face! I didn't mean to shock him, but I guess I did. We discussed the incident that happened when he was little. I told him all about Tim's close call, and my being his foreman.

The boy listened quietly. "I didn't know anything about that. I had to have been only five-years-old at the time." His mother said she remembered it well. She remembered my call to see how Tim was doing after his accident. As we parted, I asked him to say hello to his dad, who is still at Loveridge.

Those chance meetings often happen when I'm delivering papers or stopping into a store to pick up something. I enjoy seeing people I used to work with in the mines. When Gay's with me, she listens patiently, but when we get into the car, she reminds me of her dedication. "Bob Armstead, I didn't work in the coal mines, but for twenty-eight years, I never missed a morning, getting up to pack your bucket and fix your breakfast."

She is right. When I worked day shift, even if we had had a spat or an argument, I'd hear her come down and fix my lunch at 5:30 in the morning. I always had a meal waiting for me when I came home. Before she started working outside the house, she'd tell other family members who teased her about being at home, "Yes, Bob works, but I keep his house, have his meals ready, pack his lunch, and wash his clothes."

We have a wonderful marriage. I take care of her, and she takes care of me. We worked through some hard times. Though we had money problems before I went to Loveridge, I continued to hoard change just like I did as a boy. One way Gay took care of little expenses was to raid my change boxes. The first time I discovered she was getting into them, I was on the midnight shift. She called me down to a late dinner. She disappeared while I ate, but I happened to go upstairs for something. Gay still says I was trying to sneak up on her. The door to a hall closet, where I kept my rifles and my change boxes, was closed, but I heard something jingling. I opened the door, and there she was, down on her knees helping herself to my change from a cigar box. I said, "I ought to have you arrested." I wasn't aware that she knew where I hid my change boxes. We still laugh about it. Sometimes when Gay washes my clothes, she forgets to check my pockets. She'll find two to three dollars' worth of silver in the washer.

On our granddaughter's last birthday, Gay got a package together. I spied an empty cigar cylinder and remembered it was the perfect size of a dime. I filled the whole cylinder with dimes just lying around the house. We included it in the package. Our granddaughter was surprised and tickled to receive some of her grandfather's money. I never had tons of money stashed away. Choosing to be a coal miner made that impossible. Even a three-day strike affected the budget for weeks. Any period of unemployment, or menial work for low pay, sets a man back. I had nearly six years of it. Maybe that's why I keep the change lying about, so I'll feel rich.

Even with a restricted budget, we enjoyed going out with friends. Ever since I've been an adult, I've worked hard all week. Maybe I'll go out on a Saturday night. The first thing in the morning, I want my newspaper. I get my paper and a cup of coffee, and I go out on the porch to read while Gay fixes my breakfast.

Where I live now, a church sits across the street from my house, but I don't go. I decided at a young age that if I grew up to be a man, there were two things I'd always do: raise a garden and not go to church. We read so much about hypocrites and devils, and about bishops, priests, or ministers sexually harassing young boys. There's so much evil in the world, and in the church, nowadays. We see people we drank with years ago going to church. They yell, "Hi, Bob. Come on over." I smile, wave, and say, "I'll be right over," or I say, "No, I can't come today. You say a prayer for me." I never would go because I can't relate to those people, and I don't want them to interfere with me. A couple have come over and talked to me, but they won't see me in church. I had enough church as a child to last a lifetime.

I'm not a religious individual, but I often think there must be some Supreme Being. We see the sky, the oceans, and the mountains. We watch the sun rising in the mornings and give way to darkness at night. The seasons come without man's preparation. Some of us live to old age, often three score and ten, like me, yet some die in their mothers' arms.

These life mysteries cause me to wonder. I am now almost seventy-one years old, but I have always been curious about myself. I've wondered about people on Earth and where, when, and why they were chosen to be conceived and born as boy or girl, black or white, and when they were chosen to die.

I'm now in my eleventh year of retirement. I'd only been retired a year or so when I started writing down everything I could remember about my

Bob and Gay, October 1998. Photograph by S. L. Gardner.

life as a child. Then the story of coal mining in my lifetime became important. Coal mining was more than a job for me. It was a way of life. As
coal miners, my father and I lived on the edge—close to poverty and sudden death.

Circumstances dealt me some difficult times, but I have shared my
most valuable memories on these pages. Though mining didn't make me
wealthy, my choices in work and in life made me a rich man where it
counts—a wonderful family and many good friends. ∎

My Brothers and Sisters

This book of memories wouldn't be complete without further information on my brothers and sisters. For those who have an interest in knowing more about them, their personalities, and where they are now, I hope this satisfies your curiosity.

Vivian Louise, born in 1915, was the eldest of all the children in my family. She was twelve when I was born. A small, thin, pleasant girl with a warm smile, Louise helped my mother with all the household duties. Since my mother gave birth to another child every two to three years, Louise helped care for her younger sisters and brothers. A determined girl, she finished high school, graduating from the old black school in Fairmont.

She began dating the young man next door. He was also the oldest in his family with four brothers. Louise married him on our front porch in Grays Flats in the summer of 1935. While opening her wedding gifts, she found a beautiful one wrapped in thick paper. When it turned out to be a "slop pail," everyone burst out laughing. Since no one had inside toilets, one guest felt Louise needed a slop jar to carry waste water from the house. What a wedding gift! We teased her about her "special" gift for years.

Louise and her husband eventually had eight children. Those eight all have children of their own.

My sister Louise followed Christianity in our mother's footsteps and became an ordained minister at the Temple of Christ on Fitzgerald Avenue in Fairmont. She is eighty-three years old and still preaches occasionally. From her kindness to me as a child, and especially after the death of our beloved mother in 1966, I continue to regard Louise as my second mother.

James Earl, born in 1916, was our guardian angel. Being the oldest brother and the second oldest child in the family, he was fatherly to us when our dad was at work. He especially looked out for his younger sisters. Barbara Jean, our baby sister, was his little idol.

After graduating high school, James felt too young to go into the mines. Like many men all over the country during the Depression, he couldn't find work. He became interested in the Civilian Conservation Corps. Besides establishing the Works Progress Administration to put older men to work, President Roosevelt started the CCC for younger men. In the corps, the men lived in movable camps, planting trees and cleaning up state parks and roadsides as they traveled.

James volunteered to join the CCC in 1935. The government paid thirty dollars a month. According to the rules, they sent twenty-five dollars each month to the young man's parents and gave him five dollars a month for his personal use. This turned out to be good for us kids. When James came home, he'd slip us each a little change. Also, with the extra money each month, my dad gave all of us fifty cents on each payday.

Like a soldier, James wore a khaki uniform and got a pass to visit home each month. Though he couldn't come home every month, we all looked forward to his visits. And how that twenty-five dollars came in handy to help feed a large family!

When James turned twenty-one, my father got him on at the Grant Town mine. Soon after starting work, James bought his first used automobile. Since he was very flamboyant and had many girlfriends, he was always on the go. James worked in the mine for three years but couldn't cope with the underground work. He gave up the job and settled down in Detroit, Michigan.

James and his sweet wife raised six children. She passed a few years ago. He is eighty-two years old and is still living in Detroit.

Clara Mae was born in 1919. She was one hell of a workhorse! I remember her all over the place, mopping, dusting, washing dishes, washing windows—busy all the time. Though small in stature, Clara was a giant, doing more than her share of the work.

After finishing high school, she remained a homebody. After we moved to Fairmont, she did odd jobs in some of the more affluent families' homes in town. I remember her walking in the rain, ice, and snow to get to her jobs, making two or three dollars for a whole days' work. Then she worked hard at home in the evenings. After my divorce, Clara took care of my children, cooked for me, and packed my lunch pail every day for five years. When I remarried, she continued to care for my children. I thank her for that.

Mom became a diabetic in her later years. Clara nursed our mother, giving her morning insulin shots before going to work and doing the same in the evenings. At night she made Mom comfortable, watching her diet and prescribed medication.

Clara married and had two children, a boy and a girl. Her husband died while the children were still young. She worked hard and supported both their children through high school and college. Like Louise, Clara is a devoted Christian, who followed in our mother's footsteps. She's seventy-nine years old and still resides in one of the coal company homes in Grays Flats.

Edith Elizabeth was born in 1922. She was five when I was born so I'm sure we played together. What I most remember from my childhood about Edith is her thin stature. She wasn't a sickly girl, but she was frail. As a young teenager Edith tried hard to do her part of the everyday chores, but my older sisters pushed her away jokingly and told her to go sit down. She never learned to cook or clean house while growing up, but she was very dear to us.

After finishing high school, Edith went to Detroit to live with our brother James. She found employment in one of the largest hotels there, where she worked over thirty years. She married and had one son.

After retirement, Edith lived a good life before passing in 1993.

Homerzella, the bombshell of Family Stories, was next, born in 1924. She loved life and squeezed activity and excitement out of every day growing up.

After high school graduation, Homerzella chose to live in Detroit, where she obtained a license as a practical nurse. She later married, raised three sons, and moved to California, where she finished her career. I visited her on several occasions before she passed in 1992. I still love her and miss her dearly.

William Bell, born in 1926, and I were inseparable as kids. We worked and played together all through our childhood. I looked up to him as my hero. He could whistle louder, throw rocks farther, and jump higher than me. Bill never played in high school sports, but he excelled in the community. I could always depend on him. He gave me the courage to stand up for myself because I knew he would be there to back me up. As with Sam Jones, I sometimes used Bill as a threat to get my way. My sisters all looked up to him as their big brother and protector.

After leaving high school, Bill also migrated to Detroit. For several years he worked as a top-notch automobile mechanic. When I visited him, he tried to get me interested in that work, but I didn't have the ability or the interest.

Bill came home and did work for my mom. Besides being a great mechanic, he was good at household repairs. Each time he visited me, Bill would hop out of his car, leaving his luggage, and head straight for my car. Clean clothes and all, he'd throw open my hood and say, "Turn that motor on." Then he'd tinker with my engine. His wife would call out from the door, "Come in here and get changed before you do that!" And he'd call back, "No, I want to check Bob's car." That's just the way he was. With grease on his clothes, he'd straighten up and tell me what was wrong.

Bill happened to be at my mom's when I had a broken ball joint on my 1957 Buick. We worked ten to twelve hours until we got that ball joint repaired. Another time he did a complete engine overhaul. Even if I thought my car was in good shape, I could count on him to say, "I'll tune it up for you tomorrow." My automobiles were always in top running condition by the time he went back to Detroit. He was a car genius.

Eventually Bill secured a position with the Detroit Edison Company, which supplied all the power for the city. He and his wife raised two daughters. Bill is retired and still lives in Detroit. I will always admire and love my "protector."

I was three years old when Clifford Jonathan was born in 1930. My sisters fussed over him. Each of them watched out for him, but Edith took a special interest in his welfare.

School was not Clifford's favorite pastime, so after he finished the ninth grade, he went to live with Bill in Detroit for a couple of years. Clifford joined the U.S. Navy in 1948 and served for twenty-four years, retiring as a senior chief petty officer. His military service kept him away from home as he moved around the country and the world. He enjoyed traveling and especially liked getting to learn about different cultures.

The brothers, 1975 (from left): Joe, Clifford, Bob, Bill, and James.
Courtesy of William Armstead.

When he retired from the Master Jet Base at Oceana, Virginia, Clifford settled in Virginia Beach. He is currently a production manager at a large plastics corporation in Norfolk. He married and has three daughters and a son. Gay and I enjoy visiting them in their beautiful home along the beach. May God bless him and his family.

In 1933 came the last of my brothers, Josephus Emanuel. The lady who named him was a close friend of the family and a member of the church my mother helped to start. Though Josephus Emanuel was his legal name, none of my brothers and sisters accepted this long, strange name. We began calling him Joe or Joey.

When Joe was a little child, everyone, including the neighbors, began to love and pet him. He was chubby and cute with deep dimples. Though he had a smiling personality, Joe was bashful and never had much to say.

Our father fussed over him as he grew up and referred to him as the "baby boy," even after he entered high school. Joe was an outstanding football player (running halfback) and was selected to the All Black High School Sports Association.

Four of Bob's sisters, 1975 (from left): Edith, Barbara Jean, Louise, and Clara.
Courtesy of Bob Armstead.

He grew into a healthy young man with a brilliant future, but the Korean War yanked Joe's future away from him. He had applied and gained acceptance to state-funded all-black West Virginia State College in Charleston. He had paid his own tuition fee. We were so happy and proud of him. He had his clothes ready to send ahead when he received his draft notice from Uncle Sam. What a shock to him and to the family!

In the Air Force Joe chose to serve in the Communications Division. He traveled all over the United States from one base to another. I remember him talking about Edwards Air Base in California and Hickam Field in Hawaii as good duty stations. He decided to stay in the service.

Then, despite his displeasure, the Air Force shipped him to Greenland, with its six months of daylight and six months of darkness. The temperatures are very cold year round. According to Joe, his time in Greenland was nothing but cold, hard work. The only source of entertainment was the radio. Our mother heard from him once every two or three months, and we worried about him.

After a year in that cold wasteland, the Air Force sent Joe to Osaka, Japan, for four years. From there he went to Thailand, where temperatures ranged between 100 and 120 degrees. He went from a frigid climate to a sizzling one in just a few years. Joe got sick in Thailand. Following weeks of rest and recuperation in a stateside hospital, he got an honorable discharge. He had served thirteen years.

Joe's mind was never the same, as our family could readily detect. He couldn't work after his service experiences. The climate changes broke his health. As the saying goes, "Old soldiers never die, they just fade away." That's the way Joe went. He died on December 19, 1990. We all still love him dearly.

Barbara Jean, the youngest, was an April Fool's Day baby in 1937. She was our darling girl and grew up with lots of attention and spoiling, but she turned out great.

After finishing high school, Barbara Jean married and raised eight children. She joined the local church founded by our beloved mother and older sisters. Later in life she developed vision problems and moved to Wishing Well Health Center in Fairmont. I go to see her quite often or keep close to her by telephone. Although she is sixty-one years old, Barbara Jean is still our "baby sister."

We sadly miss those who are gone, but we have wonderful memories of growing up and try to keep in touch. ■

Epilogue

On December 9, 1998, Bob Armstead died at Ruby Memorial Hospital in Morgantown, West Virginia.

During the summer he had contracted a cold that settled in his chest. The cold hung on and worsened. Related coughing made it necessary for him to rest a great deal and postpone some of our sessions. Finally, on October 27, we met for a question and answer session and to discuss his last two mine experiences, Four States and Robinson Run. His cold had nearly disappeared, but he continued to have shortness of breath. I knew he had black lung and assumed that condition was simply slowing down his recovery from the terrible cold he'd been fighting.

On November 20 Bob called me from Fairmont General Hospital to tell me he had been admitted on the eighteenth and was on oxygen to help his breathing. He sounded great and said not to worry, he'd be fine. I visited him that evening in the hospital. He welcomed me with a big wave and announced to his visiting family, "There's my good friend. My tutor."

Though Bob had oxygen tubes inserted in his nose, he felt much better not having to struggle to breathe.

We had a friendly visit. I got to meet his son, Tony, and his daughter, Doris, for the first time. Bob's spirits were high. An excerpt from this book appeared in the *Times West Virginian*, just that day, November 20, in a special edition commemorating the thirtieth anniversary of the Farmington mine disaster in 1968. A copy of the article circulated the room, and Bob seemed proud of this tangible proof that his book was coming together.

Tony walked me to the elevator and confided that doctors told Bob that he had lung cancer back in October, and that he had already had one chemotherapy treatment. The doctors predicted he only had four months left. I couldn't conceal my shock and despair. Gay and I held on to each other as if our wishes would change things.

I understood why Bob hadn't told me, thinking it might affect my work on the book, but I felt so helpless. We were close to finishing. Now it looked as if Bob may not see the fruit of all those months of work. I wouldn't allow myself to think the worst and held onto hope along with his family. This hope motivated them to seek a second opinion, and they transferred Bob the following Tuesday to the cancer center connected to Ruby Memorial. Testing confirmed a tumor at the base of the trachea, that, while possibly operable earlier, had now grown and was partially blocking his windpipe.

Within a week, complications threw Bob into unconsciousness. Doctors placed him on a respirator. The evening of December 8, Bob's seventy-first birthday, his intensive-care physician asked the family if they could meet the following morning to discuss disconnecting his life support. They agreed. The family said their good-byes, and Gay told Bob they were going to put his life in God's hands. Bob died during the night, sparing his family that most agonizing decision. His family was devastated.

Bob's decline and sudden passing left a deep chasm in my spirit. I couldn't work with his words for weeks. Though I only saw him about once a month, we had talked on the phone for hours. Sometimes with the tape recorder running, sometimes not. If the tape wasn't running, I was feverishly taking notes, for he was a wealth of information.

This book was important to Bob, as a legacy in a way, but also to tell the story of coal mining from the inside. If his friends and associates remember mine-related experiences happening differently, so be it. *Black Days, Black Dust* is a record of his recollection and his viewpoint. I wasn't there. I could never have done what he did, going underground for eight hours a day, every day. I tried it once, for the experience. The roof rumbled, and I couldn't breathe until I got out of there. The experience gave me the utmost respect for those who enjoy it and make it their life's work.

This book has been a labor of joy. Though his memory was excellent, specific historical accuracy and statistics were not Bob's top priority. I made numerous calls to libraries and the UMW and visited local libraries to dig into mine reports and many reference books searching for accuracy. I thoroughly enjoyed it. All aspects of this work were fun. Sometimes I felt guilty having so much fun. I'm pleased that I could help Bob Armstead get his life story published.

Through his hardships and heartaches, Bob lived a good life. He was a good man. A real gentleman. It was an honor to know him.

S. L. Gardner

Glossary

active workings Ventilated areas in a coal mine where miners and/or machines work or travel. Also called workings.

air shaft Shaft used for ventilation. Depending on its size, may also have a cage to transport miners or a hoist for a three-man bucket.

airway Any passage in a mine that carries air.

anemometer An instrument with a revolving wheel that measures how fast air is moving through an area.

band A thin layer of sulfur, stone, or clay in a seam of coal.

bar Long wooden timbers (six by eight inches by fourteen-plus feet) used horizontally for roof support in a mine heading. Measured, cut, and placed by timber crew. See also POST.

bench Bottom part of a coal seam left after the coal above is mined.

bit The cutting, drilling, or tearing tool attached to a mining machine.

black lung Common term used when referring to respiratory diseases in miners brought on by years of inhaling coal dust. See also COAL WORKERS' PNEUMOCONIOSIS.

blackdamp A suffocating gas mixture of air and carbon dioxide, or air and too much nitrogen, that is fatal when inhaled. Occurs when ventilation is poor or non-existent, as in fan malfunction or power outages. Gob areas produce blackdamp.

blast Using explosives to bring down coal or rock.

blasting cap A cartridge, containing fulminate of mercury, with a long fuse that is tamped into a drilled hole with explosive powder. Can also be ignited by electrical current.

blow out A failed blasting attempt that blows the stemming back out the hole without shattering the coal.

boney pile See GOB PILE.

booster fan A secondary fan inside the mine used to force air further into the headings.

bottom The floor of a mine entry, heading, or room.

brass A brass tag with a miner's company number or social security number. Placed on and retrieved from a board when entering and exiting a mine. See also CHECK.

brattice (pronounced brattish) or brattice cloth Temporary, plastic-coated cloth partition hung from a mine roof to deflect or channel air currents. Also called canvas check. See also CURTAIN.

bug dust Fine particles of coal dust produced by cutting machines, continuous miners, and the longwall. See also COAL DUST.

buggy A small mine car. Nickname for shuttle car.

cage Metal or wooden platform housed in an elevator-type vertical shaft used to transport miners, supplies, and coal cars in and out of a deep mine. May travel hundreds of feet down to the mine workings.

canvas check See BRATTICE.

cap rock A two- to six-inch layer of rock mixed with coal or carbonaceous rock, located between the coal seam and the solid rock roof of a mine.

car A wheeled vehicle that transports coal and supplies inside a mine.

carbide Acetylene gas from a compound of carbon and calcium, mixed with water. Used in miners' carbide lamps.

carbide lamps Small carbide, carbon, and water mixture acetylene flame attached to a miner's cap giving off just enough light to see a few feet. Replaced in the early 1940s by safer, battery-operated units.

cartridge Waterproof paper roll packed with explosive powder used in blasting coal.

cave or cave-in See ROOF FALL.

charge Measured amount of explosive used in one blast.

check Brass tags engraved with a miner's company number used in the past to receive credit and payment for hand loading a coal car. See also BRASS.

check curtain See CURTAIN.

chest auger Manual or electric drill with breast plate used to drill holes in coal to set blasting charges.

chocks Movable, flexible metal canopy, supported on hydraulic jacks, that served as the roof-control system over the first longwall mining operations.

coal cutter See CUTTING MACHINE.

coal car Common name for funnel-shaped railroad car with a bottom that opens. Designed to transport coal. Also called hopper, coal hopper, hopper car.

coal dust Finely powdered coal. See also BUG DUST.

coal face See FACE.

coal hopper See COAL CAR.

coal workers' pneumoconiosis (CWP) Coal miners' chronic lung disease contracted by years of exposure to coal dust in underground mines. Major symptom is shortness of breath. X-rays determine severity of condition by revealing extent of spots in lungs that prevent air exchange. Can incubate in the lung for fifteen to twenty years. See also BLACK LUNG.

colliery Entire mining facility, including mine and outside buildings.

continuous miner Mining machine with sharp bits attached to a revolving drum or to rotating arms. One operator can mine up to eighty tons of coal in one hour. See also CONTINUOUS MINING and MINER.

continuous mining Process that revolutionized mining industry. In room-and-pillar mining or heading mining, one machine replaced cutting, blasting, and mining. Continuous miner rips coal from face, drops it onto its own flat bed with belt, and conveys it back to a loading machine or directly into a shuttle car. See also CONTINUOUS MINER.

conventional mining Method of coal mining in which the coal face is undercut and sidecut so that blasting brings down tons of coal at a time. Coal is then gathered from the bottom by a loading machine and loaded onto shuttle cars and moved to haulage rail cars or to conveyor systems to the outside.

conveyor belt Electrically powered, suspended or platformed, continuous-running heavy rubber belt used to move coal to the outside.

conveyor system Main line conveyor, permanently installed, moves coal to a dumping point or to the outside. Movable section conveyors interconnect to link headings to the main line conveyor.

crib Timbers laid crossways in a square, alternating layers, to form a pillar that supports the roof of a mine.

crosscut A passageway or tunnel cut between headings, often (but not always) at right angles to the main entry.

curtain Any temporary cloth or plastic material hung from a mine roof to regulate, deflect, or channel air currents. Also called check curtain. See also BRATTICE.

cutter bar Nine- to fifteen-foot flat arm on a cutting machine that cuts into the coal face using many sharp bits attached to a chain. Design resembles a huge chain saw.

cutting machine Conventional mining machine used to undercut, topcut, or shear the coal face in preparation for blasting. Able to cut nine to fifteen feet into the coal. Also called coal cutter.

dead time Unpaid time spent to do dead work. See also DEAD WORK.

dead work Work that is not producing coal, such as draining water or removing rock after a roof fall. At one time miners were not paid for dead work.

dog hole Small, privately owned mine in which the operator can chose to deny his employees UMW affiliation. Also called scab hole.

drift mouth See PIT MOUTH.

driver Mine worker who drives horses or mules in underground mining to move coal from the face to the cage for haulage to the surface.

drummy Mine roof condition that sounds loose, hollow, or weak when tested by pounding with a tool. Hollow, drumlike sound indicates gaps above the cap rock and potential danger.

entry An underground passageway used for hauling coal or for ventilation.

face The exposed area of a coal seam where miners and/or machines extract the coal in a room, heading, or longwall operation. Also called coal face.

fall See ROOF FALL.

fireboss Foreman who inspects the mine for gases.

first break See MAJOR FALL.

gob 1. Part of the mine from which coal has already been mined.
2. Coal mine waste material consisting of shale, slate, clay, and so forth.

gob area Any mine waste area underground. In longwall mining, the area where the roof support system has advanced and the roof has caved in behind it.

gob pile Common name for massive amount of mine waste brought to the surface and dumped on hilltops and into ravines. Also called boney pile, slate dump.

gobbing Practice of placing waste in mined-out areas to avoid the expense of transporting it to the surface

heading Coal mine tunnel where coal is being, or has been, actively mined.

helper One who works under a trained miner as his/her assistant.

hoist Machine used to raise and lower the cage in a shaft or to lift coal underground. To raise and lower the cage.

hopper **or** *hopper car* See COAL CAR.

hot Describes a mine that contains high levels of methane and other explosive gases.

inby **(pronounced inbye).** Toward the active workings of a mine.

inhalable dust The portion of coal dust that is hazardous when breathed in and retained in the lungs.

loader 1. Any miner who shovels coal into cars or onto conveyor belts.
  2. Miner who operates a loading machine.
  3. Loading machine.

loading machine In conventional mining a machine with crablike arms that scoops coal from the bottom and deposits it into a shuttle car.

locomotive See MINE LOCOMOTIVE.

longwall mining Mining method that revolutionized the industry in which long sections of coal, up to one thousand feet across, are mined. Shearer cuts and deposits coal directly onto conveyor system. Shields support the roof and advance the longwall. As system moves on, roof collapses behind the work area. Small crew of operators can extract more than two hundred tons in one hour.

main entry **or** *main line* A mine's main large tunnel where miners and machines move in and out and coal is transported out by cage, rail, or conveyor system.

major fall When the roof collapses for the first time behind a longwall mining operation because the unsupported roof is too massive to bear the weight of the rock above. Result is thunderous noise and a forceful escape of compressed air from the site. Also called first break.

manhole A hole cut in the side wall, or rib, of a narrow rail entry for miners to jump into in case of an emergency, for example, runaway rail cars.

mantrip Combination of mine locomotive and attached cars that transport miners from the portal or main entry into work areas by rail. Cars are open-sided, with/without canopy roof. Can also be a battery-powered, rubber-tired single vehicle, resembling a large, low dune buggy. Also called personnel carriers. See also TRIP.

mine locomotive Electric or battery-powered locomotive used in mines to haul coal cars or supplies and mantrips. Also called locomotive, motor.

miner 1. Any individual who works in a coal mine.
  2. Continuous-mining machine. See also CONTINUOUS MINER.

motor See MINE LOCOMOTIVE.

outby **(pronounced outbye).** Toward the shaft, main line, or drift opening of a mine.

pan line In longwall mining operation, large L-shaped pieces of steel that are bolted to the face in ten-foot sections. The shearer and large steel-chain conveyor ride on the pan line to move the coal out to the conveyor system.

personnel carriers See MANTRIP.

pillar Section of a coal seam left as roof support after mining. Can be a twenty-, thirty-, or fifty-foot block, depending on roof stability. Pillar may remain or be mined out, allowing roof to collapse intentionally.

pit Common term for a colliery or coal mine.

pit mouth Walk-out opening from a coal mine to the outside. Can be located in a manmade pit or at the base of a hill or mountain. Also called drift mouth.

portal Usually refers to the opening to the main entry of a walk-in or ride-in coal mine, but may refer to any entrance, including a shaft.

portal-to-portal pay Wages based on time spent from moment of entering to moment of exiting the mine, not only on hours worked. Union issue arising from miners traveling very long distances underground to their work place as mine expands.

post Long wooden timbers (four to six inches square) used vertically for roof support in a mine heading. Two are set opposite each other to hold up a bar. Measured, cut, and placed by timber crew. See also BAR.

rail or rails Railroad or railroad tracks.

red check or red tag Method used by mining company weighman to deny miner credit for a car of hand-loaded coal that contained rock or slate. Placed red metal tag on coal car, which meant "no pay." In some mines, also placed red tag on a miner's cap to humiliate him. Unethical weighmen often used this power to cheat miners, causing unions to lobby for union weighmen.

retreat mining Practice of mining out large coal pillars left after the first phase of mining, thereby allowing the roof to collapse as the operation "retreats" from the site.

return Mined out heading kept open for return air and/or escape.

return air Air that has already flowed through the mine workings and is returning to the outside.

rib Side surfaces, or vertical side walls, of a mine heading, pillar, or room.

rock dust White, powdered limestone sprayed in great quantities on mine roofs, bottoms, and ribs to eliminate the explosive qualities of coal dust. Mixes with coal dust particles to keep them apart. Critical to mine safety.

roof Ceiling of a mine entry, heading, or room.

roof fall Roof collapsing in a mine. Also called fall, cave, or cave-in.

roof working Thunderlike rumbling noise heard as overhead rock strata slips, slides, and settles to fill in mined-out areas. Common occurrence in underground mining. Can be a warning sign of a roof fall.

roof-bolter Miner and/or machine that places bolts in holes to support the roof.

roof-bolting machine Machine that drills thirty-inch- to ten-foot-deep holes into the roof of a mine and then screws long bolts with resin or glue up into the holes to support the roof. One bolt design has a device that expands against the walls of the hole as the bolt is tightened.

safety lamp A metal lamp with a flame, fueled by naphtha and protected by fine gauzes, that will change color or size if hazardous gases are present in a mine.

scab A miner who works against union orders during a strike.

scab hole See DOG HOLE.

scoop Small mine vehicle with rubber tires used to haul coal in thin seams or to clean up gob. Resembles a front-end loader.

screen System to separate coal into various sizes for marketing.

seam Solid coal deposit.

section Tunnel or series of tunnels (headings) in a mine where coal is, or is going to be, actively mined.

seepage Groundwater or rain runoff that enters mine workings and accumulates in low areas.

shaft A deep, vertical opening, with a cage and hoist, used to transport miners and supplies into and out of a deep mine and to transport coal to the surface. Can be used for water drainage and ventilation. See also AIR SHAFT.

shearer or shearing machine Longwall mining machine consisting of two rotating drums, with cutting bits and water sprayers. Moves from one end to the other and back of a five-hundred- to one-thousand-foot coal face, continually grinding coal onto a chain conveyor belt.

shield Steel unit approximately four to five feet wide weighing eight to ten tons used as roof support in a longwall operation. Consists of a movable platform with two to four vertical hydraulic jacks that control a large roof-supporting panel. Unit also has one horizontal hydraulic jack that presses the pan line against the coal face. Many units operate side by side to advance the longwall.

shooting Blasting in a mine.

shuttle car Electric or battery-powered mine vehicle with rubber tires and a built-in conveyor with a large bed used to haul coal. Moves from loading machines or continuous miners to mine cars or conveyor systems. Built to haul six to ten tons. Also called BUGGY.

skid A slab of metal or a wooden platform with a hook and chain used to move small loads. Usually transported by rail.

skip Moving a trainload of coal cars, one car at a time, to be loaded with coal. The attending loud clang as rail-car couplings jolt apart and then together.

slate dump See GOB PILE.

slope A tunnel or passageway that is carved out to get down to or up to a seam of coal.

slurry Mine waste mixed with water.

snake A curved line on a miner's paycheck stub signifying no wages are due because of his indebtedness at the company store.

snap coal Extremely dangerous mine-roof condition caused by dense, compacted coal under pressure. Unpredictable cracks and "snaps" occur as small or large chunks of coal shoot down suddenly. Roof falls may occur as pressure shifts.

stemming Material rammed into shot holes before blasting, usually wadded paper or clay.

stopping Airtight wall, created from sheet metal or concrete blocks. Built across headings or crosscuts to seal off portions of a mine and/or to segregate fresh and return air. May have built-in door or trap door.

subsidence Slump or cave-in of the earth's surface as a result of extensive underground mining. Can compromise stability of roadways and residential/commercial structures.

tamp Packing a drill hole in a coal face with stemming after a previously inserted blasting cap is in place. See also TAMPING BAR.

tamping bar or tamping rod A long, thin, copper-tipped metal pole used to ram clay or stemming into a drill hole prior to blasting coal. See also TAMP.

timbering Any use of wood for roof support in a mine, specifically the practice of installing and fitting large wooden side posts and long wooden overhead bars to secure the mine roof in a heading. Placement is every three to five feet, depending on roof conditions.

timberman Miner who sets timbers in place.

tipple Elevated structure outside a mine shaft or entrance where coal is dumped, or "tipped" in, from mine cars or a conveyor system and is then washed, screened, and loaded into railroad cars or trucks.

trip Succession of coal cars moved at one time by a mine locomotive. See also MANTRIP.

UMW United Mine Workers of America, a national labor union for miners.

undercut First step in hand-loading and conventional coal mining. Historically done by hand with a pick, removing a section of coal at the bottom of the coal face. Cutting machine replaced manual labor in the 1930s.

weighman In hand-loading era. Company-paid or employee-paid man, stationed on the surface, responsible for charting weight of coal loaded by each miner. At one time had total control of wages for loaders.

wet seal Practice of sealing off an abandoned mine entrance and installing a drainage pipe to allow trapped mine water to drain to the outside.

work practices Policies and procedures aimed toward controlling workplace hazards and promoting safety.

working See ROOF WORKING.

working wet Working in an area of the mine that has pooled water as a result of seepage.

workings See ACTIVE WORKINGS.

Suggested Resources

Books and Articles

Arble, Meade. *The Long Tunnel: A Coal Miner's Journal*. New York: Atheneum, 1976.

Brophy, John. *A Miner's Life*. Edited by John O. P. Hall. Madison: Univ. of Wisconsin Press, 1964.

Campbell, Shirley. *Coal and People*. Parsons, W.Va.: McClain Printing, 1981.

Cassidy, Samuel M., ed. *Elements of Practical Coal Mining*. New York: Society of Mining Engineers of the American Institute of Mining, Metallurgical, and Petroleum Engineers, 1973.

Coleman, McAlister. *Men and Coal*. New York: Farrar & Rinehart, 1943.

Conley, Phil. *History of the West Virginia Coal Industry*. Education Foundation, Inc. Charleston, W.Va.: Charleston Printing, 1960.

Corbin, David Alan. *Life, Work, and Rebellion in the Coal Fields: The Southern West Virginia Miners 1880–1922*. Urbana: Univ. of Illinois Press, 1981.

Densmore, Raymond E. *The Coal Miner of Appalachia*. Parsons, W.Va.: McClain Printing, 1977.

Dillon, Lacy A. *They Died for King Coal*. Winona, Minn.: Apollo Books, 1985.

———. *They Died in the Darkness*. Parsons, W.Va.: McClain Printing, 1976.

Dix, Keith. *What's a Coal Miner to Do? The Mechanization of Coal Mining*. Pittsburgh: Univ. of Pittsburgh Press, 1988.

Dixon, Phil, and Patrick J. Hannigan. *The Negro Baseball Leagues, 1867–1955: A Photographic History*. Mattituck, N.Y.: Amereon House, 1992.

Dixon, Thomas W., Jr. *Appalachian Coal Mines and Railroads*. Lynchburg, Va.: TLC Publishing, 1994.

Dunbar, Paul Laurence. *The Complete Poems of Paul Laurence Dunbar*. New York: Dodd, Meade, 1913.

Eller, Ronald D. *Miners, Millhands, and Mountaineers: Industrialization of the Appalachian South, 1880–1930*. Knoxville: Univ. of Tennessee Press, 1982.

Fedorko, Nick. "Fairmont, West Virginia: A Look at Mining, Geology, and Subsidence." *Mountain State Geology* (1986): 9–17.

Fishback, Price Van Meter. *Employment Conditions of Blacks in the Coal Industry, 1900–1930*. Seattle: Univ. of Washington, 1983.

Foner, Philip S., and Ronald L. Lewis. *Black Workers: A Documentary History from Colonial Times to the Present*. Philadelphia: Temple Univ. Press, 1989.

Gates, Henry Louis, Jr. *Colored People*. New York: Alfred A. Knopf, 1994.

Giesen, Carol A. B. *Coal Miners' Wives: Portraits of Endurance*. Lexington: Univ. Press of Kentucky, 1995.

Humanities Foundation of West Virginia. *The Mining Life: Coal in Our History and Culture*. Charleston: West Virginia Coal Life Project, 1982.

Hume, Brit. *Death and the Mines*. New York: Grossman, 1971.

Johnstone, Bill. *Coal Dust in My Blood: The Autobiography of a Coal Miner*. Victoria: British Columbia Provincial Museum, Heritage Record No. 9, 1980.

LaLone, Mary B. *Appalachian Coal Mining Memories: Life in the Coal Fields of Virginia's New River Valley*. Blacksburg, Va.: Pocahontas Press, 1997.

Lamarre, Lora. "Everettville Refuse and Portals." In *Project Summary Report*. Nitro, W.Va.: Division of Environmental Protection, Abandoned Mine Lands and Reclamation, 1994.

Lee, Howard B. *Bloodletting in Appalachia*. Morgantown: West Virginia Univ., 1969.

Letwin, Daniel. *The Challenge of Interracial Unionism: Alabama Coal Miners, 1878–1921*. Chapel Hill: Univ. of North Carolina Press, 1998.

Levy, Builder. *Images of Appalachian Coalfields*. Philadelphia: Temple Univ. Press, 1989.

Lewis, Ronald L. *Black Coal Miners in America: Race, Class, and Community Conflict, 1780–1980*. Lexington: Univ. Press of Kentucky, 1987.

———. "From Peasant to Proletarian: The Migration of Southern Blacks to the Central Appalachian Coalfields." *Journal of Southern History* 55, no. 1 (Feb. 1989): 77–102.

Lindbergh, Kristina, and Barry Provorse. *Coal: a Contemporary Energy Story*. Seattle: Scribe Publishing, 1977.

Lockard, Duane. *Coal: A Memoir and Critique*. Charlottesville: Univ. Press of Virginia, 1998.

Mattone, John G. *Coal Miner's Son*. Huntington, W.Va.: Univ. Editions, 1994.

Moore, Marat. *Women in the Mines: Stories of Life and Work*. New York: Twayne Publishers, 1996.

Morris, Homer Lawrence. *The Plight of the Bituminous Coal Miner*. Philadelphia: Univ. of Pennsylvania Press, 1934.

Nichols, Harry H. "A Brief History of Federal Mine No. 1." Loose-leaf, unofficial record of Grant Town mine history, Dec. 30, 1952. Genealogy Room, Marion County Public Library, Fairmont, W.Va.

Norris, Randall, and Jean-Philippe Cypres. *Women of Coal*. Lexington: Univ. Press of Kentucky, 1996.

On Dark and Bloody Ground: An Oral History of the U.M.W.A. in Central Appalachia, 1920–1935. Charleston, W.Va.: Miner's Voice, 1973.

Selzer, Curtis. *Fire in the Hole: Miners and Managers in the American Coal Industry*. Lexington: Univ. Press of Kentucky, 1985.

Shifflett, Crandall A. *Coal Towns: Life, Work, and Culture in Company Towns in Southern Appalachia, 1880–1960*. Knoxville: Univ. of Tennessee Press, 1991.

Smith, Barbara Ellen. *Digging Our Own Graves: Coal Miners and the Struggle over Black Lung Disease*. Philadelphia: Temple Univ. Press, 1987.

Smith, Richard C. *Human Crisis in the Kingdom of Coal*. New York: Friendship Press, 1952.

Thomas, Jerry Bruce. *An Appalachian New Deal: West Virginia in the Great Depression*. Lexington: Univ. Press of Kentucky, 1998.

Trotter, Joe William. *Coal, Class, and Color: Blacks in Southern West Virginia, 1915–32*. Urbana: Univ. of Illinois Press, 1990.

Turner, William H., and Edward J. Cabbell. *Blacks in Appalachia*. Lexington: Univ. Press of Kentucky, 1985.

Vecsey, George. *One Sunset a Week*. New York: E. P. Dutton, 1974.

West Virginia Coal Association. *Coal Facts '87*. Charleston: West Virginia Coal Association, 1987.

Williams, Bruce T. *Coal Dust in Their Blood: The Work and Lives of Underground Miners*. New York: AMS Press, 1991.

Williams, John A. *West Virginia and the Captains of Industry*. Morgantown: West Virginia Univ. Library, 1976.

Films

Matewan. Directed by John Sayles. Cinecom Entertainment Group, Inc., 1987.

October Sky. Directed by Joe Johnston. Universal Studios, 1999.

Index

Black Days, Black Dust was designed and typeset on a Macintosh computer system using QuarkXPress software. The text and chapter openings are set in Goudy. This book was designed by Cheryl Carrington, typeset by Kimberly Scarbrough, and manufactured by Thomson-Shore, Inc. The paper used in this book is designed for an effective life of at least three hundred years.